HOUSES IN MOTION

*The Experience of Place and the Problem
of Belief in Urban Malaysia*

Cultural Memory

in

the 

Present

Mieke Bal and Hent de Vries, Editors

HOUSES IN MOTION

The Experience of Place and the Problem of Belief in Urban Malaysia

Richard Baxstrom

STANFORD UNIVERSITY PRESS

STANFORD, CALIFORNIA

Stanford University Press
Stanford, California

Printed in the United States of America on acid-free, archival-quality paper

Library of Congress Cataloging-in-Publication Data

Baxstrom, Richard.
    Houses in motion : the experience of place and the problem of belief in urban Malaysia / Richard Baxstrom.
        p. cm.—(Cultural memory in the present)
    Includes bibliographical references and index.
    ISBN 978-0-8047-5891-8 (cloth : alk. paper)
    1. Sociology, Urban—Malaysia.   2. Urban policy—Malaysia.   3. Islam and politics—Malaysia.   I. Title.

HT147.M325B39 2008
307.7609595—dc22   2007050725

Typeset by Westchester Book Group in Garamond 11/13.5

Contents

Acknowledgments

Without the generosity and openness of the residents of Brickfields, Kuala Lumpur, the sustained, rigorous intellectual engagements of my mentors and colleagues, and the love and support of friends and family, this project would not have been possible. Above all I wish to thank Veena Das who, through her tireless engagement and distinctive commitment to the work of anthropology, has made a singularly decisive contribution to this study. Without Veena's exceptional combination of care and critique, I could not have brought this project to fruition. As this book is a revised version of my doctoral dissertation, I would also like to thank the other members of my dissertation committee—Paola Marrati, Michael Peletz, Deborah Poole, and Hent de Vries—for their wisdom, dedication, and friendship. In addition, I wish to thank Hent and Mieke Bal for their continued support of this work as the editors of the *Cultural Memory in the Present* series, and I would also like to express a particular debt of gratitude to Norris Pope, Emily-Jane Cohen, and the staff and readers at Stanford University Press for their time and effort in bringing this book to press.

The Wenner-Gren Foundation provided financial support for field research in Kuala Lumpur through its Individual Research Grant program. Additional financial support in connection with this project was provided by the Program in Southeast Asian Studies, Cornell University (Foreign Language and Area Studies [FLAS] grant for participation in the Full Year Asian Language Concentration and Composition [FALCON] program), the Department of Anthropology, Johns Hopkins University, and the Office of the Dean, Zanvyl Krieger School of Arts and Sciences, Johns Hopkins University.

Special thanks to the best friends a person could ever have: Todd Meyers, Brenda Peterson, Stefanos Geroulanos, and Rania Ajami. I look forward to many more years of creative mischief.

The uniquely active and open intellectual community that I have been a part of in the Department of Anthropology at Johns Hopkins University has played a decisive role in the writing of this book. In particular I would like to express my appreciation to my partners in our long-running reading group, Aaron Goodfellow and Naveeda Khan, for their inexhaustible insights, enthusiasm, and camaraderie. Additionally, I wish to thank Hussein Agrama, Jane Guyer, Sidharthan Maunaguru, Sameena Mulla, Ross Parsons, Sylvain Perdigon, Valeria Procupez, Pamela Reynolds, Isaias Rojas-Perez, Don Selby, Bhrigupati Singh, and James Williams for their friendship and encouragement during our time together in the Department. Talal Asad, Steve Caton, William Roseberry, James Siegel, and John Wolff provided invaluable support and critique during the initial stages of this project, and I thank them for their early belief in my work. Through the years many others have been equally important to this research and in my life generally, particularly Matthew Amster, Valerie De Cruz, Jim Hoesterey, Laura Kaehler, Erin Koch, Peter Quinn, Gillian Stewart-Quinn, Barney Rosset, Lisa Todzia, and Andrew Willford. I would also like to thank the undergraduate students I had the good fortune to teach during my time at Johns Hopkins, since their questions, comments, and engagements always helped me to rethink things that I thought I already knew.

Although I cannot mention most of them by name for reasons of confidentiality, I wish to express my gratitude to the many people I worked with in Brickfields and in Kuala Lumpur. Without these friends and neighbors, this project would never have seen the light of day. Many scholars, professionals, and activists in Malaysia also contributed greatly to this project. In particular, I would like to thank Raymond Lee Lai-Ming, Sumit Mandal, M.G.G. Pillai, A.B. Shamsul, Nani Kahar, Peter Kiernan, S. Nagarajan, Yeoh Seng Guan, and Kala Kovan for their invaluable assistance during the period that I conducted field research in Kuala Lumpur. I also wish to acknowledge the support of several institutions in Malaysia that assisted in the completion of this project, including Arkib Negara Malaysia, Bernama (National News Agency of Malaysia), the Department of Anthropology and Sociology and the Asia-Europe Institute at the University of Malaya, Institut Kajian Malaysia dan Antarabangsa of the Universiti Kebangsaan Malaysia, and the Economic Planning Unit of the Office of the Prime Minister of Malaysia.

Many thanks to my family for the warmth and affection they have shown me all of these years. In particular, I am grateful to my mother, Elizabeth McCabe, and also Dorothy Humbracht, Barbara Humbracht, William Matlock and Marget Johnson, Gary Matlock and Jan Thompson, and the "Hada clan" (Masaru, Osamu, and Susumu).

To Gerald Humbracht, Kenneth Baxstrom, Kiyoko Hada: nothing is more painful than the fact that you three did not make it to see this project to its end. You are missed . . .

Finally, I would like to express my deep gratitude to Mamiko Hada and to dedicate this work to her. This project would not have happened without her love, companionship, intelligence, and humor, and I am truly indebted to her for helping me create a life worth living.

HOUSES IN MOTION

*The Experience of Place and the Problem
of Belief in Urban Malaysia*

The Mysterious Incident at Jalan Chan Ah Tong Field

Jalan Chan Ah Tong field was the only public open space remaining in Brickfields by early 2002.[1] Although not officially a park or space designated for recreation by the Dewan Bandaraya Kuala Lumpur (City Hall), the vacant lot was used by neighborhood children for pickup soccer games and by the nearby Vivekanenda School for its physical education activities. Despite its abandoned appearance, the field had a strong place in Brickfields folklore. Elderly residents claimed that the field was the site where Nehru spoke during his visit to Malaya in 1937.[2] Middle-aged residents told tales of the legendary football players who honed their skills on the Jalan Chan Ah Tong field by competing in the resident-organized Deepavali Cup tournament. Many of these neighborhood legends went on to become members of the Malaysian national football team. Younger inhabitants merely claimed that they liked to have an open space to hang out, caring less about the legends than about the fact that the open field at Jalan Chan Ah Tong was the closest thing Brickfields had to a public park. Bordered on two sides by the Hundred Quarters, one of the oldest remaining government apartment complexes in Kuala Lumpur, the field was a locus of intergenerational neighborhood activity.

Residents of the Hundred Quarters awoke one morning in January 2002 to find that half of the field had been paved over with asphalt the night before. Although some neighbors noted that they heard a great deal of noise throughout the night, they thought nothing of it, as it was normal to hear the noise of construction in the middle of the night in Brickfields. Neighbors were aware of the activity, yet remained unaware of precisely what was going on right outside of their flats. By morning no visible signs of who had constructed what appeared to be an illegal car park on the field remained. The new parking lot had simply "appeared" on the site.

The audacity and speed of the event stunned those who lived around the field. The initial reaction was a numb blankness in the face of this sudden effort to convert the space into a parking lot. The event was simply unbelievable, and yet there it was. This initial shock and inertia was quickly replaced by anger over the violation of the neighborhood by strangers who felt that they could manufacture a fake development project in order to turn a quick profit. Furious Brickfields residents converged on the Dewan Bandaraya Kuala Lumpur and demanded to know who held the license to develop this space. DBKL claimed to know nothing about it and confirmed that no building license had been issued for the construction. Responding to the angry protests, DBKL sent out its investigators. By afternoon the matter was splashed all over the local newspapers, provoking outrage from Brickfields old-timers. Although the mysterious construction had only taken place the night before, football legends from the 1960s and 1970s had already emerged from the obscurity of their present to denounce the car park to reporters. Residents congregated around the field throughout the day, keeping watch. The sentries told me that they intended to catch whoever did this when they returned, presumably to set up shop and begin collecting parking fees. Those keeping watch claimed to be angry, but their demeanor was one of stunned disbelief. "This happens all the time," they repeatedly told me.

Illegal land developers read the papers and the culprits never dared to return and carry through with their plan. The labor and asphalt was a dead loss for whoever did this, but taking this loss was presumably better than being beaten up by local residents while trying to make good on the investment. Whoever laid the asphalt was clearly unaware of the history of this seemingly vacant piece of land and, in the context of the building frenzy in Brickfields that was taking place, figured nobody would really notice or care if they set up a little parking lot. In most other cases, this assumption would have been correct. The calculated risk that this mode of ad hoc development entails normally works out fine, at least for a while. Only the aura of a threatened, fading past prevented the blacktopping of Jalan Chan Ah Tong Field. DBKL, sensing a public relations opportunity, quickly sent some crews out to tear up the asphalt and then planted several trees and bushes around the perimeter. This official effort was the first time in the field's long history as a social space that City Hall had recognized it as a recreational site and contributed materially to its upkeep. The field was essentially returned to its previous state by the end of January, although some of the poor-quality asphalt remained visible under the hastily laid sod for months afterward. Despite their best efforts, the landscaping crews sent by City Hall could not fully erase the evidence of this strange event.

DBKL's quick action on the matter was appreciated by local residents, but at a distance. Many whispered among themselves that someone within the municipal bureaucracy knew about this all along. One local businessperson summarized the widespread suspicion held by local residents:

Although I don't have proof, I think DBKL knows who tried to put the car park in. I think someone down there said "go ahead, but if you get caught we don't know anything about it." It is just too suspicious. They moved too quickly afterwards to have not known something. Within a few days they had gotten rid of the asphalt and planted trees. That *never* happens in KL!

The perpetrators remain unknown.

An Introduction to Urban Life in Brickfields

I begin with this seemingly insignificant local scandal because in it we find a rich illustration of the issues of urban life and transformation that form the central concerns of this book. Specifically, these issues are the following: (1) the law and the gap between legality and local understandings of justice and relatedness, (2) the ability of local residents to form a mental image of the world that is believable and provides the possibility for action in the world and the formation of an ethical life in the context of possessing an ambiguous legal and social subjectivity, and (3) alternative avenues of engagement with the state that are generated in an environment where urban subjects find themselves formally excluded from the authoritative discourses of law and development and the formation of what are believed to be ideal, ordered urban spaces. This book addresses these issues by asking how the right to public space and community is imagined and articulated in urban Malaysia. The questions that drive the inquiry are: Who has the right to the city and public space? How, through the law and local realities, is that right determined? How is such a right legitimized or contested? And how does this right give form (or not) to urban spaces that are experienced as orderly, just spaces that generate the possibility of action in the world for individual residents?

The trajectory of events surrounding the incident at the Jalan Chan Ah Tong field unfolded in a manner that illustrates this set of complex issues in a condensed fashion. The fact that residents living near the field were vaguely aware of the construction going on right next to their homes but did not notice it as unusual is the first significant aspect of this incident. In January 2002 Brickfields was undergoing a radical change due to the ongoing construction of the KL Sentral Train Station complex and the KL Monorail public transportation system. These projects, undertaken as part of a coordinated plan for urban development in Kuala Lumpur, had generated a palpable sense of uncertainty in the neighborhood due to the speed and scale of change demanded by such a large project. Plans for KL Sentral were first made public in 1994, although major construction on the project was delayed for several years due to the Asian economic crisis during 1997 and 1998. The initial phases of the project opened in March 2001. Anchored by the station itself, designed by Dr. Kisho Kurukawa, the KL Sentral project consists of fourteen separate land parcels situated immediately west of Jalan Tun Sambanthan in Brickfields. The overview of the project offered by its developers is worth quoting at length:

KL Sentral is being developed as a futuristic self-contained city, providing the perfect live [*sic*], work and play environment. Office towers, condominiums, hotels, restaurants, retail malls and entertainment and leisure centres are all walking distance from each other within the 72 acres that is KL Sentral. Adding to this, the transport facilities offered are on par with the best the world over. Not only is Stesen Sentral the country's rail transport nucleus, and an extension of the KLIA [Kuala Lumpur International Airport], but road access to KL Sentral has been carefully thought out so as to offer the highest convenience to motorists entering and leaving the development.

KL Sentral supports fully the vision of the KL Structure Plan 2020, namely creating a metropolis that is efficient, harmonious and spiritually inspiring. Blending cutting-edge technology with soothing surrounds [*sic*], KL Sentral offers a fine, and rare, balance between fast-paced urban living and the very human need for leisure, relaxation and comfort. It is a place where you can truly exercise your body, mind and soul. But KL Sentral is more than a development that seeks to improve the quality of life of Malaysians. It is also a prominent landmark in our evolving city that symbolises national pride and prestige.

KL Sentral is being developed in phases, and is expected to be completed by the year 2012.[3]

This carefully constructed description for public consumption is accurate in its references to KL Sentral's modernity and its place in the national imaginary of development. Unintentionally, it also clearly signals the dramatic absence of Brickfields as a place within this imaginary. Explicitly designed to exclude the neighborhood surrounding it ("a futuristic, *self-contained* city"), KL Sentral, along with the related construction of the KL Monorail system,[4] had nevertheless come to define the experience of living in Brickfields between the years 2000 and 2002. While these projects sought to ignore the neighborhood, the neighborhood could hardly ignore the transformations that the projects had brought to the area.

Although they seldom articulated their goal as a slogan or organized political platform, the citizens of Brickfields consistently attempted to assert their right to the city in the face of the dislocating effects of urban development in Brickfields. This right was not fully invested in the rules and procedures of the Constitution or the Land Acts governing property ownership and transfer (although the specific operation of these statutes remained critical factors), but was predicated on the notion that the city is a space that arises out of the relationships that exist between its residents. In this conception of the right to place, local concepts of justice and proper relatedness must engage the state and the formal institutions of law. With an understanding of rights resembling those articulated by Lefebvre (1991, 1996), Mitchell (2003), and Young (1990), Brickfields residents sought engagements with the state and its proxies and among themselves that produced a sense of place commensurate with the history of the neighborhood and the moral understanding of proper living held by members of the community.

According to Lefebvre (2003), the right to the city implies the right to inhabit city spaces. I understand this to mean not only that individuals have the right to enter and circulate in a particular space but also that these spaces must be experienced as open and stable within the larger geography of the city. The experience of stability does not exclude change, but does imply that the pace and trajectory of change must be anticipatable and that the process is to some degree open to action initiated by the community itself. In this sense the right to the city is established through the possibility for individual urban dwellers to actualize an ethical, social, urban self through repetition or habits in relation to space. During the time of extensive transformation that took place in Brickfields, however, such a possibility was often blocked by interventions of the state and its proxies. This lack of possibility made living in Brickfields an uncertain, ambiguous experience for residents during the time that I conducted fieldwork there. The concrete attempts of members of the neighborhood to address their experience of uncertainty in relation to the law, the state, and the space of their neighborhood is the subject of this book.[5] Within this uncertain context of aggressive spatial and demographic changes driven by the modernizing efforts of the state, members of the community sought to establish their "right to the city" through discursive and practical strategies of dwelling in the space and using it on their own terms. Such ways of imagining the neighborhood serve to oppose the experience of being denied one's right to "place" through state practices that frame modes of habiting space that empower certain groups and alienate others (Lefebvre 1996, 2003).

Lefebvre's notion of right must be distinguished from the juridical or scientific concepts of "human rights" or "rights of citizenship" that are largely invested in the authoritative discourses of the state, the empirical judgments regarding normalcy and causality of science, or the orthodoxies of religion. Unlike such notions of rights "granted" based on axiomatic criteria of identity, Lefebvre's concept specifically refers to an ethics of establishing spaces that are not only ordered and safe but also allow for action and a concrete sense of being able to create an ethical life. This "right to the city" is not invested in the stable certainties of identity, but rather in the *potential* of individuals to realize an ethical self from a host of presubjective possibilities. This concept of right runs counter to the notion that the law can do justice through the careful recognition of identity and the subsequent creation of legal and subject categories that "recognize" or "allow for" difference. The "rights through recognition" model is insufficient to Lefeb-vre's concept; the self in this model is endowed with an essential nature that is understood as stable, singular and, if properly understood and cultivated, in harmony with nature and the world.

A number of anthropological works related to South and Southeast Asia elaborate existing local concepts of recognition and self that are tied neither to notions of rights or identity as it is commonly understood in the West. Strongly influenced by Clifford Geertz's description and theoriza-tion of the *slematan* community feast in Java as an essential space by which individuals can "see and be seen" and the centrality of this feast in the con-text of Javanese sociality generally (Geertz 1960), the work of James Siegel has consistently engaged everyday notions of recognition in Indonesia. Emphasizing domains where appearances are unrecognizable, uncanny, and mistrusted, Siegel has elaborated the complex notions of self, identity, and recognition that exist in Indonesia through an engagement with how Javanese domesticate the "strange" (*aneh*), how recognition and domestica-tion are critically linked in the Indonesian national context, and how de-sire and the uncanny circulate and serve to structure engagements with criminals, counterfeiters, and witches in contemporary Indonesia (Siegel 1986, 1997, 1998, 2006). Consistent in all of these works is a close engage-ment with precisely how one can form a sense of self that is experienced as unitary and moral, and that indexes oneself in relation to others in a world marked by appearances that are never in actuality singular, transparent, or whole. Siegel's definition of "identity" clarifies this point:

I have used the word "identity." I do not mean to imply, however, that identity is ever fully achieved. My view is contrary, therefore, to the stream of current thought that sees identity as achieved, negotiated, crafted, and in other ways the product of a self which, knowingly following its interests, invents itself. I think of it in the tradition of Hegel. There, to find a place of self-definition is to be thrown off-balance unless one can be convincingly self-deceiving. Identity exists only at the price of enormous confusions and contradictions. (Siegel 1997, 9)

While emphasizing the critical importance of forms of recognition, Siegel insists that appearances are never understood as given or singular in Indonesia. In my view, this perspective regarding the centrality of "seeing and being seen," even in contexts where appearances are mistrusted, mis-recognized, or not recognized at all, holds true in the Malaysian context as well. As I demonstrate in the present work, Siegel's insights regarding recognition and identity are very useful in understanding the complex social spaces that exist in urban Malaysia.

Although I largely agree with Siegel regarding identity and recognition, his emphasis on "confusion" and "contradiction" requires elaboration, particularly in light of Veena Das' recent work regarding the essential role of silence and disavowal in the context of returning to everyday life in the face of the catastrophic, the traumatic, and the unnamable (Das 2007). Bearing Das' insights in mind, Naveeda Khan has argued for a concept of the self as emergent from a realm of presubjective possibilities in her recent work regarding the complex relationships between the self, the domestic, and the everyday aspects of religious sectarianism in Pakistan; these possibilities are singularities that exist and, when brought to actualization, produce a "Self" or an "I." Strongly building on Deleuze's notion of the self as generated out of singularities that exist within a plane of immanence (Deleuze 2001), Khan argues for difference as being internal to being and highlights the critical importance of affirmative potentiality and the ability to move between these qualities in response to the world as an essential aspect of subjectivity. Thus, rather than understanding the self within the negative operations of crafting a unitary self out of perceived social norms (Mahmood 2001, 2005) or the presentation of multiple selves based on manifold everyday contexts (Ewing 1990, 1997), Khan effectively demonstrates how the multiplicity of potential selves ("impersonal, preindividual singularities" in Deleuze's terms) is neither evidence of a "split" self nor a condition to be masked or fully domesticated in relation to authoritative, disciplinary discourses (Khan 2006; see also Deleuze 1990, 1994, 2001). Building on Siegel's insights regarding identity and recognition in Indonesia, Khan's work serves to engage these issues without an emphasis on contradiction or confusion; this elaboration is crucial to my own argument here as to how the often disjointed experience of living in Brickfields was nonetheless reenfolded back into the everyday and notions of self as articulated by local residents.

What is under question in Khan's formulation is the notion that the self or the subject can arise out of a given state of the world. This is an important issue in relation to the question of rights and legal subjectivity raised earlier. "Recognition," even recognition of certain states of diversity between legal subjects, is granted according to a transcendental value assigned to the law in relation to nature and the real. This presumption gives rise to the notion of a "preestablished" harmony between justice, the law, and ethics that assumes that the law can properly order difference between stable, discrete subjects. When applied to specific ethnographic situations (such as Khan's example), Deleuze's notion of difference as internal to being casts doubt on the efficacy of analytic models that privilege recognition, as the detection and ordering of discrete subjects becomes a secondary operation in relation to the process of becoming through difference that Deleuze strongly asserts as the key to the production of self. Although diversity in the world can lead to multiple legal systems that are legitimate within frameworks of recognition, the idea of the *Law itself* as the guarantor of justice and ethical living is what is universalized and endowed with a transcendental status in models of recognition. Engaging with writers as diverse as Hume, Kant, and Sacher-Masoch, Deleuze consistently reminds us that we should never confuse the Law with justice or ethical forms of life and raises the uncomfortable possibility that it is *impossible* for the Law, purely by virtue of its own operation, to do justice (Deleuze 1989b, 1991b, 1997).

Considering Deleuze's consistent antagonism towards orthodoxy and opinion, it is unusual at first glance that he would turn to concepts of immanent belief and what he termed "nondogmatic" images of thought as an alternative. For some, this turn has left Deleuze open to the charge that his philosophy is "outerworldly" and out of touch with the "real world" (Hallward 2006). To the contrary, I assert that through a careful consideration of Deleuze's concepts in relation to the ethnographic evidence that constitutes the bulk of this book, such concepts provide a rich basis for the analysis of empirical data generated out of concrete engagements with this "real world." At the center of my engagement with Deleuze is his understanding of *belief* as immanent and always linked to a "brain/body/culture" nexus of experience; this is a critically important insight in relation to understanding the transformations that took place in Brickfields over the two-year period that I lived and actively conducted research in the neighborhood. I maintain that this specific example (including the analytic frameworks deployed within the study) has a generalizable value in relation to other similar sites and situations. Foregrounding belief in the manner in which I do in this book is as essential for secular modes of living as it is for the religious. For members of a specific religious faith, belief is an essential aspect in formulating an ethical life according to the will of the Divine; for secularists belief is crucial in that knowledge alone cannot make the world knowable or livable in a real sense. The internal character of this belief is the same in that its primary object in both cases is possible modes of existence in a world of difference and change (Deleuze 1986, 1989a; Marrati 2003).

This capability to act is certainly dependent upon an ordered present but also requires the creation of spaces where individuals possess the means to imagine future life and action. In Brickfields, the problem for local residents was not just that their legal rights or physical persons were being literally violated in the present, but rather that the transformation of the space had shattered the link between present experience and the possibility of future action. Not able to believe in Brickfields as their place in the world, residents lacked "resistance to the present" (Deleuze and Guattari 1994). Understood within Lefebvre's framework, the concrete outcome of this phenomenon was that Brickfields residents were largely denied their right to the city during the period of intensive transformation of the neighborhood between 2000 and 2002.

The transformation of the space of Brickfields was undertaken as a way of making the neighborhood safer, more orderly, more closely integrated with the rest of Kuala Lumpur, and better overall for its residents. The final outcome of these changes remains to be seen. It is clear, however, that the strategies deployed by the state concretely worked to rupture the sensory-motor links between Brickfields residents and their world in the present. Change always entails rupture; however, largely excluded from formal processes of law, state planning, and municipal decision making, Brickfields residents struggled to create other links with their world out of the radical, aggressive change that was taking place around them. Life in Brickfields was often intolerable for its residents during the period that I conducted fieldwork in the neighborhood. Bearing witness to changes that were sudden, unexpected, and perceived to be total, this sense of the intolerable arose from the fact that the trajectory of change and the potential for life in the new Brickfields was often literally unthinkable. For land developers, city planners, and government ministers, the process of reform was linked to a teleology of progress and "the Brickfields to come"; local residents generally had no access to this *telos* to be reached, despite official proclamations after the fact as to the future of the area. It was not enough for everyday life to be understood and lived through authoritative institutional discourses; life must be thinkable for individual residents. The "unthinkability" of Brickfields often prevented residents from forming an image of the world that allowed for action based on knowable relations between oneself and others within sensible horizons of possible meaning. Such images of livable configurations must engage authoritative institutional discourses but are not necessarily the logical outcome of such discourses. In Brickfields the state, the law, and various religious institutions did not always produce vectors within everyday life that allowed for action or agency on the part of individual subjects, often liquidating the sensible reality of the world for those caught in it (Deleuze 1991a). The outcome was *not* that Brickfields residents came to believe that they lived in a "fantasy"; individuals did not lack information in regard to the present. Rather, the problem was that they could not imagine this new world as a world of possibility or becoming and therefore could not form an image of this world that they could *believe* in.

Belief in this context is not tied in an absolute sense to religious orthodoxies, practices, or a transcendent divine sphere, although as I demonstrate in the final chapter the supernatural world remains a strong factor within this general notion. Nor is belief in this sense an articulation of a transcendent project of a revolutionary world to come. The object of belief in this context is *the world itself*. This belief is not invested in grand tropes of salvation or deliverance, but rather in the ability to establish, sense, and live through concrete links to the world. An ability to imagine a future remains important in that individuals must believe that they can, in the face of transformation, forge new links with their world in response to change or difference.

Understanding belief in the manner that I am advocating requires a revised engagement with the issue of how institutions normally associated with secularism, such as the law or the state, come into play in everyday life. William E. Connolly, in reference to the work of Talal Asad, has described this revision of the "brain/ body/culture" network[6] as follows:

[T]he practices in which we participate continue to be organized in circuits between institutional arrangements and lived layers of human embodiment, but many secularists, theologians, and anthropologists interpret such practices within a cognitive framework that ignores them, diminishes their importance, or reduces them to modes of cultural manipulation that could in principle be surpassed. . . . [M]any still construe ritual to be only a mechanism through which beliefs are portrayed and symbolized rather than a medium through which embodied habits, dispositions, sensibilities, and capacities of performance are consolidated. (Connolly 2006, 77)

My aim in this book is to address the issues that Connolly and others raise regarding the "fugitive circuit" that exists between embodied, visceral belief and the institutional configurations that shape, limit, and depend upon this circuit. *No* domain of human social life is "free" of belief, "above" faith, or can operate outside of this fugitive circuit linking experience of the world, thought, and the inevitability of change in the world at large (Asad 2003; Connolly 2005). I am not arguing that secularism does not exist as an organizing concept that operates concretely in the domains of everyday life; rather, I hope to call into question simple or fixed binaries between "secularism" and "religion" or "belief" that obscure the subtle, numerous, necessary connections that cut across each domain and link them to one another in everyday life and practice.

In this spirit, the revised understanding of the role of belief in everyday life that I am advocating does not seek to exclude or marginalize organized religious belief or concrete engagements with the supernatural and the Divine from the analysis. The final chapter of this book shifts the basis of this engagement away from a discussion of immanent belief in everyday life and engages how a Malaysian state that sought to explicitly make Islam a central aspect of rule shaped the everyday practices of a predominantly Malaysian Tamil Hindu urban community. This chapter directly addresses the specific outcomes of introducing an overt form of belief into the realm of modern governance. Dealing primarily with interventions made by the Malaysian state and civic actors regarding the problem posed by the presence of a number of unregistered Hindu temples in Brickfields, I contextualize these specific events with an analysis of how Islam's role in governance in Malaysia provided limited avenues of engagement and agency for these temples with agents of the state. Rather than quarantining faith within private domains, the explicit introduction of belief into governance produced unforeseen consequences both in terms of how non-Muslim faiths were present in the public sphere and in relation to how belief was lived at the everyday level. For Muslims and non-Muslims alike, "believing" became an essential aspect in the formation of a life within sensible realms of possibility and meaning, and operated as an important aspect of public life. By (re)introducing belief as an allowable basis for ethical life and practice, the possibilities for engaging the state and forming ethical lives at the local level often exceeded the formal boundaries of authoritative discourse regarding proper or "true" belief articulated by the state or religions institutions.

Efforts to locate Islam as a primary moral basis for rule in Malaysia did *not* automatically result in the rejection of techno-rational modes of governance, nor did these initiatives necessitate the rejection of laws and institutions associated with secular governance. To the contrary, efforts to morally ground the law and the practices of the state in Islam required an active mode of engagement with secularist understandings of proper governance. Brickfields residents struggled with competing notions of morality, justice, and the Good in understanding themselves and living ethically. The state itself faced a similar problem in seeking to reconcile a desire to "become modern" while also investing its authority to pursue such strategies within the larger domain of a divine sovereignty.

The struggle over the introduction of Islamic concepts to governance turned on the issue of how Islam could legitimately function as *authoritative* within larger discourses of governmentality.[7] Suspicion regarding this issue was not restricted to non-Muslim communities, as many Malays would openly support the notion that "Islam" was an appropriate source of legitimacy and practical techniques for the government, while also struggling with the fact that the orthodox governmental discourse of Islam generally cast their own specific beliefs regarding the world into question (Peletz 2002). Following Asad, I argue that issues of authoritative discourses related to religion and ethical life must always refer to complex internal structures that engage multiple material domains (Asad 1993, 2006). I understand such engagement as a set of possibilities that emerge out of what Asad calls "the somatic processes that authoritatively bind persons to one another, of discourse as a physical process" (Asad 2006).

Everyday practice, ethics, and belief together constitute vectors of living not only though authoritative institutional discourses but also through an experiential sense of the world as perceived by individuals. Inspired by Deleuze's concept of immanent belief, I seek to understand how individuals are able to produce a unitary image of *their* world that can be believed and is essential for the production of ethical life and selves (Deleuze 1990, 2001). In other words, how is it that belief itself comes to be a defining factor in the creation of ethical subjects and spaces of living in urban Malaysia?

The Significance of the Malaysian Case

Recent work on globalization and the production of the local constructively addresses the complex relation between diasporic communities and concepts of "homeland" (Appadurai 1996; Bhabha 1994; Comaroff 1997; Comaroff and Comaroff 1997; Hannerz 1992; Harvey 1989; King 1997; Sassen 2001). In particular, the concept of *global flow* as a mode of disrupting primordial notions of culture and practice is particularly useful for understanding the effects of mobility that have their roots in colonial histories. As articulated by Appadurai and others, globalization has created new conditions of "neighborliness" that are often framed by "a new set of global disjunctures" (Appadurai 1996, 29–41). In this body of work, the concept of the local is understood as *translocality* (Comaroff 1997), and attends to the specific ways in which any local situation will always indicate a world beyond itself. While this is a very productive way of linking colonial legacies with the processes of the modern state, it deploys concepts that are not sufficiently fine tuned to capture the distinct ways in which different kinds of mobility translate into distinctive practices and possibilities for action in the present for individuals and communities. The transformation of Brickfields generated a great deal of mobility and instability. Much of this movement, however, took place within the neighborhood or the city itself and did not entail the transnational flow of bodies at the scale that has been observed in other minority communities in Malaysia (Ang 1993; Chan and Chiang 1994; Nonini 1997; Nonini and Ong 1997; Ong 1999).

Understanding Brickfields as a translocal space brings us to my second point regarding the ethnography of postcolonial states. In particular, the complex interactions between the Malaysian state and the Hindu temples in Brickfields that I explore in the final chapter of this book require a revised understanding of the relationship between religion, the law, and urban governmentality in Malaysia. By focusing on the experience of Brickfields as an example of urban life and transformation that one can find throughout Malaysia and, to some degree, within urban Asia generally, I seek to bring into focus the variable ways in which Malaysians, both Muslim and non-Muslim, deal with social and religious difference and issues regarding the creation of a public life that is simultaneously modern and spiritual. Chakrabarty argues that social science has tended to relegate religious life to an epiphenomenal status that primarily designates religion as a private concern (Chakrabarty 2000; see also Euben 1999). An ethnographic consideration of religion, law, and urban governance in the transformation of Brickfields, coupled with Deleuze's concepts regarding belief and being, allows us to extend Chakrabarty's general insights to a context in which a state self-consciously seeks to ground its techniques of governmentality within Islamic belief and practice.

The Malaysian case is significant in regard to issues of law, governance, and religion because during the past thirty years the state has experimented with a version of modernist Islam that goes beyond the limited territorial expanse of the nation (Peletz 2002). During the years that Dr. Mahathir Mohamad was prime minister (1981–2003), Malaysia successfully represented itself internationally as a viable alternative to Western-style development. Due to the effective citation of Islam as the foundation for a progressive, modernizing mode of Asian governance, the generalizable significance of the Malaysian case is evident in recent scholarship regarding "Muslim modernities" (Eickelman and Piscatori 1996; Hefner 2000; Mehmet 1990) or "Asian modernities" (Englund and Leach 2000; Nonini and Ong 1997; Rofel 1999). By placing a non-Muslim Malaysian community at the center of my ethnographic discussion, I take the issues in a direction not previously explored. For example, the last chapter of this book argues for the possibility that the exercise of an agency rooted in notions of Hindu spirituality was possible in a context where Islam is cited as a primary moral justification for rule. This phenomenon is significant in that it challenges the seemingly bedrock notion in neo-Kantian theories of the state and of the law which presume that the only possibility for ethical agency as legal subjects lay in a recognition of difference in public life rooted in the secular, practical reason of the modern citizen. The claims articulated by these temples specifically as Hindus (rather than simply as citizens) and their ambiguous recognition by a state that often defines itself as Islamic complicates normative understandings regarding belief and governmentality alike. Most accounts of predominantly Muslim states barely mention the material situation of non-Muslim subjects, preferring to limit their analyses to what is stated in the *Qur'an* and formally codified in the *Shari'a* (Eickelman and Piscatori 1996; Zaman 2002). I seek to articulate the ways in which such a state recognizes (rather than simply annihilates) religious difference. This approach does not presume a binary opposition between the "secular" West and the "religious" Muslim Other. Scholars such as William Connolly and Diana Eck have shown that despite the constitutional provision for the separation of church and state in North America, religion continues to play an important role in public life (Connolly 1999, Eck 2001). Conversely, modes of governance that are linked to conceptions of Islam are not hermetically sealed from either ideas or desires that have their roots in Western modernity (Asad 1993, 2003; Devji 2005; de Vries 2001; Euben 1999; Majid 2000). As Connolly (1999, 2002) argues, the ideal of a secular public cannot be sustained as either an elemental characteristic of Western modernity or as an essential marker of difference in the ways that arguments about "clashing civilizations" tend to posit (Huntington 1996). The Malaysian example serves to problematize the assumption of a radical opposition between a secular West and a fundamentalist Islam.

Setting—Brickfields, Kuala Lumpur, Malaysia

Brickfields is located due south of downtown Kuala Lumpur, adjacent to Chinatown and Kampung Attap to the north, Bangsar to the west, Taman Seputeh to the east, and the Mid-Valley Megamall to the south. Consisting of roughly five square miles and with a population of 11,659, the neighborhood has the following commonly accepted boundaries: the Klang River (east), Jalan Tun Sambanthan (south), Jalan Bangsar (west) and Jalan Damansara (north and west).[8] Although the borders of any urban neighborhood are by their nature ambiguous, any reference to "Brickfields" in this work generally refers to the area within these boundaries.

Historically, Brickfields has been strongly identified with Malaysian Indian communities, particularly Tamils and Ceylonese.[9] The common-sense belief that Indians overwhelmingly populated Brickfields, however, was misleading. Although the area's largest population is the Malaysian Indian community, Brickfields has never been completely dominated demographically or culturally by this ethnic group. In strict numerical terms, the figures from the three censuses compiled since 1980 clearly illustrate the ethnic diversity of the neighborhood:

While the proportional size of the Malay and Chinese communities has been shrinking since 1980, the percentage for the Indian community has

TABLE I

Population by ethnic group, Brickfields

Year	Malay[a]	%	Chinese	%	Indian	%	Other	%	Non-citizen[b]	%	Total
1980	3,779	25	5,521	36	5,888	38	184	1	—	—	15,372
1991	4,081	29	4,096	29	5,142	37	122	1	617	4	14,058
2000	2,726	23	2,885	25	4,371	38	156	1	1,521	13	11,659

SOURCE: Ministry of Population Statistics, Office of the Prime Minister of Malaysia. All percentages are approximate.
[a] In the 1991 and 2000 censuses the category "Malay" was separate from the category "Other Bumiputera." Non-Malay bumiputera primarily refer to tribal groups (orang asli) who are culturally distinguished from Malays, although they are formally equal to Malays under the law. Since their numbers in Brickfields were negligible (70 in 1991, 100 in 2000), and because they are legally considered an equivalent group as Malays, I collapsed their numbers into the "Malay" category for this table.
[b] Non-citizens are not categorized by reported ethnic identity or country of origin. In the 1980 census there was no distinction made between "others" who were Malaysian citizens and those who did not hold Malaysian citizenship.

remained constant. Despite these decreasing numbers, both communities were substantially represented in the neighborhood, with the numbers of Chinese residents in Brickfields nearly equal to those from the Indian community as recently as 1980. What is striking is the fact that, in real numbers, the overall population of Brickfields had decreased by nearly 25 percent since 1980, reflecting the large-scale relocation of unregistered residents out of the neighborhood in recent years. Although my interlocutors nearly unanimously reported that Brickfields was becoming more crowded, the area was in fact being depopulated. The one group that showed a significant increase in numbers was that of noncitizens, reflecting both the presence of outside experts and workers affiliated with the development projects being constructed at the time, and the increased presence of an international community in Brickfields.

Organization of the Work

This book is divided into two parts. Part I, consisting of Chapters 1 and 2, details the historical context of the situation in Brickfields and Kuala Lumpur during the period that I conducted fieldwork there. Part II of this work, made up of Chapters 3, 4, and 5, contains the ethnographic findings of my research and my interlocking arguments regarding place, law, experience, and belief in relation to everyday urban life in Malaysia and the outcomes of radical change for Brickfields residents due to modernizing development projects.

The first chapter provides a summary of the prewar history of Brick-fields and the development of the area as a distinct neighborhood in Kuala Lumpur, presented in the context of the development of Kuala Lumpur as the capital of colonial Malaya. This chapter asserts that Brickfields was the outcome of social, political, and economic forces that generated and defined particular social groups that then articulated a variety of claims on the city and the neighborhood. The multiple understandings and uses of the urban space in colonial Malaya are summarized in this chapter, with careful attention given to how conflicts over the proper form of the city arose and how these conflicts were addressed by each of these groups. Highlighting how urban space was a contested terrain both in terms of colonial ideologies of proper social organization and the local meanings generated through the seemingly mundane practices of the everyday, the early history of Brickfields and Kuala Lumpur highlights the practical nature of everyday life in the colonial city.

Chapter 2 provides a context for understanding the techniques of city planning and the governance of urban space, the experience of the law, and the role of religion in the transformation of Brickfields during the years 2000–2002 that is the subject of Part II of this book. This chapter summarizes two historical processes that have transformed the character of urban life and governance in Malaysia: the state of emergency that existed in Malaya between 1948 and 1960[10] and the evolving efforts throughout the twentieth century to make Islam more central to public life. By recognizing each of these processes as moments of social and political crisis that demanded the establishment of new forms of relatedness and ethical living, Chapter 2 establishes the ground by which we can understand the divergent responses of the state and the Brickfields community to issues of urban order and moral good that emerged as central themes during the period that I conducted fieldwork in the neighborhood.

In Chapter 3 I describe the complex relationships between the state, law, and local practice that existed in Brickfields during a time of radical change that occurred due to state-sponsored urban development projects that were under way between November 2000 and October 2002. I argue that this transformation revealed a gap between the abstract rule of law and the concrete experience of the law by local subjects. The issue for Brickfields residents in the face of aggressive transitions in their daily lives was that of formulating a response to these changes that allowed for the possibility of forming ethical lives in the context of the transformation that was under way. The speed of the changes taking place and the relative exclusion of residents from formal domains of law and politics created a situation where Brickfields inhabitants often experienced the space as radically unstable and struggled to respond to a world that they could perceive, but simultaneously had a difficult time believing was real, particularly in relation to the possibility for action and agency in everyday life. This skepticism was not cognitive in the literal sense, but moral. Articulated as a desire for recognition according to broadly understood principles of justice and what were believed to be the promised guarantees of the law, these attempts to respond were often framed around anticipating events that threatened to negate local principles of justice and personhood and to generate a public space that was indeterminate and illegible for many who lived there.

Drawing upon the complex understandings of place and the practices entailed in inhabiting local spaces detailed in the preceding chapter, Chapter 4 explores the ways in which Brickfields residents, faced with the possibility of displacement, erasure, and exclusion, worked to constitute a sense of self and community through engaging a set of abstractly articulated figures of personhood. The figures that I identify, the *stranger*, the *counterfeiter*, and the *gangster*, were generated from a number of intersecting sites, including the Malaysian state, the popular media, and the discourses of self and community that circulated at the local neighborhood level. These figures, images of thought as to how the local concretely existed, provided a means by which Brickfields residents could understand events that shaped their everyday lives. These figures were objects of belief generated outside of the discourses of the state or religion, and often diverged from these authoritative discourses. Functioning as ambiguous relays between perception and action, these figures produced the possibility for individual residents to form mental images of Brickfields as a concrete space and imagine the possibility of ethical life within the neighborhood. I argue that the figures of strangers and counterfeiters gave a "face" to perceived threats to the community that were otherwise difficult to identify concretely. In contrast to this, the generalized, stereotypical figure of the gangster was the one most often associated with the neighborhood by outsiders. Although also a figure through which Brickfields residents sought to establish and understand relatedness, the gangster required local residents to engage how others characterized "them" and how these images of their "place" in turn structured that place and the possibilities for those who lived there. By considering these three figures in an ethnographic context Chapter 4 seeks to "rethink difference through connection" and establish the central place of belief in the formation of ethical forms of urban life.

Chapter 5 concerns interventions made by Malaysian state and civic actors regarding several unregistered Hindu temples in Brickfields during the years 2000–2002. These events are discussed in the context of how state efforts to make Islam more central to Malaysian public life provided certain avenues of recognition and agency for these temples, through their interactions with agents of the state and indirectly affiliated proxies such as educational and Hindu religious organizations. The problem of belief in everyday life remains a central aspect in this final chapter, shifting from the general necessity of belief in the world that is discussed in Chapters 3 and 4 to the unintended consequences of the explicit recognition of Islam as a legitimate basis for governance by the Malaysian state. I maintain in this chapter that the Malaysian government articulated a clear interest in the "proper" practice of Hinduism and the formation of a public life that was in accord with its wider notions of modernity and morality, and argue that the state's understanding of its own Islamic modernity created the possibility of articulating a ethical public life that provided a certain public legitimacy, if only partial, to non-Muslim modes of religious belief and practice.

Fieldwork

The findings of this ethnography are based upon fourteen months of field research that was conducted for this project during two periods of residence in Brickfields. Survey work for the project was conducted during November and December 2000 and the extended period of field research and data collection took place between October 2001 and September 2002. Ninety ethnographic interviews with fifty-three different interview subjects were completed during this period. The duration of these interviews varied, lasting from one hour to, in an extreme case, nine hours. When possible, a second interview was held and in several cases I conducted numerous interviews with the same subjects during the period of field research. These figures do not include numerous meetings and ceremonies attended, informal conversations, or other activities where I was a participant. These public events were nonetheless key sites of data collection and were recorded in field notes and though other modes of evidence collection, including video recording where appropriate.

Most of the interviews conducted for this project, particularly the initial interviews with individual members of the Brickfields community, were carried out in public settings. This was in keeping with the established social rhythms of the neighborhood, in that nearly all informal social contacts between friends, neighbors, and colleagues would happen in local tea shops, eateries, and food stalls. The marked local preference for conversing in public spaces required me to approach each interview with a flexibility that would allow me to follow the interview protocols that I had established in advance while also taking into account the specific sites in which individual interlocutors preferred to sit down and talk. In this context it was often difficult to predict if my interlocutor would be alone or with friends, how long I had to conduct the interview, and if it would be possible to broach sensitive topics of discussion in these settings. In most cases these variables did not, in my view, preclude frank discussion, although in nearly every case I would attempt to conduct a second, private interview in the home of the interlocutor or in some other private setting. After the initial interview most of my interlocutors consented to a second, more private interview. It was rare, however, for my interview subjects to consent to the private interviews without having met in public first.

My own experience in meeting and interviewing Brickfields residents is reflected in the theoretical frameworks and conclusions that constitute the body of this book in two ways. First, local understandings of community were explicitly linked to forms of social space that allowed for regular informal contacts in the context of eating, drinking, shopping, and generally circulating through the space at one's own pace and on foot (*jalan-jalan*, which roughly translates as "strolling" or "walking around"). As it was common for individuals or entire families to spend time every day in such spaces for the purpose of meeting others socially, my requests for interviews were often folded into the typical rhythm of the neighborhood. The established social pattern would often emerge as an explicit point of conversation during my interviews, in that efforts to reorganize the space of Brickfields around KL Sentral and KL Monorail were understood as threats to this informal mode of socializing.

Although seldom articulated as directly as the first point, I understand the second reason for this form of contact as the necessity of "seeing and being seen." Although I seldom encountered open suspicion or hostility in regard to the research that I was conducting, it was nevertheless important for my interlocutors that their contacts with me could not be coded as something fully "private" or as encounters that were happening "behind closed doors." Brickfields residents consistently had a well-formed image of who a social scientist was and what sort of work such people did and, in a context of change driven by the opinions and studies of experts who were largely inaccessible to area inhabitants, it was very important for my own contacts and activities in the neighborhood to be open and observable to the community at large. As this inaccessibility was widely understood as a form of injustice due to its failure to address the community, it was crucial that my methods and activities in the area did not inadvertently replicate this felt neglect or unfairness.

Although the expectation that most of my initial contacts with interlocutors would be in public places required rethinking certain methodological strategies that were part of the original research design of the project, this mode of engagement proved to be advantageous in a number of ways. One clear benefit is that the openness of most of my data collection allowed me to interview a roughly even number of men and women for this project. Meeting in public places and oftentimes in small groups allowed me, as a male researcher, to contact and interview women without placing potential female subjects in awkward or impossible situations socially. This is not to say that gender played no role in the course of my research; to the contrary, it was still apparent that even follow-up interviews with female subjects often could not be one-on-one encounters (as my interview with Zaina and her friend Najwa in Chapter 3 illustrates). However, as my contacts with male interlocutors often followed the same pattern, gender difference did not emerge as an insurmountable obstacle in the course of my research.

Interestingly, for the women surveyed for this project, gender difference did not consistently emerge as a separate theme in their narratives of how notions of community, law, and justice were experienced in the context of urban life in Brickfields. In part this is certainly due to the fact that the research was not originally conceived as a project centered on gender difference, and it stands to reason that a framework that more explicitly highlighted gender would yield a different result. However, in seeking a sample where female subjects were accurately represented in terms of numbers, I did allow for the possibility of a gendered dimension in the context of the experience of the urban that I sought to investigate; surprisingly, a consistent articulation of how life in Brickfields was different for women than for men did not clearly emerge in the narratives and data that I was able to collect.

All of the interviews for this project were conducted in either English or *Bahasa Malaysia* (Malay language). Often, as is often the case in everyday conversation, both languages were in use, although one nearly always tended to predominate over the other. My approach regarding which language to choose in conducting a particular interview was to deploy the language the interlocutor sought to use in conversing with me. I would always make it clear that the interview could take place in either Malay or English; as English remains widely spoken in everyday contexts in Brickfields, many of my interviews were conducted in this language. In only one instance did I interview a subject through the use of a translator, and this was due to the fact that the person who introduced me to this individual "felt" that he would be most comfortable speaking Tamil. As it turned out, this particular person was fully conversant in Malay as well and our subsequent contacts were conducted in this language and without the use of the translator.

Although most of my ethnographic data was collected in Brickfields itself, I did conduct a number of interviews outside of the neighborhood. These interviews were primarily with government officials, political and religious leaders, and property developers who had a direct stake in the area. These interviews took place in a more formal register than those conducted in Brickfields itself and most often this form of engagement did not allow for follow-up interviews or informal contacts outside of the context of the interview itself. Given the direct relevance of the data gleaned from these engagements, I have included these interviews within my overall pool. Interviews with local academics, reporters, lawyers, and other experts regarding urban life in Malaysia and the changes that were occurring in Brickfields inform the organization of this book and its conclusions but are not included in numbers cited above.

Basic population and household survey data was obtained from the Office of Population Research and Statistics, Government of Malaysia, based on census data collected by that office. Primary and secondary source materials were collected throughout the period of research, including government reports and studies, studies sponsored by private agencies, books, monographs, theses, media reports, private writings, photographs, and other related materials. A partial list of sites where secondary data was collected includes the Dewan Bandaraya Kuala Lumpur (City Hall), Perpustakaan Universiti Malaya (Library of the University of Malaya), Arkib Negara Malaysia (National Archive of Malaysia), and the headquarters of the KL Monorail Corporation.

The Founding of Brickfields and the
Prewar Development of Kuala Lumpur

Introduction

The aim of this chapter is to provide a brief history of Brickfields and of the development of the area as a distinct neighborhood in the city in the context of the founding and growth of prewar Kuala Lumpur. By examining the processes through which Kuala Lumpur was established as the capital of colonial Malaya, this chapter hopes to show how neighborhoods such as Brickfields acquired their own identity within the city. Of particular concern in this narrative are the ways in which the urban environment was differentially understood and inhabited by the colonial authorities and other social groups. This chapter will provide a summary of the multiple understandings and uses of the urban space in colonial Malaya, paying close attention to how conflicts over what constituted the proper form of the city arose and how these conflicts were addressed by each of these groups. Framing the early history of Brickfields and Kuala Lumpur in this way turns our attention to the practical nature of everyday life in the colonial city, highlighting the space of the urban as a contested terrain both in terms of colonial ideologies of proper social organization and the local meanings generated through the seemingly mundane practices of the everyday.

Since the 1960s theorists of urban development have sought to establish frameworks that distinguish the development of colonial cities from classic conceptions of the urban that broadly privilege "preindustrial/industrial" or "sacred city/market city" dichotomies[1] (Forbes 1996; Sjoberg 1960, 1965). Scholars such as David Simon, Ronald J. Horvath, and Terence G. McGee observed at that time that classic theories of urbanization did not take into account the force and impact of colonialism when applied to so-called Third World cities. While recognizing the diversity of forms that the colonial cities could take, these scholars articulated a notion of urban development in colonial contexts that attempted to account for the relations between the social and functional features of these spaces and their role in the establishment and maintenance of colonial rule (Horvath 1969; King 1990; McGee 1967; Simon 1984). In her survey of this emergent literature pertaining to colonial cities, Brenda S.A. Yeoh identifies three characteristics particular to the colonial city that are commonly cited by these theories: (1) the racial, cultural, social, and religious pluralism characteristic of colonial cities, (2) the presence of a system of social stratification distinct from that associated with the class structures of preindustrial and industrial cities in the West, and (3) the concentration of social, economic, and political power in the hands of a racially distinct colonizing group (Yeoh 1996, 1–3). In general terms, all three of these characteristics were present in colonial Kuala Lumpur. From its founding in the 1870s the city has been home to a diverse population of immigrant Chinese and Indian communities, small Malay enclaves, and British expatriates (Adnan 1997; Gullick 1993, 2000). These populations were subject to a system of social stratification rooted in nineteenth-century understandings of race that defined the social and economic terrain under which each of these groups lived and worked. Finally, although the British instituted a system of indirect rule that granted formal sovereignty to the Malay sultans, actual governance was largely in the hands of the British residents, the colonial bureaucracy, and the European economic interests operating in the colony.

While this framework is useful in formulating an analytic understanding of the organization of Kuala Lumpur as an urban configuration, its usefulness must be qualified in light of the assumptions regarding the nature of power in colonial societies and the relative stability of social categories that are evident in its logic. In particular, the assumption that an overwhelming asymmetry of power existed between stable groups of colonized and colonizers that allowed for the colonizers to largely "create" colonial cities and towns is complicated considerably in the case of Kuala Lumpur. There is ample evidence that British government officials and city planners *imagined* an urban landscape ordered by segregated living quarters, racially defined economic functions, and separate social worlds. Just as clearly, local imaginations of community, justice, and order emerged as equally critical factors in the material development of Kuala Lumpur as a city and Brickfields as a distinct neighborhood within that city.

The struggle between the colonial power and the various categories of inhabitants to define people and places is key to understanding the creation of Brickfields. Colonial power in Malaya was exercised through the imagination and the attempted imposition of definitional categories related to the social and the spatial that sought to order both public and private domains. Yet this power could not be exercised in an unbridled way. In more recent times scholars, following Foucault's insights regarding power, discourse, and discipline (Foucault 1977, 1991), have argued that local arenas of action must also be considered in understanding the development and regulation of colonial cities (Ferguson 1999; Holston 1989; Low 1999; Mitchell 1989; Rabinow 1989; Yeoh 1996). As with other colonial cities, the microprocesses of everyday life were critical factors in the formation of urban space in Kuala Lumpur.

The physical environment of Kuala Lumpur held different uses, meanings, and interpretations for the various communities who came to live there. As such, there was no absolutely dominant or privileged discourse that operated to totally define or dominate the space of the city. Spaces like that of colonial Kuala Lumpur must be seen as polydiscursive, with the operating discourses in constant flux due to everyday habitation by ordinary people who may read different meanings and usages into what is nominally the "same" built environment. Kuala Lumpur spatially reflected the desire of the colonial state to create a segmented, utilitarian space that divided the city into racial and economic domains according to prevailing understandings of proper colonial social organization (Dick and Rimmer 2003). The ability to successfully manifest this ideal urban environment was clearly linked to both the functional and symbolic aims of the British colonial empire. However, by the 1920s the continued "failure" to realize these ideals generated a great deal of anxiety and pessimism regarding the colonial project in Malaya. This "failure" clearly demonstrates that this ideal colonial landscape was never fully accepted by those who inhabited neighborhoods such as Brickfields and that, through the articulation of local notions of community and relatedness, the everyday social practice in the city challenged the idealized plan. Spaces such as Brickfields were thus never entirely subject to colonial control; on the other hand, Brickfields residents could not simply ignore the pressures generated by colonial attempts to order the space. Rather, the development of Brickfields and Kuala Lumpur demonstrates the tensions, negotiations, compromises, and conflicts that existed between social groups over time in prewar Malaya (Andaya and Andaya 1982; Blythe 1969; Butcher 1979; Cowan 1961; Gullick 1993, 2000; Heussler 1981; Roff 1994; Sandhu 1969).

Frank Swettenham, Yap Ah Loy, and the Founding of Kuala Lumpur

Brickfields has always been strongly linked to the global. Without the combined forces of British colonial power, the capital and efforts of Chinese entrepreneurs, and the labor of emigrants from South India, the place would not exist in the form it does today. Despite its contemporary reputation as a forgotten, "closed" area, Brickfields materially owes its existence to the desires of "strangers"—desires to cleanse, to build, to order, and particularly to make money. The story of Brickfields is not simply that of an autonomous community, as the area has always been an integral part of larger processes, schemes, and conflicts. Yet, as I will demonstrate in this chapter, it was precisely these wide-ranging historical processes that made the experience of Brickfields as a *local* space all the more intense for early neighborhood residents.

For all I have heard of Mr. Swettenham he will do his work well wherever he is. Is he however exactly the man for Salangore? [*sic*] Might he not drive the coach a little too fast?
—Lord Kimberley, Colonial Secretary, 1882

The Captain China is as impecunious as ever, he is a speculative, energetic and enterprising man . . . he must work.
—Bloomfield Douglas, Resident of Selangor, 1878

At first glance, it is difficult to imagine a more unusual partnership than that of Frank Swettenham and Yap Ah Loy. The former, born "outside Belper in Derbyshire," educated at St. Peter's School in York, and finding himself from 1871 attached to an evolving Malayan colonial bureaucracy, was an ambitious young officer with a passion for Malay culture and a taste for broad "civilizing" projects enacted in the name of the crown. The latter, a poor Hakka Chinese laborer who had immigrated to Malaya to work in the tin mines, had risen through a combination of contacts and guile to the position of Captain China and was primarily interested in maintaining the viability (not to mention the profitability) of his position. In the fluid social terrain of late nineteenth-century Malaya these two men were brought together by circumstance and discovered a surprising degree of overlap in their ambitions. Through the joint efforts of these two men Kuala Lumpur was established as the preeminent city in the Malay peninsula, and Brickfields came into being as a distinct neighborhood within the town. J.M. Gullick describes Yap Ah Loy as follows:

Yap Ah Loy was a typical example of the Chinese immigrants who came to seek their fortunes in the Malay States. Born in the Kwangtung province of China in 1837, he came of a peasant family of the Hakka community, which was itself divided . . . into distinct, and often hostile, "clans" (Ah Loy was a Fei Chew Hakka). At the age of seventeen, he had come to Malacca, and thence had moved on to the mines at Lukut and, after that, in Sungei Ujong (Negri Sembilan). Originally a laborer, like the rest, his ability had gradually raised him to leadership. He was at first one of the *panglima*, who were the bodyguards and assistants of a Captain China in control of a particular mining area. [B]y 1868 he had become Captain China of Kuala Lumpur. (Gullick 2000, 13)

A fuller account of Yap Ah Loy's remarkable life is beyond the scope of this work (see Middlebrook and Gullick 1989). What is important to note is that by the 1880s Yap Ah Loy had been the *de facto* leader in Kuala Lumpur for well over a decade and, in his position as Captain China, controlled both the commercial and municipal spheres of the town. During his tenure Yap had weathered natural disasters and a civil war that had resulted in the repeated destruction of Kuala Lumpur. Despite this adversity the town began to prosper, and for Yap Ah Loy it was proving to be a profitable venture. Middlebrook notes that by 1880 there were 220 buildings in Kuala Lumpur and that Yap owned 64 of them outright. His holdings constituted fully two-thirds of the urban land east of the Klang River (Middlebrook and Gullick 1989, 98). Coupled with the fact that he controlled the profitable tin mines situated at the edges of Kuala Lumpur, Yap Ah Loy's influence over the town was unchallenged until he died in 1885 at the age of forty-eight.

Frank Swettenham first set foot in Malaya in 1871, arriving from England as a cadet in the then-new Straits Civil Service. After an apprenticeship in Singapore, Swettenham was dispatched to the peninsula in 1872 where he would remain in numerous capacities for the next thirty-three years. Arrogant and overachieving, Swettenham rose fast in the Civil Service and held several important positions throughout his career, including separate terms as Resident of Perak and Selangor, as Assistant Colonial Secretary of the Straits Settlements, and finally as Resident General of the Federated Malay States. In retirement Sir Frank, who was knighted by Queen Victoria in 1897, continued to serve the British government as head of a royal commission to Mauritius in 1909 and as Joint Director of the Official Press Bureau during World War I. Swettenham also remained active in Malayan affairs from afar, exercising an influence in the Colonial Office that would remain strong forty-two years after his exit from Malaya.[2] Swettenham's amazing ninety-six years of life would be read as parody if created by a novelist; his civilizing ambition, jack-of-all-trades résumé, colorful yet "correct" rapport with "the natives," corrupt land deals, suppressed sex scandals (complete with blackmail), and bitter long-term rivalries matched the archetype of the colonial pioneer ideal so closely it is hard to believe Swettenham actually existed at all.

The Origins of Brickfields

Brickfields came into being as a discrete zone within Kuala Lumpur due to a financial venture initiated by Yap Ah Loy. In the wake of the collapse of the tin market in 1876 Yap was, in Gullick's words, "energetically seeking alternative employment for his miners." One project he undertook at this time was the completion of the unfinished Damansara Road. Another was the production of bricks, originally intended for export to Singapore. Swettenham described Yap's efforts in an 1878 report:

He has established a brickfield and kiln, and has already produced a large number of excellent bricks and tiles . . . to be sent to the Singapore market . . . hitherto supplied from Hong Kong. The clay of which these tiles is made is of a peculiar quality, which enables them to be made at once thin and light, whilst they are stronger and more durable than ordinary tiles. (Gullick 2000, 23)

As an export-oriented venture, this project was a failure due to the prohibitively high cost of shipping to Singapore at the time. The undertaking did have two lasting effects, however; the area[3] came to be generally known as "Brickfields" (identified as such by 1889 on official maps),[4] and the presence of fifteen brick kilns in the area by 1886 (Selvaratnam 2002) made it possible for Swettenham to undertake his ambitious rebuilding of the entire town of Kuala Lumpur in the 1880s.

Over the objections of Bloomfield Douglas, the British Resident for Selangor, colonial officials in Singapore (including Swettenham, who was Assistant Colonial Secretary at that time) relocated the headquarters of the state government from Klang to Kuala Lumpur in March 1880. This shift was in large part due to the fact that, unlike Klang (which appeared "deserted" and "decayed" to Swettenham) Kuala Lumpur was fast becoming the commercial center of Selangor and its active tin mining operations (Butcher 1979; Dick and Rimmer 2003; Lim 1978). This move was undertaken despite the fact that Klang was the functioning port for the region and Kuala Selangor served as the traditional center of power for the local Malay community, with the Sultan of Selangor continuing to reside there even after the colonial state government decamped to Kuala Lumpur. At this early stage it was clear that commercial interests were the first priority for the colonial authorities.[5] Until the late 1870s Kuala Lumpur itself was administered directly by local Malay and Chinese headmen with little oversight by colonial officials,[6] although this situation began to change with the formation of a Mining Board in 1878 and the arrival of a colonial magistrate in Kuala Lumpur in September 1879 (Gullick 2000, 33). For the authorities in Singapore, however, these developments were not enough to "safeguard" their stake in the area and thus the relocation of the headquarters of the state government itself was undertaken the next year.

Although the advantages of the move were clear in the minds of the colonial bureaucrats in Singapore, local British administrators were skeptical. This skepticism was due to Kuala Lumpur's growing Chinese population, as the Chinese laborers were regarded by the British representatives as unruly, violent, and beyond the direct control of the colonial state. With the recent murders of the Resident of Perak and of the district officer in Pangkor (an island off the coast of Perak) fresh in their minds, local officials set out to create a physical environment that was orderly, safe, and most of all defensible.[7]

The new government staff quarters in Kuala Lumpur were built on the high ground west of the Klang River, just opposite the "native" town but separated from it by the river itself. The plan for this complex included locating the treasury and customs offices near the river with a "defensible" police station, living quarters, and the residency itself sitting on the high ground behind the present site of the Royal Selangor Club (Gullick 2000, 34). Thus colonial officials could survey the town without being too close to it and, in a worst-case scenario, retreat to Klang via the unfinished Damansara Road that ended near the site. Preoccupied with attack, Swettenham and his colleagues designed the new residency and colonial quarter in the manner of a fort.[8]

Although seemingly a minor episode in the colonial annals, the move of the colonial headquarters from Klang to Kuala Lumpur is significant in understanding both the general manner of transforming the built environment that has become routine in Malaya and also specifically to the establishment of Brickfields as a viable, discrete area within Kuala Lumpur. First, once the decision had been taken to relocate, the move was fast and accomplished along military lines, resulting in a government complex that was primarily concerned with controlling access to, and circulation within, the space of the town. Although this was one of the few instances in which the colonial officers themselves would undertake such a move, radical reordering of entire communities would become a common feature of Malayan public life during the Emergency and in the postindependence era. Second, once the move had been accomplished, it was clear that the character of the buildings themselves had been overlooked and, after the Klang structures had been reassembled on the new site in Kuala Lumpur, it was decided that the ramshackle wooden structures were neither defensible nor properly representative of the grandeur of Her Majesty's Government. The solution to this problem, in Swettenham's view, was brick.

Yap Ah Loy's failed brickfield came to play a crucial role in making Frank Swettenham's dream of an orderly and safe Kuala Lumpur a reality. Swettenham's plans were not limited to the rebuilding of key government buildings, however, and in the wake of devastating fires in January and

August 1881 he saw an opportunity to remake the entire town (Dewan Bandaraya Kuala Lumpur 1990, 12). Appointed Resident of Selangor in 1892, Swettenham decreed that a rapidly phased mandatory rebuilding project would be put into effect that would widen local roads and expand the road system between the town and the outlying mining settlements,[9] improve drainage, and replace wooden structures with ones constructed of brick.[10] In the time since the Residency had moved to Kuala Lumpur, Swettenham had grown increasingly concerned with what his biographer describes as "the filthy habits of the Kuala Lumpur residents." His remedy to the most glaring problems of refuse and sewage removal was to instruct the police to enforce ad hoc regulations drawn up by Swettenham on the spot during his personal inspections of the town (Barlow 1995, 232). But he found this remedy insufficient, and he set about rebuilding the entire town, capitalizing on his relative independence in running Selangor's affairs. The total estimated cost of the project was estimated to be $40,354 in October 1882.

Yap Ah Loy was not the only entrepreneur interested in making the bricks necessary to rebuild Kuala Lumpur. Although his brickworks had been functioning since at least 1878, those who knew of Swettenham's plans saw an opportunity to get in on the action themselves. One person who clearly tried to break Yap Ah Loy's brick monopoly was coffee planter T. Heslop Hill, who in 1883 applied for land in what became Brickfields for the purpose of building brick kilns. He also proposed to produce the bricks on contract with the government at a set price and with a two-year monopoly. It is unclear whether or not his request was granted. Swettenham himself tried to set up a brickmaking company, with the venture registered in his wife Sydney's name. This attempt was not entirely underhanded, as Swettenham applied directly to Governor Weld for permission to purchase land for this purpose. Weld granted this permission and several leases on land in Brickfields were transferred to Mrs. Swettenham on September 12, 1883. Unsurprisingly, the seller was Yap Ah Loy, and the leases he transferred to Mrs. Swettenham had only been issued to him on the very day of his transaction with the Resident (Barlow 1995, 299, 424). The suggestion of a *quid pro quo* is unmistakable, given that the major legal obstacle to Swettenham's plans was resolving the ambiguous land claims of the Captain China.[11] As with Hill's venture, it is not clear if Sydney Swettenham's brickmaking company was ever realized and if it produced bricks for the rebuilding project.

What is clear is that *someone* in the mid-1880s was producing a massive number of bricks. In early 1884 Kuala Lumpur had four brick structures. By the end of that same year that number had increased to 234. By the end of the following year homes with *attap*[12] roofs were prohibited entirely, and at the close of 1887 Kuala Lumpur had 518 brick-and-tile structures (Gullick 2000, 45). Included in Swettenham's plans was the building of a new General Hospital, an expansion of the Pauper Hospital, a new jail with quarters for the guards, a new police station (also with living quarters), and new housing accommodations for governmental department heads (Barlow 1995, 235). Building with brick also allowed for multistoried shophouses that, in turn, allowed for a greater population density and the development of the central area as a true mixed-use zone, in that most shop owners could now house their business on the first floor of their shophouse while residing upstairs. Although this development was viewed as an improvement at the time, the rapid increase in population density allowed by the standard shophouse design (including the easy partition of the overall space for use by boarders and small businesses who were willing to rent a portion of the space) would by the turn of the century become a concern for colonial officials and leading British citizens of the town.[13] In the 1880s, however, both the British and the leaders of the Chinese community in Kuala Lumpur viewed these developments favorably.[14]

The rebuilding of Kuala Lumpur was the centerpiece of a wider plan to encourage all Malayans to settle in "properly" planned and constructed towns and villages throughout the peninsula. Worrying over the fact that few recognizable towns existed in the early 1880s, Swettenham wrote:

Efforts were made to encourage the building of villages all over the country, and round the head-quarters of every district settlers congregated, small towns were laid out, shops and markets were built, and everything was done to induce the people to believe in the permanence of the new institutions. The visitor who now travels by train through a succession of populous towns, who lands at or leaves busy ports on the coast, can hardly realize the infinite trouble taken, in the first fifteen years, to coax Malays and Chinese and Indians to settle in the country, to build a better class of house than the flimsy shanties of *adobe* structure hitherto regarded as the height of all reasonable ambition. (Swettenham 1907, 239; italics in original)

Early urbanizing projects such as the one undertaken in Kuala Lumpur were simultaneously concerned with practical and "civilizational" aspects of proper public life. To achieve these goals the Resident sought to solidify his administrative staff, particularly in the Public Works Department that had been operating without a head since the previous Resident's nephew, Dominic Daly, had been unceremoniously fired from the post in the summer of 1882 due to general incompetence (Barlow 1995, 236). A.C. Norman was eventually tapped for the position. Yet the efforts undertaken in Kuala Lumpur and elsewhere throughout the peninsula to reorder the public were not part of a master plan devised in the back rooms of the Governor's office in Singapore; rather, during these early years they were a reflection of Swettenham's own ambition and notions of what an orderly, modern Malaya should be. The Resident felt that the colonial government had set up the newly installed Residents to fail, in that they were broadly charged with creating the conditions for a properly ordered public and yet were, at the same time, instructed not to interfere too directly with the minutiae of governing the states:

The Colonial Office said the Malay States were to be wheeled into line, everything was to be done on the most approved principles, and one white man was to do it, but the means to secure this desirable end were not mentioned . . . For one white man to maintain the law—something unwritten and unknown—and preserve the peace in a foreign State of which he knew very little, initiate a sound system of taxation and get it observed, develop the resources of the country, supervise the collection of revenue so as to provide means to meet all the costs of administration, and yet "not interfere more frequently or to a great extent than is necessary with the minor details of government"[15] was surely an impossible task. (Swettenham 1907, 217–218)

The former Resident and Governor's complaint regarding the impossible situation of the Residents in the 1880s concludes with the following:

[I]t is too much to expect that one white Christian will be able to impose his will upon a Muhammadan people who have never known any outside interference. To the Malay the situation was obvious, and in the silence of the night he more than once explained to me that I and the other residents were thrown out as bait by the British Government. If the Malay chiefs swallowed the bait, they would find themselves on the hook; of course, no one would worry about the bait. (Swettenham 1907, 218–219)

Swettenham's characterization, thirty years after the fact, defensively casts the Residents as tragic heroes, charged with an impossible task of reordering a stubbornly "backward" society, battling red tape and ignorance all the while in order to achieve the dream of a developed, orderly, modern Malayan society. In Swettenham's telling, the only "honorable" course available to the Residents at the time was one of principled disobedience:

It will be understood that even from the first the Residents had exercised, or tried to exercise, an influence which could not be truthfully defined as the simple offer of advice, and when, in 1878, they were warned that if they departed from the role of advisers, they would be held answerable for any trouble which might occur, they accepted the responsibility as preferable to a position of impotence and an attitude which no native in the country could have either understood or appreciated. (Swettenham 1907, 221)

Swettenham saw himself as an agent of civilization who had to deploy modern techniques of governance to reorder the society under his charge. The dithering of politicians and recalcitrance of "natives" aside, he was duty bound to create order out of "chaos," regardless of the drastic nature of some of these methods. The quasi-messianic overtones of Swettenham's thinking are undeniable, and the clearest legacy of his approach to governance in Selangor and the other Malay States is found in their cities and the persistent, sweeping attempts to reorder the built urban environment in colonial Malaya and postcolonial Malaysia throughout the twentieth century.

The ambiguous nature of British rule in these early years proved to be an advantage for someone with Swettenham's ambition. Although in 1875 he had recommended that the vague position of the Residents be solved by annexing the four Malay states that had been parties to the Pangkor Agreement, by the time Swettenham himself had become a Resident it is clear that he had shifted his position on the matter:

[C]ertainly within a short time of taking up his post in Selangor, [Swettenham] must have realized that the advantages of independence were considerable. The Resident was by then nominally answerable to the State Council. Yet this body, particularly during Swettenham's early years in Selangor, was no more than a constitutional fig-leaf. It was headed by the Sultan, who knew better than to attempt to oppose the Resident, and its members were senior Malays and Chinese, all of whom were appointed by the Sultan on the Resident's recommendation, approved by the Governor. It met infrequently, generally after the events had occurred, to provide a rubber-stamp approval for the Resident's actions. Thus during 1883, Swettenham's first full year as Resident in Selangor, it met on only one occasion. (Barlow 1995, 258)

In other words, the Resident could simultaneously usurp the arbitrary power of the Sultan while also claiming that the exercise of such power was constitutional. Swettenham, with his personal arrogance, his hatred for "red tape," his concern for the development and "well-being" of the Malays, his love for the romantic "civilizing" pioneer,[16] and his personal ambition, regarded the situation as an open door for his plans to remake Kuala Lumpur and Malay society generally. In later years this policy would come to be referred to as "indirect rule," a cornerstone of British rule in Malaya until the end of the colonial era in 1957[17] (Andaya and Andaya 1982, 172–175).

It is clear that there was a great deal at stake for Swettenham in the rebuilding of Kuala Lumpur, and before long colonial officials were offering positive assessments of the changes in the town. By the end of the 1880s the town, which had variously been described as "squalid," "dirty," and "dangerous," was now well on its way to becoming, in the words of Governor Weld, "the neatest and prettiest Chinese and Malay town" (Gullick 2000, 45). The reorganization caused a sharp upsurge in the town's population and with it the necessity to expand public services.[18] Therefore, in the context of the rebuilding of the town, Kuala Lumpur's Public Works Department (PWD) expanded both in terms of the size of its operations and workforce and in terms of the scope of its operation. As the bricks being used in the reconstruction were originating from Brickfields, most of the PWD's daily operations came to be located in the area as well, with a PWD factory, facilities for quartering the *kerbau* (buffaloes) used to pull the night soil collectors carts, and housing for the rapidly expanding PWD labor force constructed in the area during this time (Selvaratnam 2002, 251). The factory, designed by State Engineer C.E. Spooner and opened in 1894, contained a timber depot, brick and tile kilns, and metal and woodworking departments. Most of the bricks and prefabricated metalwork required for government building projects until 1910 were made in this factory,[19] and although its exact location within Brickfields remains a mystery it is generally presumed to have been situated on Brickfields Road at the current site of the YMCA and the (now vacant) Railway recreation ground[20] (Kuala Lumpur Municipal Council 1959, 19). Given that the vast majority of municipal laborers were Tamil immigrants (specifically brought to Malaya to work in the factory), the area quickly became the town's "Indian Quarter." Furthermore, as the government bureaucracy expanded in response to the growth of the town, a steady stream of low-level government clerks and bureaucrats began to arrive from Ceylon. Housing Asian staff with British officials on what had become Bluff Road and Federal Hill was considered improper. Therefore, most of the Ceylonese staff took up residence in modest government bungalows that were constructed on the edges of the area that was by 1895 officially being referred to as Brickfields. Although the brick kilns had ceased operations by the 1910s the neighborhood was settled as the headquarters of the daily municipal operations of the PWD and a neighborhood of "Indian"[21] clerks and laborers.

The imagination of Brickfields as an "Indian" area was further solidified with the coming of the railroad to Kuala Lumpur in 1886.[22] The decision to build a railway between Kuala Lumpur and Klang was made in 1883 during Swettenham's tenure as Resident, although it was Acting Resident (1884–1888) J.P. Rodger who pushed the project to its realization (Dewan Bandaraya Kuala Lumpur 1990, 15). The fact that Rodger was able to accomplish this despite the projected cost of the project being nearly double the annual revenue of the entire Selangor government[23] indicates his persistence and the broad faith in modernizing technologies that was already evident in the governance of the state.[24] It became the second operating railway in peninsular Malaya when Governor Weld and Sultan Abdul Samad made the inaugural forty-three–minute journey from Klang to Kuala Lumpur on September 15, 1886 (Gullick 2000, 55–56).

Most of the laborers working on the construction of this railway were Tamils. As the construction crew had to be mobile, government contractors only provided temporary housing for these laborers, a practice that was continued as the construction moved to what was then the end of the line in Kuala Lumpur. The railway line entered Kuala Lumpur through Brickfields. Thus, many laborers erected temporary housing in the area, and as it was decided that the depot, godowns (warehouses), and repair shops required for the continued operation of the railroad should be located permanently in Brickfields, the population of the area quickly swelled with the influx of railway workers taking up residence there. Although over time lower-level bureaucrats were provided with permanent housing by the railway in Brickfields,[25] most laborers had to fend for themselves when it came to accommodations. This situation generated the first colonies of unregistered dwellings in Brickfields. As the railway expanded in the 1890s (including a spur line cutting to the east across the center of Kuala Lumpur and lines extending north to Rawang and south to Seremban), the services of the laborers continued to be in demand in the general area of Kuala Lumpur, leading to the permanent establishment of Brickfields as the "neighborhood of choice" for many railway workers[26] (Gullick 2000, 57–58).

The creation of Brickfields as a primarily "Indian" space became a matter of policy in 1890s Kuala Lumpur. The official imagination of Brickfields as an "Indian reserve" was manifested in the creation of religious institutions for the various Indian communities in the town from 1895 with the formal recognition of the Sasanabhi Wurdhi Wardhana Society,[27] followed in 1902 by the consecration of the Sri Kandaswamy Temple and in 1907 by the founding of the Sri Vivekanenda Ashram. Each of these institutions was established by leading members of the Malayan Indian community and their ability to function was dependent on formal recognition from the colonial government.[28] Requests for land and facilities were channeled through a colonial bureaucracy that was motivated primarily by a concern for spatial and social order and economic development in the rapidly growing town.

The Sasanabhi Wurdhi Wardhara Society traces its origins to a meeting held by local Singhala Buddhists on February 4, 1894 (de Silva 1998, 24). This meeting was held for the purpose of founding a Buddhist society and temple in Kuala Lumpur to serve the rapidly growing Buddhist community from Ceylon. The minutes of the meeting, as summarized by de Silva, indicate that Brickfields was already imagined as a proper site for such an institution, as they record:

1. that there was a need for a Buddhist temple in Kuala Lumpur, as there were over 200 members of the Singhalese community in Selangor, the majority being Buddhist;

2. that it was beyond the means of the Singhalese Buddhists to purchase an allotment of government land (about two acres) needed for a temple site;

3. that the site desired be located at *Batu Limabelas* [Brickfields] in the vicinity of the PWD factory where the majority of Singhalese lived; and

4. that the Buddhist priests would be got down from Ceylon for the supervision and running of the temple and for the administration of the last rites for deceased Singhalese Buddhists prior to interment. (de Silva 1998, 24)

Based on these resolutions, a petition was drafted requesting a grant of two acres of state land for the purpose of building a temple, and was submitted to C.E. Spooner, the State Engineer. Spooner, seen by the community as the official who would be most likely to respond positively to the request due to his extensive experience in Ceylon (and perhaps also due to the fact that he had personally been responsible for bringing a number of Singhalese staff members over when he was reassigned to Malaya), passed it on to A.R. Venning, the State Secretary, for consideration. Venning, like Spooner, viewed the proposal favorably, and he referred the matter to the Collector of Land Revenues with a proposal and sketch plan for the temple grounds to be located on a lot at the official boundary of the town. The collector reported back that "I have been dealing with this Section lately and can find no objection to the proposal. Reserve might be gazetted under Section 5 Land Code. (I have proposed to the Surveyor to throw the land unalienated in the Section outside town limit *in order to facilitate the factory scheme*)" (de Silva 1998, 30; emphasis added).

For the collector the proposal was advantageous in light of plans to further develop the now-open PWD factory. In a context of de facto racial segregation already evident in Kuala Lumpur,[29] and given that the pronounced majority of PWD workers were either Tamil or Singhalese, it is not a surprise that the official would casually link the request of a Singhalese religious organization with the development of the area as an industrial zone. From the point of view of both the community and the state government it made perfect sense to locate the temple close to the PWD factory, and the proposal gained initial approval on May 5, 1894, without additional internal debate. Ground was broken on construction of the new temple on August 25, 1894, with C.E. Spooner's wife doing the honor of laying the foundation stone. Emphasizing the tie between the Singhalese community and the PWD factory, coverage of the groundbreaking ceremony in the *Straits Times* commented that the temple was not "one-hundred yards beyond the PWD buildings" (de Silva 1998, 40).[30]

The Selangor Ceylon Tamil Association had similar concerns when they purchased a plot of land at the end of Scott Road sitting on the banks of the Klang River in 1901. As an anonymous author in the *Centenary Celebration Guide* notes, the association bought this land with the aim of constructing a temple due to the "central position it occupied in relation to the government quarters in which most of the Ceylon Tamils lived then" (Sri Kandaswamy Temple 2002, 160). Scott Road, constituting the northern border of the neighborhood, was by this time a busy area lined with government bungalows and shops catering to the needs of the growing Brickfields Indian community. Although the land was officially purchased in 1901 (with the "Vel" of Murugan, the deity of the temple, installed on January 16, 1902) there is some evidence that the association was able to purchase the land due to the fact that an unregistered Murugan temple already occupied the site. The temple today recognizes 1902 as the year that official worship began at the site, with the original temple construction being completed by 1909[31] (Sri Kandaswamy Temple 2002, 160).

Religious institutions continued to be established in the Brickfields area, including a Catholic Church in 1904 and the Vivekanenda Reading Hall in 1907 (Dewan Bandaraya Kuala Lumpur 1990, 45). The presence of these institutions, primarily serving immigrants from Ceylon educated in English-medium colonial schools, indicates a rapid process by which Brickfields was constituted as a discrete site within the town. Coupled with the government housing being constructed around the PWD factory and the railways complex (on the west side of Brickfields Road, directly across from the factory) and the appearance of a number of permanent two-story shop houses along Brickfields and Scott Roads, the area's designation as the "Indian Quarter" was now taken for granted.

Early Attempts to Centralize Urban Planning

Despite the efforts of colonial city planners and municipal officials, by the turn of the century it was clear that Kuala Lumpur was not developing in the manner that they had intended. As early as 1902 problems familiar to present-day residents were being identified and discussed in the local press. One resident wrote:

Kuala Lumpur is not an ancient city, yet we already find that in the very outset of her development, the arteries of her traffic are incapable of adequately performing the functions of which, in the beginning, they were deemed sufficient. . . . It may be that Kuala Lumpur was not originally expected to blossom out so rapidly as she has done, that the growth has, in a very short time, outstripped the ideas of those who were called upon to cater for the future, but the fact remains that the federal capital of these rapidly developing States finds herself thus early called upon to undo as economically as possible the work of the past. (Dewan Bandaraya Kuala Lumpur 1990, 39)

Swettenham's vision of a peaceful, efficient, orderly city was not being realized. In fact, as the above writer clearly indicates, these problems were due to the early successes that Swettenham and the colonial bureaucracy had in their efforts to reconstruct the town in the 1880s. The major problem was overcrowding, as Kuala Lumpur's population continued to grow at an astounding rate. In 1891 the town had 19,020 inhabitants; by 1901 that number had grown to 32,381 and further jumped to 46,718 by 1911 (Sidhu 1978, 13). Corresponding with the rise in population, land values had skyrocketed, with city lots that sold for $1,000 in 1889 selling for upwards of $50,000 thirteen years later (Gullick 2000, 177). As was the situation in Singapore at the time (Yeoh 1996), municipal officials in Kuala Lumpur found themselves handcuffed by the combination of unacceptable (by their standards) population densities and the prohibitive cost of reordering the built environment in order to promote the hygienic, orderly town that was held to be ideal by the standards of the time.

As in the early 1880s, Swettenham felt that a radical rebuilding project was the only way to alleviate the infrastructural strain. In 1902 Swettenham, as Governor and High Commissioner of the Federated Malay States, appointed G.T. Tickell President of the Kuala Lumpur Sanitary Board. Tickell proposed a bold, "Napoleonic"[32] plan to free up space in the central zone by opening each existing town block with the creation of "back lanes," rationalizing city roads and opening up new areas at the city limits to construction. His plans, when presented to the Sanitary Board, outraged the "unofficial" (i.e., Asian) members of the board to the point that none of them would second the motion that the plan be considered at a higher level.[33] Tickell's prohibitively intrusive and expensive proposals angered the Resident of Selangor, H.C. Belfield, to the point where he officially opposed their enactment and encouraged Tickell to withdraw his "outrageous" proposal. Much to Belfield's horror, however, Swettenham supported Tickell's plan, although neither man would remain in Malaya long enough to put the proposals to the test. Swettenham departed Singapore in October 1903. Without his benefactor Tickell found himself edged out of his position on the Sanitary Board and he subsequently resigned from the government entirely in 1904[34] (Gullick 2000, 176–178).

Although the plan was quickly defeated, the "Napoleonic" drive to radically alter the existing built environment as a way of addressing social issues remained a factor in most major city planning initiatives undertaken in Kuala Lumpur throughout the twentieth century. While it is true that Swettenham could not force another radical rebuilding project on Kuala Lumpur in 1902–1903, its defeat should not be taken as a signal that city planners and government officials were not prepared to deploy radical means to achieve their goals in the shaping of the built environment and the communities that inhabited such spaces. Swettenham and Tickell miscalculated in that their proposals were prohibitively expensive and that the primary landowners in Kuala Lumpur (many of whom were members of the very Sanitary Board that Tickell originally presented his plan to) would bear the brunt of the cost without an appreciable return. Although anticipated public reaction to the plan also seems to have played a part in the proposal's defeat, the main issue was that the unofficial members of the board did not feel a similar urgency in "cleaning up" the town and, without a clear goal beyond the general commitment to "safe" and "healthy" conditions, they would not accept such a radical plan. Like landowners in Singapore, the elite in Kuala Lumpur saw no need to address questions of public order in the ways that municipal officials advocated. As I argue in Chapter 2, only under the greatly transformed social conditions brought about by the Japanese Occupation and the Emergency in the immediate post–World War II period would the "Napoleonic" urge of colonial planners again come into play in the development of urban space in Malaya.

Civilizational Anxiety and Urban Order in Kuala Lumpur

The first four decades of the twentieth century saw relatively few shifts in urban planning and development in Kuala Lumpur. Unlike the planned transformations envisioned by Swettenham and Tickell, the town grew in a piecemeal fashion; most changes in the urban environment came in the form of realizing plans long on the board, such as the completion of the large government office complex, the construction of a new railway station, and the continued development of the rail and road system throughout the state. By now firmly established as the capital of the Federated Malay States (as it had been since 1895) and clearly the commercial center for the peninsula, Kuala Lumpur was an enigma to many at the time, neither fully a "city" nor properly a "town." One *Malay Mail* correspondent, struggling to characterize Kuala Lumpur's personality, wrote in 1909, "I fear it is impossible to describe it" (cited in Dewan Bandaraya Kuala Lumpur 1990, 55). The population of what was now the major peninsular city continued to grow, with 46,718 reported residents in 1911, increasing to 80,424 by 1921. This persistent population growth, fueled by Malaya's rubber trade, led not only to increased population densities but also to several annexations of land at the edge of Kuala Lumpur, including the annexation of Sentul, a second railway and industrial zone (again, heavily populated by Indians) to the north of town, in about 1905 (Dewan Bandaraya Kuala Lumpur 1990, 50).

Unlike the early days of command and control reconstruction in Swettenham's style, these moves were not part of a comprehensive plan to manage city growth. Early moves to centralize city planning and related municipal functions had stalled and the Sanitary Board remained the leading authority in these matters. Despite persistent pressure to centralize these functions in a separate department (given that the Sanitary Board's primary function was to ensure that municipal services were available in already existing neighborhoods), it was not until 1921 that an actual City Planner position was created by the board, and even then the Planner's role was much more that of a consultant than an actual player in the local government.

Brickfields was now firmly established as simultaneously the "Indian Quarter" and the industrial zone for the city. As with the other areas in the city, complaints were mounting as to the area's "out of control" character. An anonymous writer to the *Malay Mail* in 1915 noted with alarm that "drunken brawls" and "surly rickshaw coolies" were bound to "stare one in the face" nearly every evening on Scott Road. The writer continued: "Lo and behold, what meets your eyes next is a whole herd of cattle, standing stock still in the centre of the roadway, and as you halt and think that it looks very much as if you won't get home till morning, the tolling of a bell makes you wonder what is going to happen next" (Dewan Bandaraya Kuala Lumpur 1990, 80).

A sense of panic is evident in this (presumably) European's description of Scott Road. Taken by itself, the panic seems a bit out of proportion to the scene, as relaxing rickshaw pullers, docile *kerbau* standing around waiting to pull night soil carts around the city, and the ringing of the bell at the Sri Kandaswamy Temple hardly seem to signal chaos or inspire terror. Yet Brickfields was not turning out as planned. The unease of failed expectations is clear in this writer's lament, which begins with the statement that there were "a few things which we people of Scott Road have to make the best of, and have done so for some time past." Clearly the writer was exasperated, expected more by way of order and efficiency, and was offering this description of Scott Road as an example of what was wrong with the city generally. For Kuala Lumpur's European community in 1915 the genial disorder of Scott's Road was a signal of a larger malaise, and perhaps a more catastrophic miscalculation. Seven years later, the unease evident in the anonymous writer's account was still palpable in a startling editorial that ran in the *Malay Mail*:

Thirty odd years ago we had no cold storage in Kuala Lumpur, no electric light, no water laid on, no motor cars, no cinemas, no book club, no weekly dances, but, thank goodness, we did not feel as if we were living in a London suburb. Life was more primitive and vastly more interesting than it is to-day. Look at the faces around us. Has the "advance" of civilization made tended to make them any happier? Rather the reverse. Social life has become more of a sham, business has become more of a cut-throat game and the officials are now mostly tied up to office tables with red tape.

Referring to the earlier leaders such as Swettenham, the writer bitterly observed:

Some of these mighty are now in obscure retirement; others are dust. No man is to be envied. The end is the same for all. (Dewan Bandaraya Kuala Lumpur 1990, 85)

Some of this bitterness can be explained by the recent experiences of the First World War and the postwar dip in the rubber market, bringing tight economic times to Malaya.[35] Yet European residents of the town were also rethinking the strident, persistent faith in the techniques of colonial governance. In the context of city life, persistent, intractable problems of urban development in Singapore, Penang, and Kuala Lumpur were not being addressed to the satisfaction of the British expatriate community. Although each of these cities was carefully planned from the beginning, the dreams of orderly, efficient, Southeast Asian urban spaces were being confronted with the realities of governing an active, heterogeneous population whose own notions of proper living seldom conformed neatly to the "Garden City" ideals advanced by colonial officials. In this atmosphere, problems of population, traffic, floods, and sanitation seemed more sinister than simply the outcomes of well-intentioned failures. Street scenes that the *Malay Mail* described as "interesting" and "comical" in a series of articles published in 1913[36] became indicators of failure and a source of fear by the early 1920s.

A Second Attempt to Create a Town Planner

In this uneasy atmosphere campaigns to bureaucratize the town planner position and urban development gained new life. The first order of business within this strategy was the passing of specific legislation intended to regularize urban development and the creation of formal positions within the colonial government to enforce these laws. The question of an FMS-wide Town Planning Enactment came up in the Legislative Council proceedings as early as 1912, and the following year the Chief Secretary was claiming in response to inquiries regarding the proposal that a Town Planning Committee had already been authorized for Kuala Lumpur (Goh 1991, 35). It appears that little concrete action was taken during the next few years, however, as the matter continued to surface in debate in the Legislative Council, with the queries becoming progressively more strident and alarmist. Under pressure, the government charged the Kuala Lumpur Sanitary Board with the drafting of a Town Improvement Bill (the board largely copied from the recently gazetted Ceylonese Town Improvement Ordinance) that was finally passed into law, without much debate, as the Town Improvement Enactment of 1917. However, the enactment hardly addressed the issues brought before the council, as it provided no funds for project development, enforcement, or the hiring of staff (Goh 1991).

It was not until 1921 that the Enactment was given some actual force. This force came in the form of Charles Compton Reade, who was appointed

Town Planning Advisor to the FMS in February of that year. Reade, a crusader and advocate of the "Garden City" model of urban planning,[37] had been working in a similar capacity in Australia for a number of years, and had also authored an influential book entitled *The Revelation of Britain: A Book for Colonials* (1909) advocating the aggressive pursuit of "modern" urban planning ideals throughout the British colonial empire. Although Reade was nearly ousted from his position before he had even begun,[38] he set to work on a careful survey of Malayan towns for the purpose of drafting comprehensive planning schemes.

Reade's survey "revealed" a number of interesting points regarding urban development in Malaya. He noted that the rapid growth of towns over the last thirty years had led to an inadequate road system, an unorganized pattern of land use, overbuilding, and "the multiplicity of coloured peoples, each with their own differing interests and indigenous problems" (Reade 1922, 164). Although not intended as a direct swipe at Swettenham and his earlier efforts to rationalize growth in Kuala Lumpur and in other Malayan towns, Reade's findings imply that Swettenham's original efforts to rationalize town planning had failed.

Based on his previous experience in Australia, Reade felt that it was one thing to draw up town plans or suggestions for future development (such as the Town Improvement Enactment of 1917), and quite another thing to have the means to implement policy on a consistent and rational basis. According to Reade it was essential that comprehensive legislation be drafted and passed before he proceeded to formulate specific plans, which led to the Town Planning Enactment of 1923. Significantly, this legislation gave the town planner executive powers in the planning and development of urban sites (Goh 1991, 41). The final document closely resembled American town planning legislation with its reliance on strict zoning procedures, and covered a wide range of activities including road improvement, land alienation for national projects, beautification, and control of major waterways.

It was an ambitious move on the government's part to invest so much control in town planners and in Reade. Ambition aside, this legislation also proved to be a failure, as the formal centralization of power in the town planner immediately raised the concerns of competing divisions within the colonial bureaucracy and amongst leading landowners in Kuala Lumpur and Penang, most of whom were leaders of the Chinese community. Reade, sensing the difficulty of convincing these quarters that radical steps needed to be taken, staged a number of "Town Planning Explanation and Catalogue" exhibitions in order to educate the population at large and build some momentum for his plans. These exhibitions, carefully crafted to elucidate the benefits of rationalized urban planning in England and America, were impressive disappointments, as they did little to rally residents to Reade's cause. Defeat was nearly total with the passing of the Town Planning Enactment of 1927, a watered-down version of the 1923 legislation that, aside from retaining the zoning proposals, reverted back to the generally "advisory" character of the 1917 law. Reade hung on for three more years in Malaya, presumably drafting town plans for major urban centers,[39] but exited the country in 1930 with the situation more or less the same as when he arrived.

The fallacy of Reade's plan was the fact that he attempted to formalize the executive power that figures such as Swettenham wielded by default within the government bureaucracy. Although Reade attempted to create a division that formally possessed the powers it needed to carry out its work and was adequately integrated with existing divisions, his planning reveals a logic of totality that was proving to be both unpopular and generally a failure elsewhere in the FMS and Crown Colonies.[40] Reade misjudged the insecurity and ambiguity commonly felt by key colonial officials and European residents of Malaya regarding the trajectory of their "civilizing project." The planner also did not realize the extent of the Chinese landowners' power to directly influence government policies, particularly those related to land use and ownership. As with Tickell before him, opposition from this quarter was a key factor in undermining Reade's proposals. One way to view Reade, like Tickell, is that he anticipated the centralized, quasi-military direction that urban planning would take in postcolonial Malaysia but attempted to enact his plans at the wrong time and through the wrong means. The bureaucratization of Swettenham's command-and-control model would require a more directly militarized governmental structure, however, and a series of crises in the realm of the everyday that would open the field for a more centralized, authoritarian mode of city planning.[41]

The Japanese Occupation would set the stage for such a shift. Japan's stunning military blitz of British Malaya between December 1941 and March 1942 and subsequent occupation of the peninsula is well known, and has been exhaustively recounted by other scholars (Cheah 1979; Chin 1976; Kratoska 1995, 1998; Sato 1994; Shiraishi and Shiraishi 1993; Tarling 2001). What is important here is the fact that the Japanese military authority had its own interest in rationalizing urban planning in Malaya, and during the occupation replaced the British colonial apparatus with one more subject to the centralized control of the military authority, designed to harmonize the functions of urban planners with the military goals of the Japanese Imperial Army. While the British abolished these institutions and attempted to revive the prewar apparatus upon their return to Malaya in September 1945, an important trend of centralized, authoritarian control had been established and would serve as a model for the planning and governance of towns during the Malayan Emergency (1948–60).

This centralization of authority was many years off, however, and during the first four decades of the twentieth century Brickfields continued as it had in years past as the center of municipal work and the home of lower-level civil servants and PWD laborers. As befits an established neighborhood, these years saw the founding of a number of schools (St. Mary's, Kishan Dial, Methodist Girls School, Lasalle, and St. Teresa's), businesses (including the first petrol station in Kuala Lumpur on Anthony Road, the Government Toddy Shop, Soon Huat Sawmill, and Lin Seng Rice Mill), a popular cinema (Prince's Cinema, later known as the Lido Theatre), and the Young Men's Christian Association (YMCA). The boundary of the neighborhood crept southward, although during these years growth was restricted to roughly the east-west border represented by present day Jalan Travers (then Travers Road) and Jalan Berhala (Temple Road) with the Hundred Quarters,[42] with the Brickfields Road/Travers Road roundabout being the southernmost point for local buses and the border between Kuala Lumpur proper and "the ulu" (outback). This boundary was determined largely by the fact that the land to the south was too swampy for development, with a stream running from the nearby Bungsar Estate due west along the southern edge of Brickfields and emptying into the Klang (which at that time ran in a long, looping S shape through the marsh).[43]

Some other changes caused concern for municipal officials. In particular, local bureaucrats and planners viewed the growing unregistered *kampung* areas in the heart of the neighborhood as major problems. Although most accounts date the establishment of large urban *kampung*s to the time immediately following the Japanese Occupation, it is clear that a number of large *kampung* settlements had been established in Brickfields by the 1920s, including *Kampung Khatijah* and *Kampung Cina*. These unregistered communities were clustered around the PWD factory, the Railway Workshop and godowns and the *kerbau* stockade, which is not surprising given that most of the residents were employed by one of these concerns. Thus, by the interwar years Brickfields had an established "order" that consisted of a number of larger institutions connected by a hodgepodge of narrow, mostly unpaved roads and trails snaking through the neighborhood. These institutions tended to be located on one of the established roads (Brickfields Road, Scott Road, Temple Road) and were surrounded by a growing network of improvised, quasi-permanent *kampung* complexes. As these three roads roughly constituted the borders of a rectangle (with the Klang itself constituting the fourth side), the appearance was one of established, "legitimate" buildings surrounding a large, seemingly unified tangle of "squatter" homes. For many, particularly British officials, police officers, and middle-class "border" residents, venturing into the heart of Brickfields had a fearful, dangerous quality.[44]

This tangle of makeshift development was exactly what the earlier planners had hoped to avoid. The edgy, fearful quality expressed by the *Malay Mail* writer in 1915 coalesced into a much more specific notion of the "character" of the neighborhood and its residents. Although a number of neighborhoods in Kuala Lumpur experienced similar patterns of development during this time, Brickfields was assigned a central place in discourses of urban disorder and danger that were becoming commonplace. The seemingly chaotic jumble of shanties, cow pens, Hindu temples, Buddhist shrines, and winding paths that surrounded "legitimate" homes, businesses, and places of worship took on an air of vague danger. If there was one neighborhood that exemplified the breakdown of Swettenham's original efforts in the minds of pre-Occupation colonial officials in Kuala Lumpur, it was Brickfields.

Conclusion

The early history of Kuala Lumpur and Brickfields was marked by a complex and dispersed set of relations and negotiations between the municipal authorities of the town and the Asian and European communities regarding the creation, use, and representation of the urban built environment. This terrain of interaction was characterized by conflict and compromise between those with the formal power to make and regulate the urban environment and those for whom this space constituted and framed their concrete lived experience in the everyday. This chapter has highlighted the intersections between colonial authorities (who sought to create an orderly city based on wider understanding of proper social life and the techniques of governance available to them in their attempts to manage this ideal order) and Brickfields residents (whose local understandings of order, justice, and the Good shaped their attempts to make the built environment useful for their own purposes).

While it is apparent that the power to shape the character of local neighborhoods in Kuala Lumpur asymmetrically favored the colonial authorities, their attempts to manipulate and "reform" Asian communities through the construction of planned urban spaces was limited by a number of factors. In the colonial administrative sphere, it was clear that while the language of reform[45] was a key discursive factor in the planning and administration of urban space in Kuala Lumpur, this discourse was internally in competition with concrete economic factors and disagreements over the material form that a colonial government guided by the ideal of "indirect rule" should take. Thus, while the role of experts and the desire to diagnose and solve the "deficiencies" of Asian modes of living was widely recognized, the formal administrative structures required to dominate the urban sphere were never fully developed in prewar Kuala Lumpur. This early pattern of urban governance, marked by the disproportionate influence of charismatic leaders coupled with underdeveloped bureaucratic structures and processes, continued to shape the development and administration of Brickfields and the city during the early years of the twenty-first century.

Attempts to construct and later remake Brickfields were also limited by the engagements, conflicts, and compromises evident in local accounts of everyday life between the colonial authorities and the predominantly Indian and Chinese communities that lived there. While prewar Brickfields was marked by the "representations of space" of city planners, architects, and colonial officials (Lefebvre 1991), the lived spaces of everyday life are also critically important to our understanding of how the neighborhood was formed in the late nineteenth and early twentieth centuries. While the built spaces of the colonial city were sites of control, local communities were often able to engage these sites in order to advance their own claims on the space. While these claims were only indirect engagements with the colonial state, but as the worried commentators of the 1910s and 1920s recognized, these engagements often had a political dimension present just below the surface of what were seemingly problems of overcrowding, "improper" use of space, or the unintended heterogeneity of certain local neighborhoods.

The empirical heterogeneity of Brickfields was clearly problematic for colonial officials and members of the European community familiar with the neighborhood. Beyond the perception of spatial disarray, Brickfields also represented a dangerous demographic disorder. These fears were linked to broader concerns regarding precisely what kind of place the British had created through aggressive immigration policies a generation before. By the 1930s the presence of an almost equal number of Malays and Chinese in Malaya, with a substantial number of South Indians also present in the colony, was fretfully debated in official circles and was also an issue for the nascent nationalist movements forming within each of these communities, particularly for Malays. Until this time, Chinese and Indians were regarded as temporary immigrants, ignoring the fact that increasing numbers from these communities were Malayan-born and had no means or intention of returning to their "home" countries (Roff 1994, 110–111). Colonial officials and Malay nationalists alike looked upon these demographic realities with unease in the 1930s. Many predicted violent, large-scale communal conflagrations in Malaya's future as a result of this diversity. Worse still in the case of Brickfields was the fact that the area was populated by various Indian communities alongside a visible, established Chinese presence.[46] Measured against an ideal of "ethnic quartering," Brickfields seemed dangerously promiscuous to many.

Conflicts over city space that emerged during the colonial period are important factors in forming an understanding of the present situation in Brickfields. While every urban neighborhood "produces its own space" (Lefebvre 1991), the particularities of how Brickfields as a space has been produced over time are important to bear in mind as we consider more recent attempts to transform the neighborhood. Saying this should not imply, however, that there is an unbroken historical trajectory between prewar Brickfields and the current situation, as the situation in the immediate postwar and postcolonial period in Malaysia brought about a number of changes in the techniques of governance available to the state in the formation and control of urban space. In the following chapter we turn to a discussion of the transformation of urban governance in the immediate postcolonial period due to an evolving understanding of proper public life in independent Malaysia and its particular impact on urban living in Brickfields.

2

The Malayan Emergency, Islamic Reform, and the Trajectory of Urban Governmentality in Kuala Lumpur

Introduction

Nearly all accounts of Malaysian politics and society stress that the political system that has evolved in the country is one dominated by the strategies of elite groups that form alliances in order to rule.[1] Elite political groups in Malaysia are always ethnic groups in this model, linking any analysis of governance and the state to the interactions of discrete ethnic communities represented in government by the leaders of communal political parties. Noting the ethnic diversity of postcolonial Malaysia, political theorists marvel at the relative political stability the country has enjoyed since independence, and attribute this "success" to the fact that the original Alliance coalition[2] has been able to negotiate problems of governance among its members in a manner that retains the separateness of ethnic communities yet facilitates negotiation and accommodation of larger national goals.

The influential work of Gordon Means articulates this understanding of Malaysian politics most clearly.[3] Basing his analysis on the works of Enloe (1973), Horowitz (1985), Lijphart (1977), and Milne (1981), Means summarized the characteristics of an elite accommodation system as follows:

> 1. that each ethnic community is unified under a leadership which can authoritatively bargain for the interests of that community; (2) that the

leaders of each community have the capacity to secure compliance and "legitimacy" for the bargains that are reached by elite negotiations; (3) that there is sufficient trust and empathy among elites to be sensitive to the most vital concerns of other ethnic communities; (4) that public mobilization on "ethnically sensitive issues" is kept to a minimum to enable the elites to deal with these issues in a bargaining mode; and (5) that representative institutions accept their diminished role of merely "ratifying" the product of elite bargaining as appropriate for resolution of these issues. (Means 1991, 2)

As a model for understanding Malaysian politics from a macro perspective, the elite accommodation framework is an effective analytic vehicle for coming to terms with the complex political realities of postcolonial Malaysia. In particular, the often top-down orientation of Malaysian governance and the relatively diminished emphasis on the rights of citizens as individual legal subjects that shapes relationships between individuals, communities, and the state are incorporated into the model. This model does not, however, account for the accommodations and negotiations that take place across communal boundaries at the neighborhood or community level. Nor does this model effectively account for the specific bureaucratic, legal, and coercive techniques of governance deployed by the state in the formation and administration of particular spaces and populations. With elite representatives of discrete, stable ethnic communities placed at the center of the analysis, the microprocesses of governance and multiple registers of the law, the state, and relatedness that exist at local levels become "by-products" of the larger political system.

Although these descriptions of Malaysian political life are often insufficiently attuned to the nuances of social life that constitute this realm, it is not my intention to "disprove" the saliency of ethnicity in Malaysia or argue against the importance of elite negotiation at the highest levels of government. Rather, it is the premise of this chapter that a clearer understanding of the Malaysian state and public life is possible only when we fortify macro-level frameworks of state formation with a detailed analysis of the social forces that challenge and constitute the social at local levels. While the works cited above offer rich accounts of Malaysian political life, it is essential to foreground several aspects of recent Malaysian history that are often displaced in these narratives in order to make sense of how such larger forces come to bear on specific spaces and communities.

The goal of this chapter is to provide a context for understanding the techniques of city planning and the governance of urban space, the experience of the law, and the role of religion in the transformation of Brickfields during the years 2000–2002 that is the subject of Part II of this book. To this end, I will provide a summary of two historical processes that have transformed the character of urban life and governance in Malaysia: the state of emergency that existed in Malaya between 1948 and 1960 (hereafter referred to as "the Emergency") and the evolving efforts throughout the twentieth century to make Islam more central to public life. By recognizing each of these processes as moments of social and political crisis that demanded the establishment of new forms of relatedness, these historical summaries seek to establish the ground by which we can understand the divergent responses of the state and the Brickfields community to issues of urban order and moral good that emerged as central themes during the period that I conducted fieldwork in the neighborhood.

An analysis of the Emergency is essential because the strategies deployed by the Malayan government to combat the violent insurgency mounted by the Malayan Races Liberation Army (MRLA) and the Malayan Communist Party (MCP) established parameters of legal subjectivity and techniques of interventionist state rule that persist to this day. Providing a summary of Islamic reform movements and long-term debates regarding the place of Islam in public life is required in order to better understand how questions of "the Good" and the moral authority to rule have become increasingly salient in any discussion of development and modernity in Malaysia. Therefore, this chapter is divided into two major sections, one each devoted to each set of issues and events.

The Emergency, 1948–60

The Emergency and Postcolonial Malaysian Governmentality

The Emergency was the making of modern Malaya. The state became a presence in the lives of many Asians for the first time. The militarisation of society it necessitated created closer structures of authority. Violence, although in the short term it disintegrated existing loyalties, forced the pace of the creation of new ones. It condemned Malaya to communalism, sometimes literally by the physical separation of populations through resettlement and regroupment. Yet the main motif of colonial government was a sustained attempt to dissolve these old attachments and to re-create community through loyalty and a sense of obligation to the colonial state, articulating a multiracial Malayan identity . . . Diverse strategies—social welfare, community development, cultural patronage—and the technological revolution that accompanied state expansion, especially the creation of a vast propaganda machine—were employed to this end. However, in many ways technology—in the shape of enhanced road communications, printing, even cinema—empowered Asians. Everywhere, the new enthusiasms these colonial initiatives were intended to arouse, began to advance identities of a different kind (Harper 1999, 8).

T.N. Harper's thesis is clear: the techniques of governmentality developed through the prosecution of the military campaign against the MCP provided the blueprint by which postcolonial Malaysia[4] would pursue its aims of state building and modern development. These techniques were oriented toward the creation of the modern Malayan citizen and a public sphere that would simultaneously cultivate and support the "right-minded" agency of such citizens within the limits set by the state. This is not particularly unusual in and of itself; one can argue that every modern state attempts to do this. What is significant about the Malayan case is that these techniques were so closely tied to an overtly military form of discipline that by the end of the Emergency traditional distinctions between "military" and "civilian" life were difficult to sustain. Harper recognizes this when he writes, "War was the midwife to a new colonial orthodoxy; a hybrid between the older tradition of Malayan scholar-administrators and social welfare ideologies" (Harper 1999, 8). The Emergency found the sweeping, "civilizing" visions of nineteenth-century figures such as Frank Swettenham linked to the contemporary techniques of the specialist. In the realm of urban planning the Emergency provided the conditions for change that Charles Reade unsuccessfully sought nearly twenty-five years earlier;[5] the will to formulate bold plans to reorganize the physical space and reshuffle the communities that inhabited those spaces, as well as the material means to systematically promote a discourse of order and habit that would be "taught" through the simultaneous use of persuasion and force.

Offering a comprehensive narrative of the events that took place during the Emergency is beyond the scope of this project. Numerous detailed accounts of the period have already been written (Coates 1992; Harper 1999; Jackson 1991; Leary 1995; Lim 2000; O'Ballance 1966, Sarkesian 1993; Short 2000; Stubbs 1989). Rather, it is my purpose here to illustrate several critical aspects of the Emergency, particularly regarding matters of governance and the ordering of urban space that remain critical issues in Malaysia to this day. Therefore, my account of the Emergency is highly selective, focusing on the transformation of public life and spatial order during the twelve years of the conflict.[6]

The decisive innovation of the British response to the armed rebellion of the MCP and the MRLA was to treat the conflict as a law-and-order issue rather than purely as a military one (Sarkesian 1993, 168). This strategy has had a lasting effect on governmental practices in Malaysia ever since. Taking notice that the efforts of the relatively small number of combatants were materially supported by a large group of landless Chinese peasants living on the edges of the forest,[7] the government developed a comprehensive "hearts and minds" strategy that sought to use military techniques to reorder social life. The primary outcome of this strategy was the forced relocation of nearly 500,000 Malayans, mostly landless Chinese, into "New Villages." These New Villages were built from the ground up in close proximity to established urban centers, requiring not only military power to force this population to move, but also a bureaucratic apparatus that could handle the sudden appearance of several hundred new "towns." This strategy, pursued after nearly three years of ineffective military counterstrategies, was a pillar of the Briggs Plan. Formally a report to the British Defense Co-ordination Committee, this plan was unofficially named after its designer, Lieutenant General Sir Harold Briggs. Briggs was named Director of Operations in Malaya in February 1950 and submitted this report in May of that year.

Sarkesian summarizes the Briggs Plan as follows:

[It] confirmed that civil government was primarily responsible for responding to the revolutionaries. The plan placed emphasis on resettlement and the New Village program combined with an integrated civilian police-military system of planning and operations. It established "war by committee" and stressed counterrevolutionary operations within a system of laws and regulations. (Sarkesian 1993, 71)

Stubbs highlights the perceived need to streamline the decision-making processes in the civilian government: "Briggs consolidated a co-ordinating structure which gave the civil administration, the police, and the army the chance to meet regularly and to co-operate. This structure had the additional benefit of bypassing the often unresponsive state administrations and gave the Federal Government more flexibility in putting its policies into effect." (Stubbs 1989, 99) For Briggs the conflict had to remain an issue of civil order. In order to effectively combat the MCP, however, the machinery of civilian government had to be restructured to more closely resemble that of a military chain of command. Although efforts to implement Briggs's plan began almost immediately after it was made public in 1950, it was not until the appointment of General Sir Gerald Templer as High Commissioner for the Federation of Malaya that these reorganizing efforts would have their fullest impact. Appointed in the wake of his predecessor Henry Gurney's assassination on October 6, 1951, Templer issued an Emergency Directive upon his arrival in Malaya in February 1952 that made the Briggs Plan official policy. This directive formalized Briggs's request regarding a unification of civilian and military chains of command and declared that Templer, while remaining the civilian head of government, would also "assume complete operational command over all armed forces assigned to operations in the Federation" (Coates 1992, 205–206). Civilian officials who directly reported to the high commissioner were assigned responsibility for the execution of directives within the Briggs Plan, with the chief secretary assuming full control of the New Village initiative. This new configuration simultaneously bypassed both the Far East Command in regard to military concerns and the state and local governments with respect to municipal issues.

The unification of civilian and military functions had wide-ranging effects throughout Malayan society. Two related effects are particularly important: (1) the more precise identification and enumeration of discrete populations within Malaya, and (2) the ability to isolate, relocate, and resettle several of these populations. Although intended to address the armed resistance of the MCP and the "problem" of rural squatters and their support for the Min Yuen (the logistics arm of the MCP), these effects continue to have an impact on the character of state interventions in the urban sphere.

Efforts to address the "squatter" problem predated the Briggs Plan[8] In 1948 a committee chaired by the Chief Secretary of the Colonies, Alec Newboult, examined the problem and made a number of recommendations in its February 1949 report. Coates summarizes the principal recommendations as:

a. wherever possible, squatters should be settled in areas already occupied by them;

b. where this was not possible, they should be resettled in an alternative suitable area;

c. any squatter refusing settlement or resettlement should be repatriated;

d. emergency measures to deal with the security problem of certain areas should be supported by administrative measures designed permanently to reestablish the authority of the government;

e. legal means should be introduced to provide a summary process to evacuate squatters. (Coates 1992, 87)

These recommendations served as guidelines for the Briggs Plan and the mass relocations during Templer's tenure as High Commissioner. By 1949 it was obvious to the colonial government that the efforts of the MCP and the MRLA were closely tied to the support of unregistered rural households through the informal networks of the Min Yuen. Prior to the implementation of the Briggs Plan, the government possessed neither the data to identify the demographic characteristics of this population more definitively, nor the legal authority to move them. Although some haphazard relocation efforts were initiated as early as October 1948, the process had been unsatisfactory, as the police were unable to control the original sites and many residents hid or escaped undetected. Government relocation procedures did not allow residents to carry along their personal belongings, and the new sites were little more than fenced compounds without amenities or a plan to make the sites permanent settlements. Upon "release" many of those relocated in these early efforts would return to their original areas. Lacking the legal means to prevent this, the government could do little to stop relocated residents from returning; it found itself in the position of not knowing with any certainty who had been relocated, who had evaded relocation, and who had, upon being moved, returned to start again. Many government officials suspected that the relocations in late 1948 actually increased local support for the Min Yuen and the MCP.

Without empirical data regarding this population, however, this was only conjecture.

By passing Emergency Regulation 17D in January 1949, the government gained the legal means to detain and relocate designated populations, prohibiting their return to the original sites (Coates 1992, 87). In the sixteen relocation operations that took place in 1949 a greater effort was made to count and track individuals subject to transfer, although these initiatives were still relatively crude and motivated primarily by the need to "show results" rather than to compile extensive demographic data regarding the target populations.

Although the resettlement efforts of 1949 point to the evolving development of a style of governmentality that was systematic in terms of identifying and controlling specific populations, these police/military actions remained haphazard, particularly in regard to what the characteristics of the resettlement site should be. At best, the refugees could hope to find a fenced enclosure with a few buildings and facilities already provided. More often the areas were little more than large, open-air holding pens. Briggs recognized that the formal consolidation of civilian and military governmental operations would not be enough; there would also have to be a comprehensive, regularized system of transforming these holding pens into permanent settlements, or "New Villages." Coates summarizes Briggs's recommendations for the establishment of these villages as requiring "(a) protection; (b) radio communications adequate for security purposes; (c) resettlement long huts and other buildings; (d) a reception and administrative control organization; (e) intelligence agents placed among [the resettled community]" (Coates 1992, 88). Noting that constant governmental intervention and oversight would be necessary in the months and years following relocation, Briggs also emphasized that police posts, schools, dispensaries, cinemas (primarily for propaganda purposes) and other "social welfare" institutions were necessary after the "domination of security forces" for the New Villages to become "socially effective." With the arrival of Templer in 1952, the Briggs Plan was set into motion along these lines with the goal of establishing a "framework of security" throughout the peninsula. Once it was agreed that the plan was the best way to address the MRLA (which had made significant gains from 1948 to 1951 in its efforts to dislodge the British from Malaya) its implementation was swift. By the end of 1952 there were 509 established New Villages with a total population of 461,822—nearly a seventh of the entire Malayan population at that time (Jackson 1991, 20). Landless Chinese peasants were not the only population targeted for resettlement, as a smaller number of *orang asli* tribes were also resettled during these years.[9] Alongside the government policy of "regroupment" of estate workers in outlying areas, scholars offer a conservative estimate of 500,000 Malayans relocated due to the Briggs Plan.[10]

The numerous histories of the Emergency that have emerged after the formal end of the conflict in 1960 generally credit the Briggs Plan with the defeat of the MRLA and the destruction of the MCP. This interpretation is presently emphasized by the Malaysian state, and although the threat of communism is now widely regarded as a straw man in contemporary political debates, the state seldom misses an opportunity to point out that it can trace its history to the defense of Malaya against communist tyranny. Harper summarizes the legacy of the Emergency in this way:

In the shadow of the Communist insurgency the state became a more ruthless and authoritarian instrument of political power. It embedded a powerful rationale of anti-subversion in the official mind and it carved out restraints on political contest. This was a central feature of the mind-set of the post-colonial bureaucracy. The political crisis and communal terror that shook the polity in 1969 seemed to vindicate its anxieties. In this sense, the legacy of British rule was immense. It bequeathed a police force possessed of a unique combination of paramilitary force, security intelligence apparatus, and prosecuting power . . . Colonial policy, we have seen, lurched between authoritarianism and a missionary adherence to the rule of law. Malaysian politicians were reactive to the same stimuli and a strict legalism surrounded the apparatus of suppression. (Harper 1999, 378–379)

Harper asserts that much of the legislation currently in force in Malaysia is a direct result of the Emergency, including the Internal Security Act of 1960, the revised Sedition Act of 1969, the Essential (Security Case) Regulations of 1975, the amended Societies Act of 1981, and the amended Official Secrets Act of 1986. All of these laws, according to Harper, have "added to the momentum of the Barisan government's long period of incumbency [and have] created a constrained role for political opposition" (Harper 1999, 379). I would add the National Land Code to this list in light of the enactment of the New Development Policy (NDP) in 1971 and a continuing contemporary policy of forced relocations in urban areas. Under this set of statutes, aggressive moves to eradicate squatters and reorder urban space were undertaken legally and without extensive formal processes allowing for local input. Because individuals and organizations are subject to strict rules regarding their legal recognition in the public sphere (Societies Act), are limited in the critiques they can publicly offer (Sedition Act), lack direct access to census data, project proposals, assessments, and other official reports necessary to make a effective intervention (Official Secrets Act), and are subject to detention without charge or trial (Internal Security Act), it is little wonder that the state seldom needs more than a copy of the latest edition of the Land Act and a team of bulldozers to initiate urban development projects.

The Generalization of a New Order

Most oral accounts by Brickfields residents assert that the Emergency did not have a substantial impact on the neighborhood. For the duration of the period there were no major developmental or reformist initiatives there. With the government's focus on eradicating the MRLA through the control of the rural Chinese population, most traditional urban development initiatives were shelved during the 1950s. Combined with the fact that preparations were under way throughout the first half of the decade for Malaya's independence from Britain, the focus in Kuala Lumpur was to institute a political system that allowed Malayans themselves to "take the reins" from the British, which they did on August 30, 1957.

Brickfields did, however, experience a great deal of change during this time. The Kuala Lumpur municipal election of 1952 is an example of how an evolving form of municipal governance in the city had a direct impact locally in the area. Although the municipality had come into existence in 1948, for the first four years it was governed by an appointed body. For colonial authorities the municipal election was regarded as a test. Could Malayans "properly" participate in the governance of the country? With the trend toward communally based political parties by then established, it was an open question for the British whether or not Malayans could negotiate "primordial" community identifications in public life.

For this initial election Brickfields was part of the Bungsar Ward,[11] grouped in the same constituency as Bungsar and several Malay *kampungs* located on the edge of the city boundary, including *Kampung Kerinchi* and

Kampung Abdullah Hukum. Compared with other areas, Brickfields was part of the most ethnically diverse ward of the twelve demarcated by the colonial government. As a result, candidates for the seat in this ward were unable to campaign solely on a communally based platform, as Malays, Chinese, and Indians were all strongly represented in the district. Understood in light of this diversity, it was not a surprise that the Bungsar Ward elected the only independent candidate among the twelve during the 1952 election.[12] British fears of communal violence and "chaos" in the municipal sphere were proven to be unjustified, as the leading Malay and Chinese political parties—the United Malays National Organization (UMNO) and the Malayan Chinese Association (MCA)—formed an alliance and coordinated which candidates stood for election in each ward. This strategy allowed the coalition parties to solidly defeat their primary rival, Dato Onn's Independence of Malaya Party (IMP),[13] and the formal cooperation between the two major communal parties is now regarded as the origin of the Alliance[14] that has (with the addition of the MIC and a revolving number of smaller parties over the years) ruled Malaya/Malaysia since its independence in 1957 (Ongkili 1985, 94).

Overt transformations in Brickfields during the 1950s were primarily limited to the political and governmental sphere, because a stronger municipal form of local governance was instituted by the colonial authorities as part of their preparations for Malayan independence. The radical spatial and societal transformations taking place in the context of the Emergency were directed at rural Chinese and *orang asli* communities and did not appear to involve urban neighborhoods such as Brickfields directly. Many Brickfields residents who remember the Emergency reported that the neighborhood was "quiet" and "not really affected" by the operations taking place in the countryside and in the New Villages established a few miles south of the area. Locally there was no fighting, no heavy police presence, and no obvious attempts to reorganize the neighborhood physically.

The Persistence of the Squatter

The Emergency did have some influence in Brickfields, however. One clear change related to the Emergency was the continued growth of unregistered dwellings in local *kampung* areas. Because much of the actual violence of the Emergency took place on rural rubber estates, many former estate workers made their way to Brickfields. Although the area had always had a large population of laborers and working-class Tamils, until this time most of these residents did not originate from the estates. Seeking to escape the violence, many Tamil estate workers left the plantations and settled in the network of unregistered *kampungs* at the center of Brickfields.

The population of the *kampungs* also increased because many long-time railway workers were reaching retirement age and, upon leaving their jobs, were setting up unregistered homes in Brickfields and Sentul. Although the FMS Railways[15] provided housing for their workers, retirees were forced to vacate their quarters. Most of these employees had lived in Malaya for decades and their repatriation to India was not a viable option.[16] Without the means to purchase property of their own, many of these retirees settled in illegal urban *kampung* areas (Sidhu 1978, 64).

The "squatter problem" reached an even greater level of intensity in the late 1960s, when the government introduced legislation requiring all noncitizens to obtain work permits, regardless of how long they had previously been in Malaya. This law primarily affected the nonskilled labor force remaining on the rubber plantations, forcing many of these laborers out of work entirely and leading to a great number of them being repatriated to India. Those who avoided deportation made their way to the cities to attempt to set up a small business of some kind, as petty traders were exempted from the legislation. As before, this renewed exodus found the populations of primarily Indian neighborhoods such as Brickfields and Sentul swelling with migrants from the rural areas (Sidhu 1978, 65).

The importance of these trends would become clear by the late 1960s and early 1970s, as the issue of squatters remained a primary concern of the state well after the end of the Emergency. Although the MCP and the MRLA were well under control by the early 1970s, the specter of the "squatter" remained as the primary symbol of social disorder. By this time Brickfields was home to one of the largest unregistered residential colonies in the entire city. This fact made the area subject to an intense program of development and reordering that has, in fits and starts, continued to the present.

The "squatter" was a resilient figure of social disorder for government officials, city planners, and academics during the late 1960s and 1970s.

Academic works, reports, and public presentations dating from that time reveal a grave concern with unregistered households, taking for granted that such household configurations were the cause of crime and the breakup of families, hindered the development of a properly "modern" work ethic, and were generally unhealthy for all city dwellers, whether they actually lived in these *kampungs* or not. The summaries of meetings to formulate a comprehensive "draft structure" plan for the city of Kuala Lumpur bears this out, with the squatter problem occupying a great deal of concern on the part of planners and officials. One researcher writing in 1977 explicitly linked the squatter with problems of the nation when he wrote: "It cannot be overemphasized that the problem of 'squatting' as a manifestation of urban poverty, and its attendant implications are growing in magnitude and seriousness and therefore will continue to pose a very serious problem to the nation unless effectively tackled" (Ishak 1977, 111).

Taken in the context of the early years of the NDP, the linkages between squatting, poverty, and national disorder are unsurprising. Most of the literature produced by social scientists connected to the state characterized the problem in this manner throughout the 1970s. Despite the call for a more systematic effort on the part of the state to "eradicate" squatting, however, researchers and policy makers also argued for a "hearts and minds" approach to the problem. M.K. Sen, consultant to the Town Planning Office, regarded squatting as a complex social phenomenon that required a multifaceted approach. Presenting at the KL Forum '73 Sen stated:

The problems of squatters should not be viewed merely as a contest between law and lawlessness. Though squatting is illegal, a strictly legalistic attitude towards it will not help to overcome the problem, as very often, squatters have no other alternative and had they been given one, they might not have flouted the law. A large majority of the squatters are prepared to conform to the law, if given a reasonable opportunity to do so, and particularly with regard to the provision of land and housing. (Sen 1973, 32)

Sen's characterization of the problem summarizes a sentiment regarding squatters that was becoming more common with policy makers and academics at the time. Chiding civil authorities for the increasingly brutal tactics of urban *kampung* clearance, Sen continued:

Squatter areas are not as disorganized and insecure as their physical appearance normally suggests. The value system of squatters is still very traditional and conservative. There is also considerable political participation by squatters and as their settlements grow older, there tends to be a gradual replacement of traditional practices with a new kind of settlement structure and organisation based on urban values reflected through labor and trade unions and political affiliations. (Sen 1973, 25)

In Sen's analysis squatters were "rational actors"[17] who would respond to proper inducements to lawful behavior on the part of the state. Sen's call for a deeper understanding of unregistered communities and the forces involved in their existence did not lead him, however, to question the overall framing of the issue in state discourses. To the contrary, he felt that the complexity of the problem made it more serious and potentially threatening than people believed. Although rational actors, Sen believed that squatters were still very suggestible and were coming under some bad influences:

There is evidence . . . as can be proved by the authorities, that squatter areas are the breeding grounds of considerable social problems particularly gangsterism, criminal acts, juvenile delinquency, prostitution and other social evils . . . With [a] value system emphasising personal and family improvement, community solidarity, conformity with social norms and identification with the common good, it is very difficult to dismiss squatter areas as evils in society and that all social and political problems stem from them. Very often however, it is their exposure to the existence of other social organisations such as labour unions, student organizations, political factions etc. that contribute to their hostility from time to time. (Sen 1973, 24)

Sen's assessment echoes the conclusions of the hasty evaluations of the Chinese rural poor conducted in the 1940s and 1950s under the aegis of the Briggs Plan. As with the earlier plan, it was in the interest of the state to separate this population from the bad influences of their environment and to provide a comprehensive alternative to their current way of life that illustrated the "error of their ways." Unlike most other comments on the squatter problem at the time, Sen addressed the question of the legacy of the Emergency, albeit in somewhat disingenuous terms:

There is another specific reason for squatting in Kuala Lumpur, which is due to the effects of the Emergency and Communist insurgency during the period 1948 to 1960. Large numbers of people moved to the urban centres for the security it afforded. Many of these people had hitherto been living on the peripheral areas and as the threat of communist hostility grew these people were forced to move to more secure areas. The exact number that moved during this period is however, not available. (Sen 1973, 20)

Sen's misrepresentation of the process by which the relocation of Chinese rural poor took place is breathtaking due to its implication that this population moved willingly to urban areas in search of security. Sen cites no statistics, studies, or evidence of any kind to support his assertion; he actually goes on to claim that the exact numbers are unknown, even though the government worked very hard to improve its methods of keeping track of rural populations.[18]

This reading of the Emergency is central to what Sen and others suggested regarding the squatter problem in the 1970s. According to many local experts at the time, the Briggs Plan was effective because it improved the everyday living conditions of the rural poor and provided a clear rationale for the reordering of their lives. Once they fully understood it, targeted individuals willingly submitted to the plan, as they realized that it was in their "best interest" to do so. Similarly, Sen characterized urban squatters as immature rational actors who had not been properly exposed to the logic of the state's plans. If he had entertained the possibility that the logic of the state itself could be rejected, much of what he then proposed regarding unregistered households in Kuala Lumpur would have fallen apart. The coercion of the Emergency *had* to disappear for Malaysian urban planners in the 1970s, even if the dangerous figure of the squatter remained very much present. Furthermore, as Sen and others made clear, this figure endured in places such as Brickfields.[19]

The entreaties of Sen, Ishak, and others had their effect on state policy, as exemplified by the first Kuala Lumpur Draft Structure Plan published in 1982. The preparation of a comprehensive plan for the purpose of guiding urban development was motivated by a provision in the Town and Country Planning Act of 1976 that required the municipal authorities in all Malaysian cities to prepare structure plans. Ironically, Kuala Lumpur was the only major city exempt from this act because it had been designated a federal territory in 1972 and was not covered by the law. Despite lacking the legal authority to do so, the Dewan Bandaraya Kuala Lumpur (City Hall) was the first authority to prepare such a plan[20] (Goh 1991, 84). This document sought to give a comprehensive picture of contemporary urban life in Kuala Lumpur and recommend policies to improve the urban sphere that would be drafted into law. As with earlier documents, squatters were a primary concern in the Draft Structure Plan.

The impact of a "hearts and minds" approach was evident in this document. Rather than treating the problem as a criminal issue, the Draft Structure Plan made it clear that DBKL regarded squatting as a broad socioeconomic problem:

The majority of squatters have no other solution to their housing problem. Squatting is the only alternative. As a community, the squatters are fairly united and perceived that their continual existence depends on their unity. The squatter labour force has been an indispensable source of manpower for the city's growing economy. Nevertheless, because of their unplanned, unsanitary and congested conditions, the squatter settlements are regarded to be inappropriate in the urban modern setting. Thus, there is a need for solutions. (Dewan Bandaraya Kuala Lumpur 1982, 117)

Compared to the negative citations by Sen, Ishak, and others of municipal attitudes, this statement was "progressive" in its tone. Although more humanistic in tone, the Draft Structure Plan articulated an ideal urban order that had been a prominent part of municipal thinking since the time of Frank Swettenham. These disciplinary aspects are clearer in the specific recommendations of the plan, including:

> SQ 1: THE AUTHORITY SHALL PROVIDE HOUSING TO SQUATTER HOUSEHOLDS.
>
> SQ 2: STUDIES ON INDIVIDUAL SQUATTER SETTLEMENTS SHALL BE CARRIED OUT.
>
> SQ 5: THE AUTHORITY SHALL CONTINUOUSLY TAKE ACTION TO ELIMINATE SQUATTER LANDLORDS
>
> SQ 7: THE AUTHORITY SHALL SET UP A PERMANENT SQUATTER DEPARTMENT TO DEAL WITH ALL SQUATTER RELATED PROBLEMS AND TO COORDINATE PROGRAMMES FOR SQUATTERS. (Devon Bandaraya Kuala Lumpur 1982, 120–123; capitalization in original)

The recommendations of the Draft Structure Plan were rooted in the now well-established notion that squatters must be eliminated and that they must be properly brought around to the idea that this process is for their own good. Coupled with the precedents established during the time of the Emergency and a legal apparatus that overwhelmingly favored the state in matters related to land, the municipal government enjoyed a great deal of latitude in dealing with communities such as Brickfields when attempting to realize radical urban development projects. The Draft Structure Plan's explicit emphasis on the continuing need to reorder the space of the city rationally, in order to alleviate problems of traffic, decrease high population densities in the central urban core, and organize zones in the city designed to facilitate single-use space, set the conditions for the transformation of Brickfields that took place during the years 2000–2002. What the plan, and the law itself, did *not* provide in this context was convincing moral arguments as to how the rule of the state was linked to a broadly accepted notion of the Good in the context of governance. This missing moral justification for rule would have to come from elsewhere. In recent years many have looked to Islam for this moral force.

The Evolving Role of Islam in Malaysian Public Life

Islamic Reform Movements in Colonial Malaya

Although little noticed at the time, the appearance of a new Malay-language periodical in 1906 explicitly marked an important debate that was evolving regarding the nature of politics in Malay society and the role of Islam in public life. Beginning with the publication of its initial issue in Singapore in July 1906, *Al-Imam* (The Leader) established the terms of a public debate that continues to this day regarding these two issues. Primarily concerned with the condition of the Malay community and with promoting a reformist message that simultaneously called for an openness to the technological innovations of the West and an Islam "cleansed" of the errors and impurities of Malay customary practices, *Al-Imam*'s first issue articulated a consistent theme that the journal would continue to present for the next quarter century (Roff 1994, 56–67). Precisely determining the size and nature of the journal's readership is difficult. Roff maintains that the majority of *Al-Imam*'s audience came from the small but growing class of urban Malays and religious educators who were exposed to Islamic debates taking place in Mecca (Roff 1994, 65). Although numerically small, this group of educated Malays was beginning to occupy positions of authority in the colonial bureaucracy and was by the 1920s and 1930s particularly influential in the educational sphere. Therefore, while *Al-Imam* never attained a large popular circulation, its influence regarding religious, political, and social debates in the Malay community is considered to be decisive in generating the *Kaum Muda* (Young Group) reform movement.[21]

Al-Imam advocated a platform for reform that linked education, economic development, and self-awareness within its understanding of the "true Islam." Malay customary practice (*adat*)[22] was understood as an obstacle to progress, and *Al-Imam* consistently criticized the ruling elite and the *ulama* for perpetuating an imperfect form of Islam. To address this issue the journal consistently published articles proposing a revised system of education that emphasized Islamic doctrinal instruction, language training in Arabic and English in addition to Malay, and the teaching of modern educational subjects alongside instruction in religious and moral matters. *Al-Imam* also published long articles regarding proper moral conduct, child rearing, the history of Islam, and analyses of disputed matters of religious interpretation that emphasized the need to return to the *Qur'an* and *hadith* literature in the consideration of these issues (Milner 1995). In keeping with its internationalist orientation, the journal freely mixed original articles with translations from Arabic sources abroad, and featured news stories from the Islamic countries of the Middle East and other parts of Asia (Roff 1994, 57–59).

During the twenty-five years of its existence *Al-Imam*'s efforts to set the terms of the debate regarding the role of Islam in public life were generally limited to exhortation over action. Although *Al-Imam* advocated a strong Muslim presence in the public sphere, and the reforms called for by the journal were often critical of the Malay rulers and the religious elite, the direct confrontation with these groups that the writers for *Al-Imam* sought did not occur until the question of nationalism more explicitly emerged in the political debates of the 1920s and 1930s (Milner 1995). Known as the *Kaum Muda,* this group of young nationalists challenged British rule by attacking the Malay traditional elite, who by this time functioned as uneasy partners with their colonial rulers. Using a critique of customary authority similar to that articulated by *Al-Imam* from 1906, the *Kaum Muda* came into direct conflict with state religious authorities over a number of political, social, and doctrinal questions. Roff describes the character of these disputes as "on the one hand, an attempt by those Muslims with a more intensive experience of metropolitan Islam to purify ritual and belief from purely local innovations and on the other, an attempt by urban-centered Muslims to reformulate Islam in response to the economic and social pressures of contemporary life" (Roff 1994, 79).

With their strident critiques of *adat* and their insistence on the equality of all individuals before Allah, the *Kaum Muda's* dual critique of established religion and the traditional elite was understood as having subversive intent; it generated a loose reactive faction, the *Kaum Tua* (Old Group).

Although the conflicts between the *Kaum Muda* and the *Kaum Tua* were still rooted in disputes over religion, the increasingly strident rhetoric and expanded scope of the discussions indicates the overtly political dimensions of the debates. Where the editors of *Al-Imam* were careful to avoid directly attacking Malay elites, religious authorities, or the British in their articles, newer journals such as *Seruan Azhar* (Voice of Azhar) and *Pilehan Timour* (Choice of the East) reflected a new generation of nationalists who engaged concepts of Pan-Malayanism and anti-colonial struggle alongside the issue of religious practice. For this new generation, colonial rule was as much an impediment to progress as religious error. In the politicized environment of the 1930s, the *Kaum Muda–Kaum Tua* cleavage over religious issues became a more general dispute over the symbols and bases of authority in Malay public life (Nagata 1984, 13). Complicated by the influence of the loosely socialist orientation of Indonesian nationalist movements, the issue of national independence and social reform was less frequently expressed through idioms of Islam by 1940.

The ambiguous status of Islam in Malayan public life surfaced as an issue during the attempt by the British to form the Malayan Union[23] upon returning to the peninsula after the Japanese Occupation, and throughout the Emergency in the 1950s.[24] In the protracted negotiations leading up to Malayan independence in 1957 the public role of Islam was debated as a constitutional issue (Fernando 2002). The formal solution reflected in the final document was to declare that Islam was officially the religion of the federation, but that religious freedom generally was a fundamental right of citizenship. The first prime minister, Tunku Abdul Rahman, summarized the understanding of Islam's role held by the Malay elite when in 1958 he stated that "this country is not an Islamic state as it is generally understood; we merely provide that Islam shall be the official religion of the state," implying that Islam's formal place in government was for ceremonial purposes (Ahmad 1978, 55). Although not everyone shared Tunku Abdul Rahman's offhand understanding of Islam as cultural ceremony, organized political action intended to interject Islam into government and politics was limited to local and state politics until the late 1970s and the emergence of the *dakwah* movement.

Dakwah

Like the *Kaum Muda* before them, the *dakwah* movement that emerged in Malaysia during the late 1970s was not a unified movement led by a single organization. Rather, the *dakwah* movement refers to an assemblage of ideas, trends, activities, and organizations that seek to promote Islam. Although the state, particularly during the later years of Prime Minister Mahathir's tenure, sought to absorb and co-opt many of the reformist ideas of the movement, *dakwah* groups generally have little institutional or traditional basis for their authority (Nagata 1984, 81).

Most scholars view the *dakwah* movement as one of the most powerful means in contemporary Malaysia to articulate opposition to government policy and critique traditional modes of authority (Chandra 1987; Husin 1993; Kessler 1980; Milner 1986; Nagata 1984; Peletz 2002). The appeal of *dakwah*'s "call" to everyday Muslims in Malaysia, however, has its limits. Primarily an urban-based movement led by highly educated members of the growing Malay middle class, its fundamentalist zeal for purifying Malaysian Islam of the influence of *adat* and its palpable mistrust of local religious authorities has alienated many ordinary Malays (Peletz 2002). Exhibiting what Nagata characterizes as "a strong streak of fundamentalism" while rejecting traditional modes of scholarly authority within Islam, *dakwah* organizations often exhibit "an extreme devotion to atavistic forms of Arabism, some of whose connections with Islam are tenuous and the result more of historical coincidence than theological requirement" (Nagata 1984, 86). Unlike reformist movements in Indonesia such as the *Muhammadiyah*[25] who sought to innovate local Islam in conjunction with contemporary economic and technological developments (Geertz 1963; Hefner 2000; Peacock 1978), Malaysian *dakwah* groups often advocate a return to a golden age of Islam as articulated by Islamic intellectuals such as the Pakistani scholar Maulana al-Mawdudi.[26] Extolling the virtues of "Arabic" Islam over local understandings of faith and proper religious practice exacerbates the rift between the cosmopolitan leaders of *dakwah* organizations and local Malay communities that resent being unfavorably ranked against "foreigners."

Given the strident critiques of the government that *dakwah* organizations have persistently articulated since the late 1970s, the Malaysian state's initial reaction to these groups was highly negative. Seeking to reject the *dakwah* message as extreme and "un-Islamic" and weaken the political impact of the largest organizations, the government deployed a multileveled strategy of suppressing the groups themselves through surveillance and periodical arrest of the leaders and the establishment of competing religious institutions whose aim was to bring a "more correct" form of Islam to the fore of Malaysian public life. This complex set of responses was necessitated by the clear popularity of *dakwah* groups by the early 1980s among the urban Malay middle class and the temporary effectiveness that organizations such as the *Angkatan Belia Islam Malaysia* (ABIM—in English, Malaysian Muslim Youth League) and *Darul Arqam* (House of Arqam) were having in organizing schools, businesses, and in some cases entire communities along *dakwah* reformist lines.[27] Responding to the limited success that *dakwah* organizations had in subverting state authority by setting up institutions that bypassed government regulations and control, the Malaysian government moved quickly to transform its own institutions within an Islamic framework (Nagata 1984, 158–184).

As the place of Islam in Malaysian public life was debated and reformulated throughout the 1980s and 1990s by the state, opposition political parties such as Parti Islam Se-Malaysia (PAS), and *dakwah* organizations, the issue of the Islamic state emerged as a central question. The government's position on this question evolved during the final two decades of the twentieth century. Syeikh Mokhsein, a member of the National Religious Council of the Federal Territory, stated in 1980 that while he supported the notion that Malaysia should be an Islamic state in principle, the nation itself was "not ready" for such a radical change. His suggestion to *dakwah* reformists calling for an Islamic state was "to wait" and strive in the meantime to alter the present form of governance to resemble an Islamic ideal more closely (Nagata 1984, 98). Likewise, the larger *dakwah* organizations were cautious regarding the call for an Islamic state in Malaysia. While the leadership of ABIM openly expressed their admiration for the Iranian revolution, they took care to emphasize that Iran, Libya, Pakistan, and Syria were all inappropriate models of governance for Malaysia, and avoided direct calls for revolutionary change. In Nagata's words, ABIM "constantly referred to ideals but rarely the details" (Nagata 1984, 98).

The fact that the emergent Malay middle class that benefited the most from interventionist socioeconomic restructuring strategies initiated by the government such as the New Economic Policy (NEP)[28] was also the group for whom the *dakwah* resurgence was most felt highlights the material reasons for this caution. A.B. Shamsul summarizes these tensions:

The "dakwah-isation" of the Malay new middle class has highlighted the "neo-liberalist" tendencies within it, particularly its internal contradictions. On the one hand, it is highly in favor of the continued expansion of the market and promotion of aggressive individualism, thus making it hostile to tradition. On the other hand, its political survival depends upon the manipulation and persistence of tradition for its legitimacy, hence its attachment to conservatism, notably in areas concerning the nation, religion, gender, and the family. (Shamsul 1999, 103)

Desiring a greater role for Islam in governance and public life yet also the beneficiaries of state efforts to restructure the economy to the greater benefit of Malays, moderate factions with the *dakwah* movement sought to work within the state for change. Many of these moderates found employment in the private and public sector and joined the ranks of UMNO, succeeding in "mainstreaming" Islam within the everyday functions of the state (Shamsul 1999, 102). While the emergence of this new middle class exacerbated tensions between Malays and non-Malays (particularly the Chinese community) and heightened class divisions within the Malay community itself (Peletz 2002, 8–9), the influx of beneficiaries of the NEP and NDP who favored both the capitalist market and a greater role for Islam in public life generated a unique mode of governance in Malaysia that pushed the state to ground its established interventionist "style" in a discourse of the Good that fused capitalism and Islam.[29] This set of circumstances increasingly framed discourses of the Good and the morality of the state's conduct through the 1990s and culminated with the controversial announcement by Prime Minister Mahathir that Malaysia was "already" an Islamic state on September 29, 2001.

Religion, Moral Authority, and the Issue
of the Islamic State in Malaysia

Prime Minister Mahathir's announcement[30] was highly controversial and widely opposed by many Malaysians. Because there was no plan to replace the secular legal system with one based on *Shari'a* law, most scholars, commentators, and leaders of the opposition dismissed the announcement out of hand as inaccurate and representative of a dangerous political ploy on the prime minister's part (Lim 2002; Noor 2002; Peletz 2005). These widespread objections are important to mark; the fact that the announcement was not accompanied by legislation in Parliament intended to formalize Malaysia's status as an Islamic state meant that the prime minister's announcement lacked the force of law. It would be a mistake, however, to dismiss his pronouncement as unimportant, as the conditions that made the declaration possible have been evolving for some time. My interest in the announcement here is not to "prove" or "disprove" the prime minister's claim, but rather to examine the context behind the statement and the trajectory of Mahathir's thinking in the course of linking a reformist Islamic agenda with a well-established interventionist mode of governance.

According to Mahathir, Malaysia has been an Islamic state for some time.[31] This statement is consistent with Mahathir's personal view of the history of Islam, particularly the history of the great Muslim dynasties of the past and the rise of the *ulama*. Mahathir has consistently expressed an idiosyncratic view of modernity, on which it has already come and gone once for Muslims. For Mahathir, a developed, modern society is one that does not limit itself strictly to "Islamic" matters but rather strives to develop in all fields—science, literature, trade, etc. "True" Muslims will not reject science, technology, or wealth, and Mahathir cites Muslim dynasties of the past (such as the Ottoman Empire) as being models of both Islam and modernity. In this reading, Muslims were the first modern people. Yet, Mahathir asserts, these Islamic empires regressed when they allowed for the development of the *ulama* as an institution separate from worldly concerns. In his telling, as the *ulama* grew in its power it sought to separate the practice of Islam from the realms of science, commerce, and art, narrowing the scope of what is permissible in Islam. In an April 1997 address at Oxford Mahathir clarified his interpretation of Islamic history:

Unfortunately, with the advent of the Muslim jurists and the so-called reformists, studies other than those specifically related to religion and its practices were frowned upon and eventually proscribed. With this the Muslims regressed. True, it was the abuses and deviations from the teachings and practices of Islam, particularly by the elites which brought about the reform movements and the ascendancy of the Muslim jurists. (Mahathir, as quoted by Martinez 2001, 222)

According to Mahathir, as the power of the *ulama* increased over time the Muslim world became more backward, inward looking, and vulnerable to Western nations who learned "how to be modern" from Muslims. Therefore, the blame for current problems of inequality and underdevelopment in most Muslim nations lay squarely with these nations themselves. Mahathir includes Malaysia in this category. This understanding of Islamic history is convenient for Mahathir for several reasons. First, pursuit of material wealth is not understood as un-Islamic. Rather, one *must* pursue wealth in order to be a good Muslim. Second, when practiced properly, Islam is the best guide for running a modern state. Therefore, it is not necessary to separate Islamic law and practice from the functions of the state. The implication is that the institution of the *ulama* is redundant in a true Islamic state. Third, Islam is not inward looking, but seeks to make connections with the outside world, including connections with non-Muslims. Such openness[32] also allows non-Muslims living in a Muslim state to prosper, even as a category of citizen that distinguishes them from Muslims.

Throughout his career in public life it was clear that the prime minister had little patience for the long tradition of debate in Islamic jurisprudence (*tafsir bil ma'athur* in Arabic, *hukum fiqh* in Malay), and his open distain for members of the *ulama* and for *dakwah* groups who challenged his policies based on their own interpretations of Islam is well known. Contrary to practices of scholarly disagreement (*ikhtilaf*) in interpreting Islam, the government often interpreted any criticism of its policies as an "insult against Islam," using the fact that it is against the law to slander, mock, or otherwise insult Islam in Malaysia[33] to stifle most discussion of these issues (Martinez 2001, 219). The fact that the everyday practices of the state were often understood through this broadly religious discourse of governance made it increasingly difficult to talk about issues of development, of government policy, and of citizenship without reference to religion.[34] Yet the substance of what constituted an "official" and hence acceptable interpretation of Islam was unclear. Formal government bodies charged with promoting an understanding of Islam often produced books and pamphlets that seldom referred directly to the *Qur'an* or *Hadith* literature in the course of promoting an agenda of modernization and economic development. Regarding the most important of these government agencies, *Institut Kefahaman Islam Malaysia* (IKIM—Malaysian Institute of Islamic Understanding), Martinez notes:

Some IKIM articles over the years and up to the present have little or no reference to the Qur'an, *ahadith* literature (tradition and sayings of the Prophet Muhammad; sing. Hadith) or the *shari'a* (Islamic canonical law). These articles just describe a particular government programme, proposal or perspective in great detail, in the context of general statement about Islam or Muslims. (Martinez 2001, 235)

Despite the lack of clear definition, the notion of "deviance" was quite central to this governmental discourse and was used in a variety of ways, including the discrediting of legal political parties such as PAS and the suppression of more radical *dakwah* groups such as *Darul Arqam*.

Contrary to popular accounts in the media, attempts to reform government practice along Islamic lines were not uncritically accepted by the population at large. Non-Muslim Chinese and Indian communities were clearly alarmed by these initiatives. Additionally, the Qur'anic interpretations offered by Mahathir and many government intellectuals placed them at odds with many independent Muslim intellectuals and theologians both in Malaysia and throughout the Muslim world.[35]

There is significant evidence that there is a great deal of opposition within the Malay community to Mahathir's claim that Malaysia is already a modern Muslim state. Peletz argues that "ordinary Malays" (his term) are ambivalent about attempts at Islamic reform originating both from the state and from *dakwah* groups formally outside of the government. Noting that reformists both inside and outside of the machinery of the state tend to belong to a highly educated urban middle class (the *Melayu Baru*), Peletz traces an ambivalent, if largely unelaborated, unease on the part of ordinary Malay Muslims regarding the logic and imagined outcomes of these reforms, particularly in terms of the reformists' consistent attack on the local customs and beliefs subsumed under the rubric of *adat* (Peletz 2002).

Adat is a broad concept that refers to the "local customs" of Malays. Although *adat* is a concept that ranges across Malay communities, it also marks certain contrasts between local communities. It generally refers to a distinctive set of local practices, such as *adat perpatih* as commonly practiced in Negeri Sembilan, or variants of *adat temenggong* found throughout the rest of the peninsula and further localized through reference to "Kelantanese *adat*," "Terengganu *adat*," and so forth.[36]

Adat refers to more than notions of kinship and ancestry, referring also to local beliefs and practices regarding the origins of the world and humanity, the relationship of humans to nature and to the spirit world, and the proper forms of sociality between individuals, families, and communities. Wazir Jahan Karim states that *adat* functions in a complementary fashion with abstract notions of morality, order, and justice found in Islamic codes. She writes:

[*Adat's*] framework of ideas and influences about "morality," "order," and justice is "popular" compared to Islam's formal scripturalism. It is through adat that state, regional, or community preferences of custom and practices continue to be maintained and it is on these levels of social interaction that deep-rooted sentiments of origin (*keturunan*) and community sharing (*perkauman*), kinship and affinity (*kekerabatan dan persaudaraan*) and social rituals (*adat istiadat*) serve to maintain and strengthen values of cohesion and identity. In this aspect, Islam, with its more worldly provisions of inter-ethnic affiliation, maintains the more symbolic function of cohesion, elevating "folk-culture" to a "great tradition." (Wazir 1992, 15)

Although Wazir implies a hierarchy of authority in her statement ("folk culture" elevates to "great tradition"), she captures some of the complexity of the relationship between *adat* and Islam for ordinary Malays. The division she makes is an analytical one, however, and although *adat* varies from region to region, it is consistently imagined by local Malays as being directly rooted in Islam and the *Qur'an* and therefore the proper observance of *adat* is locally the same as the proper observance of Islam.

Mahathir's public statements exemplify official attitudes toward *adat* and its specific practices, highlighting how *adat* observance was often evidence for Islamic reformers of the irrationality and irreligion of ordinary Malays. Writing before he became Prime Minister, Mahathir stated:

The value concepts of Islam in Malaysia are affected by the much older faiths of the Malays. Some, especially animism, have a much greater hold on the rural than the urban Malays. The influence of these faiths is therefore still considerable in the rural areas, and at times it runs counter to Islam. Apart from religious faith, Malay civilization has thrown up a comprehensive and rather formidable code of behaviour and forms of ceremony which go by the name *adat* or custom. *Adat* itself appears to be influenced by the past and present religions of the Malays, *but there is a considerable portion of it which appears to be unique and quite unrelated to any faith*. (Mahathir 1970, 156; emphasis added)

For Mahathir *adat* did not represent diverse understandings of conduct, practice, and the world originating from within Islam, but rather was a mixture of pre-Islamic belief and practice separate from any established religious faith. According to Mahathir it was a failure on the part of Malays that *adat* was not recognized as being at variance with the "substance" of Islam: "To outwardly bend with the wind is the adherence to form as prescribed by *adat*. In the Malay code of behaviour, form is so important that it is preferred to actual substance" (Mahathir 1970, 158). *Adat* for Mahathir represented devotion to form at the cost of being religiously correct. In keeping with his training as a physician, Mahathir's final word on the subject clearly pathologized the ordinary Malay:

By and large, the Malay value system and code of ethics are impediments to their progress. If they admit this, and if the need for change is realized, then there is hope; for as in psychiatry, success in isolating the root cause is in itself a part of the treatment. From then on planning a cure would be relatively simple. (Mahathir 1970, 173)

Absent from Mahathir's discussion of Malay values and *adat* in *The Malay Dilemma* is the notion that proper observance of Islamic principles is the key to addressing the problems of development and the formation of a public life in Malaysia. At the time Mahathir wrote this book his concerns were primarily the genetic characteristics of "the Malay race" and how Malays could address the economic and political inequities facing the community in the wake of the May 1969 riots in Kuala Lumpur.[37] *The Malay Dilemma* continually refers to genetics and the somatic, with society imagined as a body subject to "illness" and responsive to the diagnostic techniques of the physician.

Mahathir did not always hold such a disdainful view of *adat*. In his 1962 article "Adat and Islam," Mahathir described an integrative and complimentary relationship between the two, focusing on the social value of flexibility and compromise in Malay society generally (Martinez 2001, 219). By the time Mahathir became prime minister in 1981, however, his thinking regarding the relationship between Islam and *adat* had shifted. In his 1986 book *The Challenge,* Mahathir claimed that "Islam is one of the most powerful influences in replacing bad values with good ones" (Mahathir 1986, 98). His discussion of *adat* and Malay values entitled "A System of Values and the Malays," was, aside from a greater emphasis on Islamic correctness, essentially the same as what was offered in *The Malay Dilemma,* albeit in a slightly less abrasive and overtly biologic tone.

Despite their differences regarding many aspects of Islamic doctrine, *dakwah* reformers understood *adat* in a fashion similar to Mahathir. Noting that many practices associated with *adat* involve the appeasing of local spirits and paying homage to long-dead ancestors, *dakwah* groups viewed *adat* as sinful (*dosa*) and bordering on polytheism. Established local practices such as the *kenduri* (ritual feast) and having the bride and groom perform the *bersanding* (sitting in state) during weddings were characterized as wasteful and out of character with proper Islamic observance. The *kenduri* was particularly troublesome for the reformers, in that it was seen as highly ostentatious and a burden on poorer Malays due to the excessive cost that such feasts tend to incur. Moreover, the *kenduri* was held not only to cement social ties among neighbors (*slamet*) but also to bring pleasure to the spirits of deceased ancestors (*roh arwah*).

Islamic reformers made the cleansing of *adat* and the reform of local religious practices a top priority. This priority has been a staple of Islamic reform movements on the Malaysian peninsula long before the current upsurge of *dakwah* activity. Peletz writes:

Since the late nineteenth century and during the past few decades in particular, core symbols of Malayness long subsumed under the rubric of adat—and in some cases that of Islam as well—have been denigrated by Islamic resurgents on the grounds that they are pre- or simply un-Islamic and, as a result, have had their legitimacy undermined. In some cases, moreover, the psychological and sociological scope and force of such symbols have been drastically undercut, and the ritual and other practices associated with them have ceased to exist. At the same time, there has been a dialectically related process entailing the development and expansion of Islamic symbols and idioms, a process that has clearly advanced (though it need not do so) at the direct expense of adat both as an institutional framework and as a system of symbols and meanings. (Peletz 1997, 256)

Yet *adat* persists as a decisive aspect of everyday life for ordinary Malays. Peletz identifies the problem when, referring to Carol Laderman's

(1993) work regarding *Main Peteri,* a (now defunct) genre of shamanistic performance formerly popular in Kelantan, he writes:

On the one hand, owing largely to opposition cast in Islamic terms, certain long-established rituals are no longer performed. On the other hand, many of the sanctified beliefs and postulates encoded in such rituals retain their wide currency and are, for many villagers, still thoroughly compelling. The more general dilemma is that while Islamic opposition to local *adat* has intensified in recent decades, these very same *adat* (or certain features of them) still comprise important, if increasingly devalued, components of cultural identity among ordinary Malays in Kelantan, Negeri Sembilan, and elsewhere, particularly as they help demarcate and reinforce the boundaries of local communities and differentiate locally defined groups of Malays both from one another and from outsiders as a whole. (Peletz 1997, 258)

Although primarily in reference to Laderman's account of *Main Peteri,* Peletz's observations are generalizable to Malaysia as a whole. While Peletz and Laderman focus on the role of *adat* in rural sociality, *adat's* importance remains strong in urban centers such as Kuala Lumpur as well. Despite the concerted attacks on *adat* in terms of both its logic and subsequent practices, this form of local knowledge continues to influence how many Malays conceptualize the world and their place in it.

Religion and Public Life for Non-Muslim Communities

This particular discourse of Islam and governance has, despite Mahathir's protests to the contrary, made it more difficult for non-Muslim communities in Malaysia to articulate a substantial stake in governance. Despite continual references to the idea that Islam allows for freedom of worship for non-Muslims and that compelled conversion to Islam is *haram* (forbidden), it was also clear that the rights of non-Muslims were limited in the official version of what an Islamic state should be. The 2001 publication (subsequently withdrawn) of a booklet entitled *Malaysia Adalah Sebuah Negara Islam* (*Malaysia Is an Islamic State/Nation*)[38] by the Ministry of Information made it clear that while an Islamic government can appoint non-Muslim ministers, these ministers must carry out their duties in strict accordance with Islam and can ultimately only support the policies of the Islamic rulers. Furthermore, the terminology deployed to refer to non-Muslims in the booklet (primarily the term *zimmi* or *dhimmi*, which has a pejorative connotation) indexed these communities as a class apart from (and, by implication, lower than) Muslims. At best, non-Muslim religious practice would be tolerated at the level of private belief.

The booklet's understanding of religious tolerance as rooted in private belief resembles the understanding of religious diversity articulated by the British during the colonial era. The idea, first articulated in the Pangkor Agreement of 1874, that the Malay Sultans would retain authority over matters pertaining to the culture and religion of the Malays resembles how the Malaysian state officially regarded non-Muslim religious practice (Andaya and Andaya 1982; Chai 1967; Cowan 1961; Sadka 1968). This resemblance was superficial, in the sense that during colonial times religious practice was relegated to the realm of the cultural and the private primarily due to the idea that religion should remain separate from government. The Malaysian government in the early years of the twenty-first century, committed to a state that functioned in accordance with Islam, could not shunt aside the question of the truth of the *Qur'an* in dealing with non-Muslim communities. Still formally bound by the secular Merdeka Constitution of 1957 and the fact that nearly 35 percent of Malaysia's population is non-Muslim, the Malaysian government was faced with the contradiction that while Islam is the official religion of the Federation the state must also guarantee some semblance of equality under the law to communities who do not recognize Islam as the basis of governance.

Conclusion

This chapter has sought to provide the necessary historical context for understanding the character of urban development, the law, and the place of religion in the transformation of Brickfields during the years 2000–2002. The summaries of the Emergency and Islamic reform movements in Malaysia during the twentieth century represent social and political transformations that established forms of association and process that marked Brickfields during the time that I conducted fieldwork there. The divergent responses of the state and the Brickfields community to issues of urban order and moral good that emerged as central issues during a period of great change and instability in the neighborhood had their roots in the historical transformation of the modes of governance that are described here. Although presented here as separate narratives, the development of distinctive modes of governance and law and the intense debates regarding the nature of the Good in society and the proper morality of rule should not be understood as mutually exclusive processes. As Part II of this book demonstrates, questions of legality, governmental technique, and the moral justification of rule were all crucial domains within the local space of Brickfields at the dawn of the twenty-first century.

Law, Justice, Disappearance: The Experience of Place in a Time of Radical Transformation

Introduction

You can't stop development projects, right?
—Francis, Brickfields Resident

In this chapter I am interested in tracing the complex relationships between the state, law, and the role of belief in everyday life that existed in Brickfields during a time of radical change occurring in the neighborhood. I wish to analyze these relationships in the context of two related state-sponsored urban development projects that were under way in Brickfields between November 2000 and October 2002. These two projects revealed a gap between the promise of law as a set of regulations and the experience of the law by local subjects. For Brickfields residents it was these development projects that constituted their direct encounters with the law and brought them face to face with its arbitrariness, uncertainty, and unpredictability. The rapid construction of the KL Sentral train station and the KL Monorail transportation network was conceived not only as a way of providing development to a "backward" neighborhood but also as a means of bringing about orderly forms of spatial and demographic organization perceived to be lacking in the area. These attempts to organize urban space along techno-rational lines, rooted in a particularly Malaysian mode of governmentality, sought to simultaneously produce a more modern and more properly spiritual public. The particular modes by which the state pursued this organization, however, created a situation in Brickfields that made it difficult for residents to locate their place as local subjects in relation to the state's ambitious plans.

The primary focus in this chapter is the relationship between practices through which the state lays claim to space and the forms of life deemed proper to such spaces. This approach highlights the dispersed character of these practices and seeks to analyze the relationships between the technical worlds of city planning and development, the political worlds of governance and the law, and the social worlds of residents (Foucault 1991; Rabinow 1989, 2003). One effect of the dispersed, relational character of the transformation of Brickfields was that the law and the power of the state were often not experienced directly as the oppressive regulation of daily life. Rather, the issue for Brickfields residents in the face of rapid transitions in their daily lives was that of formulating a response to these changes that allowed for their recognition in the course of the transformation that was under way. In Brickfields local reactions to state development projects were generally not motivated by actions felt to be directly oppressive, but rather were in response to the local experience of living in a public space that was indeterminate and illegible. The frequent inability of Brickfields residents to bridge gaps between law and justice and between experience and authoritative discourses that claimed to provide meaning to life in the neighborhood shook their *belief* in the possibility of forming ethical, knowable ways of living. It is for this reason that I understand the primary issue regarding everyday life in Brickfields as a problem of belief rather than within the dialectic of oppression and resistance. This chapter details the specific ways in which a general belief in the world was undermined and, in extreme cases, shattered due to the aggressive changes taking place in the neighborhood.

In this chapter I highlight several events where the support voiced by Brickfields residents for the modernization projects pursued by the state was in conflict with their direct experience of the execution of laws regarding the acquisition and use of land in urban settings. In these moments the rapid and seemingly arbitrary nature of the state's actions in annexing land, demolishing existing structures, and relocating residents clashed with local understandings of justice and due process. Local principles of life and the desired character of human relationships that simultaneously sustain and limit the state's implementation of the law were commonly experienced by residents as having been disregarded during these events. The lack of acknowledgment persistently cited by residents was not due to the illegality of the state's actions; rather, a gap between formal legality and local principles of justice arose that made the actions of the state appear indeterminate and unjust even though these actions were taken in accordance with the law.

Many theorists claim that visions of social order and association depend on the interplay between concrete legal rules and local principles of human association that prevail in different domains of social life. These arguments maintain that law as a system of rules is always balanced by "counterprinciples" that link local understandings to a wider legal framework. This formulation recognizes that legal principles are imbedded in custom and habit, and that therefore the law is simultaneously a site of restraint and possibility. This tension is the ground by which the law is recognized as legitimate in the everyday; it thus generates the possibility for individuals to be recognized as legal subjects (Sarat, Douglas, and Umphrey 2003; Sarat and Kearns 1993; Unger 1986). For example, Unger has argued that the legal principle of contract is accompanied by a penumbra of non-contract that allows for an "intuition" to be formed as to which kinds of contracts are legitimate in the first place (Unger 1986; see also Durkheim 1984). Similarly, Das has argued that markets in human organs are often considered illegitimate even if the exchange takes place between consenting parties. Although the rules regarding transplants assume both partners enter the contract on roughly equal terms, informal sentiment regarding such exchanges is that this abstract equality is impossible to achieve and thus constitutes an exploitative exchange (Das 2000).

The existence of multiple, mutually constitutive domains of law that interact and reshape one another has generally been referred to as "legal pluralism" by anthropologists who examine legal phenomena. Broadening the tight local focus of early anthropological studies of law by Malinowski (1985), Gluckman (1955), and Bohannan (1957), studies of legal pluralism consider the interconnectedness between formal domains of law and other social orders; they attempt to expand the scope of analysis to consider how local spaces may be vulnerable to influences located far outside their immediate worlds. Expanding on Geertz's suggestion that law is a structure of meaning linked to symbols as well as concrete practices (Geertz 1983), works of this type have been particularly successful at understanding the complexity of legal systems both in the West (Arthurs 1985; Benda-Beckmann and Strijbosch 1986; Greenhouse 1986; Merry 1990) and in postcolonial nations (Bowen 2004; Comaroff and Roberts 1981; Engel 1978; Nader 1990; Rosen 1989; Witty 1980). The concept of legal pluralism, with a particular emphasis on dispute processing,[1] also generated attempts to formulate a comparative theory of law that would allow for comparisons between "Western" and "non-Western" legal systems (Pospisil 1971, 1978; Snyder 1981). Although much of this work was later criticized for being overly reliant on rational choice-making models of behavior, the study of disputes as a mode of understanding and comparing legal processes across communities and regions continues to exert an influence on the ethnographic study of law (Merry 1992; Moore 1978, 1986, 2001; Starr and Collier 1989).

Brickfields residents voiced a number of principles regarding the proper development of urban space, particularly the principle that the state and property developers working on the state's behalf should be subject to clear legal formulas regarding the alienation of land. The majority of people I interviewed supported the notion that the government must have the ability to acquire land and reshape the built environment of the neighborhood in order to "modernize" the area. For these same residents, however, their relative exclusion from legal processes regarding which specific sites were to be annexed, timetables, compensation, and community review was understood as unjust and arbitrary.

A second principle that was evident in the narratives of Brickfields residents was the assertion that long-standing residents were entitled to some form of recognition based on their history in the area. This principle was voiced in reference to both long-time residents who had some legal standing to occupy their space (such as renters) and to those who had for many years illegally occupied sections of government land. According to the Malaysian Torrens system of land regulation (discussed in detail later in this chapter) the only parties who have legal standing in matters related to land ownership and development are the state and the titled owner of the land; however, local articulations of justice and association demanded a consideration of personal histories and ties of association developed between neighbors over time as well.

The actual force of these principles in Brickfields was mixed between 2000 and 2002. In certain instances the state and its proxies acted in a manner that partially recognized the expectations of local residents, particularly in terms of providing low-cost housing for residents who illegally occupied parts of the neighborhood. Although not legally obligated to do so, the state worked with local residents and property developers to ensure that displaced residents had new homes to occupy when they were evicted from their homes in Brickfields. Seeking to avoid both the political fallout of ousting the neighborhood's poorest residents[2] and the problem of potentially creating thousands of homeless city residents, the Dewan Bandaraya Kuala Lumpur (City Hall) negotiated settlements with illegal residents that allowed them to move to apartments located throughout the metropolitan area. While the prospect of remaining in Brickfields was generally disallowed, most displaced residents were offered some form of compensation provided jointly by the state and the property development corporations that were involved.

Local principles and beliefs also came into play as a restraint on the state in relation to the numerous Hindu temples that served *kampung* communities. Again, although these temples had no legal claim to the land that they occupied in Brickfields, several were able to negotiate settlements that allowed them to move to nearby sites and remain in the neighborhood. The complex interplay between local notions of justice, beliefs regarding the Divine, and the Malaysian state's own concern with articulating modes of governance that are partially rooted in religious principles is the subject of Chapter 5 and will not be dealt with at length in this chapter.

Despite these specific examples, the overall recognition of local principles of justice and association by the state and its proxies was weak during the transformation that occurred in Brickfields. In particular, the expectation that institutions responsible for urban development and governance should pursue their projects according to clearly defined legal standards that recognized the stake of the community at large was almost entirely absent from the actual process. This was *not* a problem of the state acting illegally; rather, the narrow legal definition of who had a recognizable stake in issues regarding property created a situation where the state, property owners, and developers could proceed legally and yet be perceived as acting arbitrarily in relation to the local community. Echoing Young's (1990) assertion that rights and concepts of justice consist of institutionally defined rules constituting possible social relations and action within a given field,[3] Brickfields residents often sought to assert a claim to the space of the neighborhood through attempts to gain recognition from the state by a wider applicability of these rules. The issue was not that of always evading the state through local practice, but rather how to gain recognition under the law for local actors excluded within the formal process. Lacking a clear set of rule-based relationships relative to land, Brickfields residents often found it very difficult to articulate notions of rights or justice related to place.

> The buildings are moving!
> —Francis, Brickfields Resident

The sense that the state would fail to recognize local understandings of justice and due process was widespread in Brickfields during this time. The uncertain gap between what was *legal* and what was *just* for local residents was evident in the specific times when the property developers and their construction crews would enter the neighborhood and begin their work. The sudden appearance of workers and the rapid disappearance of residential and commercial buildings were experienced as unexpected events even though local residents could, to a limited degree, anticipate these disappearances. Thus, both the narratives of anticipation articulated by many in Brickfields and the direct experience of the law in these events were linked to an experience of *time* that was simultaneously structured and disrupted by the legal actions of the state in the course of pursuing development projects in the neighborhood.[4] Sticking to the letter of the law without recognizing local principles of justice in pursuing these changes created a situation in Brickfields where "everything seemed to be happening at once," a palpable sense that the temporal promises of the law (such as the provision of a structured process by which the actions of the state are planned and reviewed) and the rhythm of everyday life were unacknowledged in the course of the transformations that were under way. Lacking a clearly sequential process rooted in the law, the physical transformation of Brickfields was often experienced as *disappearance* rather than as *change* by local residents.

Disappearance in modern urban life is often explained as a consequence of speed (Abbas 1997; Harvey 1989; Virilio 1991). This is correct, but speed must be understood as an intensely local phenomenon. The development projects that were producing local events marked by disappearance in Brickfields had been making their way through legal and bureaucratic channels for years. At the level of policy, speed was not the issue. It was only once the pursuit of these ventures reached a local environment that had little access to the history of the project that the world seemed to speed up. It was in these moments that the link between the experience of "buildings that move" and the unstoppable force of "development" became apparent. For Brickfields residents the unstable, sped-up environment was the concrete product of a mode of development that refused to recognize them as proper subjects with a stake in the process. The fact that entire buildings seemed to disappear "suddenly" was understood as difficult to anticipate concretely, unstoppable, and unjust. Thus, though residents of Brickfields desired the "modernity" that state-sponsored development projects offered to them, often the experience of that modernity was marked by indeterminacy and the concrete sense that one was fast becoming lost in one's own neighborhood.

> You cannot stop development.
> —Datuk Bandar (Mayor), Kuala Lumpur,
> quoted by Dr. Kurukkal, Brickfields Community Activist

Deborah Poole has characterized this indeterminacy as being caught between the "threat and guarantee" of the law. Referring to the unpredictable character of juridical paperwork in Peru, Poole notes that the materiality of the Peruvian state for everyday people is not necessarily located in territorial boundaries but rather in a "highly mobile, tangible, and embodied space through which the power of the state is felt as the slippage between threat and guarantee" (Poole 2004, 38). A similar situation existed in Brickfields during the time I conducted field research there. To understand the materiality of the state at local levels better, Poole asserts that issues of "time and mobility [are] in some senses even more central than space to the twin problems of margins and the exceptions that inhabit (and constitute) those margins" (Poole 2004, 37–38). This is a critical insight in understanding precisely how the state emerges materially for Brickfields residents in the form of exceptional events and their anticipation on the part of local residents. Those who lived and worked in Brickfields often articulated a narrative of anticipation that marked the promise of the law in relation to an ordered regularity of daily life that, far from being resisted, was often sought out in the face of the *aporetic* moments produced through the pursuit of development projects intended to properly order everyday urban life.

Indeterminacy in the space between the law and local understandings of proper human association has not always produced the effects that are the subject of this chapter. Until recently this indeterminacy was not always understood as a threat in Brickfields, but rather was often viewed as an *opportunity*. The gap between law and legal process at the local level was the space that made the formation of nominally illegal urban *kampung* communities possible. For decades, both colonial and postcolonial authorities openly tolerated local understandings that the use of open government land by the city's poorest residents was both just and necessary. During this time principles of justice articulated by neighborhood residents were partially recognized by the state, making the space between legal formulas and local principles of justice a site of ambiguous agency and possibility for many and a source of stability in relation to change in the community (Goh 1991; Nagata 2001). One aim of this chapter is to mark how this relationship shifted in the years 2000–2002.

In more recent times the space between threat and guarantee in Brickfields has become the zone where the law materially emerges for residents through the state's power to act legally and yet be experienced as acting unjustly at the same time. The state's avoidance (intentional or not) of local principles of justice and understandings of the law meant that this zone was experienced as a juridically empty space of disappearance. The specific events in which these disappearances took place reversed the typical formulation of state power as restraint, regulation, or limit. In particular, these moments were perceived as a momentary disappearance of local orders by many who were caught in the interstices between regulatory guarantees that acknowledged residents as legal subjects and the threat of exception that these events represented in local narratives. Such events pointed to the formation of increasingly unstable local spaces where the velocity of exceptional events did not compel individuals to evade the limits of the law but rather to search those limits out actively, as a mode of reinscribing themselves in the flow of time and the sociality of the city that emerged from the ability to formulate a sense of self and the world in the context of the present.

The Land Acquisition (Amended) Act of 1991

The set of statutes that dominated the trajectory of everyday life in Brickfields between the years 2000 and 2002 was the laws related to the owning and transfer of land. The exercise of power through the Land Acquisition (Amended) Act of 1991, a revision of the Land Acquisition Act 1960, is a critical factor in understanding how the Malaysian state was able to exercise its authority and undertake a systematic reorganization of urban space. The terms of the act, a subset of regulations under the National Land Code of 1965, allow the state to pursue its plans without substantial challenges in the form of judicial review (Harding 1996, 247). The specific provisions of the act regarding definitions of state authority and public interest and its relatively open-ended procedures regarding community review foster an experience of the law that confounds attempts on the part of citizens to link local understandings of justice with the actual use of Malaysian land laws by the state. Thus, appeals to the judiciary for clarification or relief regarding the actions of the state were rare.

As in many former British colonies, land law in Malaysia is based on the Torrens system. Aspects of the Torrens system were introduced in the Federated Malay States on a state-by-state basis, beginning with Perak in 1879. By 1911 these separate state enactments were replaced by two sets of uniform land statutes, the FMS Land Enactment of 1911 and the FMS Registration of Titles Enactment of 1911[5] (Salleh 2001, 9). These regulations replaced prevailing Islamic land codes and Malay customary law in force in the years before the British established administrative control of the peninsula, codes that remained in force until superseded by the Land Code of 1928. The 1928 code was replaced in the postcolonial era by the National Land Code of 1965. Salleh Hj. Buang describes the overriding concern of the Torrens system:

Under the Torrens system the register reflects all the facts material to the registered owner's title in the land. These material facts refer to the name of the proprietor for the time being, the land which has been alienated, its area and location, its survey plan and its boundary limits. The Torrens system has thus endowed the register with the attributes of a mirror of sorts that can reveal all the necessary particulars relating to the land that would interest a potential purchaser or chargee. (Salleh 2001, 14)

The sanctity of title and its "mirror" effect places the register (the title document for the individual land owner) at the center of all claims and transactions, effectively working to exclude context or extenuating circumstances once the facts of the register have been duly recorded. This notion has been consistently upheld during the review of litigation challenging the centrality of the register, with the federal court judge Ajaib Singh's declaration that "under the Torrens system, the register is everything" (*Teh Bee v. K. Maruthamuthu* [1977] 2 M.L.J. 7). Any challenge to the supremacy of title is formally allowed only under certain limited circumstances, including statutory exceptions cited in section 340(2) of the National Land Code of 1965[6] and allowable exceptions under Malay custom or *adat*[7] (Salleh 2001, 17).

The provisions of the National Land Code of 1965 firmly circumscribe precisely who can make legal claims regarding the ownership, alienation, and use of land. With the exception of certain claims made in the name of Malay custom, the only parties formally able to address the status of specific tracts of land are the registered owner(s) and the state. Furthermore, given the clarity spelled out in the statutes and reflected in subsequent judgments by the Malaysian courts, certain branches of the government are more able to determine ownership and use of land than others, with the federal executive and state authorities possessing a great deal more latitude in such matters than the Malaysian judiciary itself. In effect, community or individual claims based on legal notions such as adverse possession or possessory rights (allowable under the 1928 Code) are strictly disallowed.

Legally registered property owners, while formally granted a series of rights under the Code, are ultimately considered entirely subordinate to individual state authorities in legal matters related to land. Formally, it is the state authority, and not the federal government, that is considered the ultimate owner of land in Malaysia.[8]

As the absolute owner of State land, the State Authority has wide powers of disposal conferred upon it by section 42 of the Code. These powers include the power to alienate State land, to reserve State land and grant leases of reserved land, to permit the temporary occupation of State land, to permit the extraction and removal of rock material from any land other than reserved forest and to permit the use of air space on or above State land or reserved land. (Salleh 2001, 39)

Under the provisions of the Land Acquisition (Amended) Act of 1991, the state authority can, without provision for judicial review, easily alter or invalidate any previous disposition of land in the name of the "general public good." This act further expanded the state's already broad rights in the alienation and acquisition of land. Specifically, it provides that the state authority can, for what it deems the public good, acquire land that is "needed by any person or corporation for any purpose which in the opinion of the State Authority is beneficial to the economic development of Malaysia or any part thereof or to the public generally or any class of the public" (Land Acquisition [Amended] Act of 1991, s.3[b]). The Act goes on to decree that "where any land has been acquired under this Act, whether before or after the commencement of this section, no subsequent disposal or use of, or dealing with, the land, whether by sale by the State Authority or by the Government, person, or corporation on whose behalf the land was acquired, shall invalidate the acquisition of the land" (s.68A). In other words, the judgment of the state authority is final in matters pertaining to either the alienation or acquisition of land. Harding notes that the overall effect of statutes written in this way is "effectively to remove land acquisition from judicial scrutiny and from the conventional restriction that acquisition must be for a public purpose." The wording of the law makes it exceedingly difficult to argue that any given acquisition by the state authority would not be "beneficial" to economic development and to the public (Harding 1996, 248).

Once the state authority deems land originally alienated to an individual or corporation necessary for acquisition, the deeded owner has no recourse to challenge this decision. While the Land Acquisition (Amended) Act of 1991 makes provision for the fair compensation of affected owners, outright refusal is essentially impossible and the compensation award is shielded from judicial review. Formally, in cases where the land acquisition is compulsory and undertaken over the objections of the registered owner, the authority must enact a law stating the purpose for the acquisition and the compensation due for the land. Due to the wide latitude that state parliaments and government ministers themselves have in matters related to the acquisition of land, this requirement is in practice a formality (Harding 1996, 248). Section 8(3) of the act states that a declaration by the state authority in Form D (Declaration of Intended Acquisition) is "conclusive evidence that all scheduled land referred to therein is needed for the purpose specified therein,"[9] and any additional legislation pertaining to the land in question nearly always tends to adhere to this circular logic. In the rare instances of judicial review, the outcome has been much the same, as evidenced by the decisions[10] in *Yew Lean Finance Development (M) Sdn. Bhd. v. Director of Lands and Mines, Penang* [1977] 2 M.L.J. 45, and *Syed Omar bin Abdullah Rahman Taha Alsagoff and Anor. v. Government of Johore* [1979] 1 M.L.J. 49, both of which upheld the state authority's near-total right of declaration in matters of acquiring land.[11] Only in rare instances has any challenge to this right been upheld, and only then in cases where the authority has absolutely neglected to follow the loose procedures outlined in the statutes regarding notification and compensation.[12]

The state authority is formally able to act more or less at will in matters pertaining to land. The legality of efforts by the state to acquire and use land as it sees fit is seldom a question in that there are relatively few procedural mistakes or violations that can be made in the formal absence of procedure itself. Thus, the primary issue for communities that suspect that their land may be of some use or interest in the execution of development projects is *not* the relationship between legality and the practices of the state. Rather, the overriding concern for the community is that the state and its agents will not recognize local understandings of justice and neighborhood life. Most business owners and residents in Brickfields were either legal renters or unregistered occupants of their land and could therefore make *no* formal claims on the state regarding its plans to reorder the physical environment of the neighborhood. Lacking a clear legal process to follow, most contacts with the state therefore assumed the form of an *event*, largely absent of the bureaucratic formalities that work to constitute individual subjects and their relation to the state in contemporary contexts. Without the sense of time that often defines legal and bureaucratic processes, individuals living and working in Brickfields were confronted with the *aporias* of disappeared (or hastily erected) buildings, blocked walkways, or entirely new traffic flows. In such moments it was literally difficult to imagine a future, a sense of "what comes next" rooted in what has just passed.

The Desire for Engagement

Although during most of 2002 large sections of Brickfields resembled a war zone due to the heavy construction going on, a recognizable pattern of spatial reorganization emerged. As KL Sentral station and the KL Monorail neared completion, these effects became clearer to local business owners and residents near the station. In the absence of community forums, legal proceedings, or public announcements as to what changes were in store, rumor became the primary form of information that circulated regarding what was going to happen in the near future.

Local reliance on hearsay, rumor, and guesswork was recognized by many residents to be an inadequate mode of information sharing regarding the changes taking place. While often residents were quick to improvise in the face of uncertainty, the idea that rules and procedures governing land and its development should be accessible to the public (and ideally would produce uniform, consistent outcomes) was often expressed; at times it was pursued through individual or collective efforts to engage the state. Brickfields residents explicitly conceptualized this local legal arena as a "semi-autonomous social field" (Moore 1978) where they would be able to assert local meanings and rules in the context of a broader terrain of law that governed the actions of the state and the developers. Although the law was often felt to be intrusive, alien, or remote, Brickfields residents often sought to engage the law rather than evade or ignore it. This mix of mistrust and desire has been noted in a number of other ethnographies that describe local engagements with the law and the state in places as diverse as Egypt (Ghannam 2002), Mexico (Nader 1990; Parnell 1989), Turkey (Navaro-Yashin 2002), Peru (Poole 2004), Indonesia (Sullivan 1992), and Lebanon (Witty 1980). The task in Brickfields, however, was finding a space of engagement through a set of land statutes that largely ignored or explicitly excluded community input. Similar to the situation Fleming (1996) details regarding ambiguity in the highly contested land laws of Mozambique, attempts to articulate local concepts regarding land as a resource, as a vehicle for personal and social identity, and as a domain of morality and proper association were often frustrated in practice. The indifference of officials and the fact that there was no clear-cut way in which to express these concepts within the rules of land tenure and alienation that governed the actions of the state and its proxies generated a confused, fearful rumor mill regarding development in Brickfields. As Dr. Kurukkal's example illustrates, attempts to address this situation concretely entailed personal risk and failure despite a great deal of effort.

Dr. Kurukkal[13] operated a small clinic on Jalan Tun Sambanthan that was situated directly across from KL Sentral. As he made clear to me in our interview, his clinic was experiencing some serious problems. He attributed these difficulties almost entirely to the KL Sentral project and what he termed the "haphazard" attempts to make Brickfields more palatable for tourists and government ministers. Dr. Kurukkal had observed similar effects due to development projects in his own neighborhood, Taman Hijau.[14] Working with his neighbors, Dr. Kurukkal formed the Taman Hijau Residents Association (THRA). As his clinic was located in Brickfields and this area had no community association of its own, the THRA had occasionally contacted developers and government officials on behalf of Brickfields residents. Despite his experience in community organizing and his occasional contact with City Hall, Dr. Kurukkal admitted that he did not have much more information regarding the situation than the average person on the street.

Dr. Kurukkal could not say for sure why the station was located in Brickfields or what the future plans were for the area. In general, he feels that most development projects in Malaysia are entirely "money driven,"[15] and therefore feasibility becomes "someone else's problem." Lacking a clear process by which the public could participate in the planning process, most local residents were "resigned to their fates, because if you make a complaint or register a concern, chances are the authorities will move against you rather than the contractors. So people are scared to say anything!"

Dr. Kurukkal's work with the THRA began several years ago when DBKL wanted to shift 18,000 unregistered residents from other areas around the city to Brickfields.[16] When local residents went to DBKL to complain they were told by the Datuk Bandar (Mayor) himself that "you cannot stop development." This was his only response, according to Dr. Kurukkal. Due to what concerned residents felt was a near-total disregard for community needs and sentiments on DBKL's part, Dr. Kurukkal and others set out to familiarize themselves with local laws and policies and try to find alternative means of organizing collectively in order to have a say in what was happening, whether invited or not. Even in cases where the land has not been formally rezoned or acquired by the state, there are problems. Dr. Kurukkal cited a number of cases where reluctant landowners suddenly find that their land has been revoked due to "violations of the Land Act." The provisions of the amended act are not well known or understood, and therefore residents are often unaware that they are violating the law in some way.

The THRA tried to "provide constructive criticism" to authorities by keeping track of what was going on locally and by knowing the law. There is relatively little legal process to master, however, regarding the procedures by which the state acquires land for what it deems the "public good." This fact exposed organizations such as the THRA to the accusation that their efforts were in violation of much more detailed and stringent laws regulating political activities and social activism, including the Internal Security Act of 1960, the Societies Act of 1966, the Official Secrets (Amended) Act of 1986, and the Sedition Act of 1948. In light of the fact that organizations more openly critical of the government, such as the Support Committee for Urban Pioneers (Kuala Lumpur) and Save Our Selves (Penang), pursued strategies that mixed organized public protest and attempts to seek relief through the courts for unregistered urban dwellers, the THRA anticipated that it would come under scrutiny and was always very careful to conduct itself in a manner that would not threaten the police or DBKL. Taking great pains to prevent its abolition as an "illegal organization," the THRA sought to represent its efforts as "assistance" to the government rather than opposition, despite the fact that more radical groups had gained much more publicity for their cause and occasionally were successful in delaying or derailing plans to demolish urban *kampungs*.[17] The THRA, while concerned about the plight of urban *kampung* residents, did not make this its central issue and openly sought to distance itself from political groups who made "urban pioneers" their primary focus. The effort to differentiate the THRA from other community activist groups was mainly accomplished by maintaining a close relationship with the Brickfields police. The THRA always invited a police officer to attend its meetings and provided the Officer in Charge of Police District (OCPD) with a transcript. It was also legally registered, as required by the Societies Act.

Generally, relations with the local police "have been good" according to Dr. Kurukkal. "The OCPD is an old friend of mine from the army," he noted. Yet in the next breath, Dr. Kurukkal reversed himself:

RB: So, you have never been bothered by the police?

Dr. K: Oh, no, not really. [Pause] Well, the Special Branch has come to see me and told me that what I am doing is illegal and threatened to take action against me, but I told them to just go down to the Brickfields police station and confirm that everything is legal. I haven't heard from them much after that. I just think the Special Branch can't do its job. They didn't even check, [they] just assumed we weren't legal.

RB: This didn't seem like intimidation to you?

Dr. K: Actually . . . I have never thought of it. Perhaps they were just trying to pressure me a bit.

It had not occurred to Dr. Kurukkal that a visit from the Special Branch would be unusual. Although the provisions of the Societies Act are quite clear as to how civic associations must be registered with the state, the fact that community groups must, by definition, address themselves to areas of the law that do not provide for regulated contacts with appropriate state agencies exposes any organization of this kind to charges of subversive conduct. Individuals working in such associations are well aware of this situation and *anticipate* the charge of subversion by the police. Avoiding the appearance of subversion is thus an ever-present task for community organizers. Therefore, visits from the Special Branch of the kind that Dr. Kurukkal described are often not understood as intimidation. For Dr. Kurukkal, a former army officer, the state appeared in such instances as simultaneously just and corrupt, driving both his continued belief in the efficacy of engaging the law through its own procedures and his nearly automatic willingness to accept modes of surveillance and discipline that characterize the modes of governmentality particular to the rational organization of land and urban space in Malaysia.

Dr. Kurukkal's experience with the Special Branch in his efforts to address the state was *not* characterized by a direct confrontation with a state that was proceeding in a manner contrary to the law. His contacts with the state as a community organizer were clearly marked by a regularity that, while not necessarily governed through formal procedures, was nonetheless structured around the principle that local communities should have an acknowledged stake in the course of everyday life in the city. Clearly, however, this acknowledgment came more concretely from the police in the form of surveillance than from engagements by DBKL officials. Without a clear means to intervene in the legal processes concerning land management, Dr. Kurukkal and his group found themselves forced into an engagement with the state on an entirely different legal register.

Anticipating this possibility from the beginning, much of the group's efforts were turned toward avoiding being identified as political subversives. These efforts produced a certain form of recognition from the state that allowed them to continue their efforts, but their original goal of articulating local principles of justice and association to the state and its proxies remained largely unfulfilled. The goal of having an impact on the trajectory of development in Brickfields was, even for this group of urban professionals, out of reach. The inability to imagine a future for the neighborhood was as acute for them as for anyone else.

Dr. Kurukkal only hinted at this difficulty during our interview. When asked what he imagined the future of Brickfields to be, he plainly stated that he did not know. "I just see problems, that's all." Dr. Kurukkal had a clear investment in shaping a particular kind of future for Brickfields and the surrounding neighborhoods. His terse, noncommittal response alluded to the difficulties that the reorganization of the urban environment presented for those caught up in it. His neighbor Janet,[18] whose business was located a few doors down from Dr. Kurukkal's clinic, was more willing to try to describe an immediate future for their neighborhood.

Janet owned a photography shop located on Jalan Tun Sambanthan, directly across the street from KL Sentral Station. Her business had been in operation since the mid-1970s. Originally it was located at the corner of Jalan Tun Sambanthan and Jalan Scott in a building that no longer exists. She moved to the present location in 1979. The business was originally a partnership with her brother, although she was the sole proprietor in 2002. The original location was a busy one due to the presence of a government office in the Suleiman Building (still existent) next door. At that time, Janet did a brisk business in passport photos and other photographs required for official government registrations and transactions, such as registering a birth or obtaining an official Identity Card (IC).

Over time Janet's clientele changed because she cultivated a reputation as an excellent wedding photographer with the Indian community throughout Kuala Lumpur. Although in 2002 Janet provided a number of photo services, her primary customer base was newlyweds and their families. Most of Janet's customers were Indians from other neighborhoods, although she built her reputation through her work with many of the middle-class Indian families that lived in Brickfields in the 1970s and 1980s.

> J: Although I am a Chinese [*sic*] almost all of my customers are Indians. When I started my business Brickfields was 90 percent Indian, so it is only natural. At first I was doing IC photos, passport photos, developing . . . things like that. But later I started to do the weddings. I do a really good job for them, so they tell their friends. Now I do a lot of weddings. Don't do much of the other stuff anymore-lah.
>
> RB: Why did you choose Brickfields to start your business?
>
> J: Well, I live so close by [in Bangsar]. I grew up here . . . it is home.

Janet's reputation kept her business going. Walk-in customers for film developing and passport photos had almost completely disappeared. In response to a changing order in the neighborhood, she forged links across ethnic community lines in order to ensure the viability of her company. Invoking "home" as the primary mode of belonging in this context allowed Janet to utilize everyday social connections to build her enterprise.

In Janet's view, the opening of KL Sentral had damaged her business. She felt powerless to do much about it, as she had never been afforded the opportunity to voice her views on the subject or to learn about the plans beforehand.

> J: There was never a public meeting, nothing! I learned about it from talking to friends or through the papers. I was shocked—there was very little warning!
>
> RB: Did you feel like you could say something to the developers or to DBKL?
>
> J: No, I don't want to lose my business! If they feel like you are making fight-fight [trouble], an inspector is down here and your license is gone!

Janet's description of the oftentimes arbitrary power of City Hall, property developers, and the police expressed a common sentiment in Brickfields. The threat of liquidation due to the capricious exercise of inspection and citation under the Land Act and regulations governing commercial enterprise was a persistent fear for business owners in the neighborhood. The strategy for avoiding the unwanted interest of the state was therefore *not* to remain in full compliance with the law, as it was generally believed to be impossible to do so, but rather to avoid the attention of state agents as much as possible. Thus, despite the occasional efforts of groups such as Dr. Kurukkal's association, open hearings regarding the large-scale projects under way in Brickfields were generally *not* sought, nor was the relative lack of information (not even an announcement) directly addressed by most merchants in Brickfields. Such demands had no formal standing under the law and such encounters with state agents were regarded as quite dangerous for any individual who might happen to raise concerns.

Materially, the fact that nearly all of the businesses in Brickfields occupied rented shophouses or offices placed them at a further disadvantage. Janet was well aware that she was in a weak position because she did not own the building that she occupied. The desire to own the building she occupied was tempered by a more general anticipation of the disappearance of her business:

I wanted to buy 15 years ago, but he [the owner] wouldn't sell. Then, buildings like this one were going for RM100,000, but not now—several million. When I first moved in it was two-story, but he renovated and is now four stories. May not matter, though. The building across the way was taken without compensation from the owner, old Chinese man. They do this all the time if it suits them.

Janet was referring to the process by which the state alienated the land for the construction of the train station. Although in most cases the previous owners of the land were compensated for their loss according to the procedures laid out in Section 3 of the Land Act and Section 8(3) of the Land Acquisition [Amended] Act of 1991, it was the stories of troublemaking landowners who found their property arbitrarily seized due to "code violations" or in the name of "public interest" that occupied the imaginations of the business owners that remained.

Janet's image of the future was not optimistic. Citing a fear of disappearance that was rooted in the fear that the state would strictly execute the law without acknowledging local public life and principles of justice, Janet worried that the physical topography that sustained the particular character of Brickfields as a community would evaporate:

J: All of these buildings here [on Jalan Tun Sambanthan] will be gone. Maybe we will be here for a little while longer, but eventually we'll have to pack up and move. That's the way it is. It won't be a neighborhood like this any more.
RB: Does this worry or scare you?
J: Yes [Looking away—barely audible whisper].

Dewan Bandaraya Kuala Lumpur

Community complaints regarding the difficulty of gaining an audience with DBKL officials are not exaggerated. The relatively open-ended formal procedures outlined in the law regarding the acquisition and use of land by the state meant that there was no great urgency on DBKL's part to field questions from anyone. Goh Ban Lee summarizes the general situation:

In Malaysia, where power is very concentrated and centralised in the hands of a few people and the culture of sharing power is almost non-existent, it is very difficult to envisage a situation where the public can participate effectively in the development plan making process. It is not only a case of the politicians and the planners not willing to share power, it is also a case where the citizens themselves are not able to make effective representations, having been denied the opportunity to do so for so long. (Goh 1991, 116)

Goh's characterization of the relative lack of public input in decision-making processes regarding urban development is generally accurate. What his description leaves out, however, is the very real ambiguity that government officials themselves face when engaged in the process of planning and executing urban planning initiatives. The general lack of procedure that hampers civic efforts to intervene in the process can also represent a zone of indistinctness for officials, forcing them to exercise a great deal of bureaucratic discretion, particularly when dealing with requests or demands from the public. Moore (2001) points out that anthropologists of the law have usually paid scant attention to the role of judicial discretion in legal systems. This insight also holds true for much of the literature regarding rule-based bureaucratic systems. Although a number of historical studies regarding government bureaucracy address issues of discretion and ambiguity as exercised by public servants (Cohn 1996; Messick 1992; Mitchell 1989; Rabinow 1989), there are very few ethnographic accounts that explore this issue in great detail.[19] Yet, as my own encounters with government officials illustrate, the issue of how bureaucrats make decisions when the proper application of rules or laws is unclear was an important one to consider in the context of urban development in Brickfields.

When I requested an interview with DBKL regarding my research project, Dr. Lim,[20] a high-level official in the Master Plan Department of

DBKL, agreed to see me, but introduced himself by stating "I've only got about ten minutes, so tell me what you want."

> RB: Does DBKL have a guiding philosophy or more broadly defined goals in planning how the city should look and what development projects should be pursued or not?
>
> Dr. L: City planning in KL is primarily a reactive process. Our planning is really a way to rationalize megaprojects such as KL Sentral. We don't always have a lot of influence until after a big project is under way.
>
> RB: So you are saying that it is the vision of the developers that counts the most here? It's not the local communities or DBKL . . .
>
> Dr. L: [Interrupting] Local communities do not, frankly, have much say in what is happening, or is going to happen, in their neighborhoods.
>
> RB: But there seems to be quite a lot of concern in DBKL documents like the Draft Structure Plans that the public doesn't really participate in this process.
>
> Dr. L: Well . . . there isn't really a process for communities to voice their opinions or complaints. Sure, sometimes there are public hearings, but this isn't really effective. Most people don't know what is going on.
>
> RB: How do you feel about that?
>
> Dr. L: I've already told you what my job is. Do you have any more questions, because I have to go now.

Dr. Lim asked me to submit my questions to him in writing. The questions I subsequently forwarded were very specific, dealing primarily with timetables for ongoing projects, plans for specific city blocks in Brickfields, and projected changes in vehicular and pedestrian traffic flows. Most of all, I wanted to discuss (or better yet, obtain) DBKL impact studies regarding the KL Sentral and KL Monorail projects. The direct, detailed questions drew a response from one of Dr. Lim's assistants, Mr. Seow.[21] Interestingly, the communication was initiated due to a case of mistaken identity. The communication took place over the telephone and in English:

> Mr. S: I have your inquiry here . . . your set of questions. Are you a consultant?
>
> RB: No, I'm an anthropology graduate student. Currently I am doing research for my doctorate in Brickfields. I included some of my bio information on the fax, I think . . . at the top?

> Mr. S: Yes, I saw it . . . are you sure you aren't a consultant? Academics don't ask detailed questions like this. Why do you need such detailed information?
>
> RB: Well, I spoke with [Dr. Lim] and he instructed me to be as precise as possible. Also, my work involved the impact of large development projects in the neighborhood, so knowing the details of the project is important to my findings.
>
> Mr. S: Yes, ok . . . [Dr. Lim] asked me to handle this, but I looked at your list and thought that you were a consultant.
>
> RB: Ah, I see. No, no . . . just for my research. I'm not working for a company or anything.
>
> Mr. S: Well, alright . . . hmmm . . . you know, I can only answer a few of these you know. Most are not my department . . .

Seow's primary responsibility was in the traffic division. Although he ruled out addressing most of my written questions, Seow did answer a few of them:

> Mr. S: Ah, here you ask about impact studies. Well, DBKL does do some of its own research, but our studies are quite small. So we tend to rely on the studies that developers submit.
>
> RB: So you don't do independent studies to check against those submitted by the developers?
>
> Mr. S: No, not really. We don't have the resources. To tell you the truth, I don't really trust what those guys give us. In fact, I think that most of their reports are simply bullshit! Still, in many cases it is all we have to work with.
>
> RB: Why do you think that? Do you think they are inaccurate?
>
> Mr. S: Well . . . I don't know. It doesn't matter. Most of these projects are done deals anyway. Especially the ones you are asking about.
>
> RB: Are these reports public?
>
> Mr. S: No way!
>
> RB: So I couldn't get a copy of them or a summary for research purposes?
>
> Mr. S: [Laughing] I don't think so.

In the absence of laws or guidelines governing their contacts with the public, *any* outside inquiry regarding DBKL policies or plans presented officials with a problem. In our brief telephone interview Mr. Seow avoided answering most of my questions directly. Yet this avoidance was expressed alongside a barely concealed desire to talk. Certainly, this was in part due to my own position as a foreign researcher seeking information, and it is safe to say I was able to gain greater access to DBKL officials than that afforded to Brickfields residents. Nonetheless, despite the relative failure of my attempts to gain empirical information from these officials regarding ongoing development projects in Brickfields, their ambivalent fear of my questions and desire at the same time to provide some answer to them is significant. *Every* request for clarification or information regarding their work outside the internal channels of the state generated an experience *aporia* much like that of local residents. Although government bureaucrats are often understood locally as the "instruments" through which the state exercises its power, my encounters with these men and women were shaped by many of the same forces that limited the agency of individuals in setting the trajectories of everyday life in spaces such as Brickfields. Dr. Lim articulated the bind very well when, addressing my request for information from his department for research purposes, he replied, "There aren't any, but we have to be careful. If we give out something that someone doesn't want us to, we can be accused of giving out official secrets."[22] Violating the Official Secrets Act is a heavy price to pay for acting in the absence of formal rules and procedures. In this context Mr. Seow's incredulous "No way!" response to my probing for access to internal impact studies made more sense, as the release of information to a researcher could easily be defined as a crime. As with Dr. Kurukkal and his community group, officials at DBKL had to anticipate the possibility that their acknowledgment of parties not formally recognized by the legal procedures in place could lead to an engagement with the law as criminals rather than as citizens or representatives of the state or community.

Dr. Lim and his assistant alluded to the fact that the decision-making process within DBKL is sharply circumscribed by ministers in the Office of the Prime Minister and by property developers allied with those officials. They did not state this directly during our brief interviews. They did, however, make reference to the fact that DBKL must often act according to information that they do not credit. Both men cited the reactive nature of their work and underscored the fact that they were primarily concerned with enacting plans that were already approved, rather than assisting in the formulation of these development projects. Mr. Seow mentioned several times that he had no confidence in the reports of property developers, and implied that he and others in DBKL were well aware that property developers file misleading reports in order to justify their projects. "I must say that I don't have very much confidence in these fellows," Mr. Seow restated toward the end of our conversation. "They have the bottom line in mind and that's it." Aside from his acidic complaints, Seow did not articulate a broad critique of the process. He disclaimed responsibility for the outcomes of his actions by citing the "real powers" (in this case the Office of the Prime Minister) that directed him to act in particular ways. He did this in a way that strikingly resembled the ambiguous understandings of agency, recognition, and justice articulated by Brickfields residents regarding their own futures and their relationship to agents of the state.

Endgame—*Kampung Khatijah*

Throughout most of its history, upwards of half of the residents in Brickfields have lived in unregistered dwellings. Since 1998, however, almost all of the unregistered residents of Brickfields have been relocated to low-cost flats in other parts of the city. Although this is not the first time that Brickfields has experienced large-scale relocations (such as the large shift of *Kampung Khatijah* residents in 1982 to make way for Palm Court Condominiums), these relocations have dramatically transformed the neighborhood, as more than 1,500 families were relocated between 2000 and 2002. By my own estimate, fewer than 100 unregistered dwellings remained in Brickfields as of September 2002.

One Saturday morning in November 2001 Brickfields awoke to find a wide swath of *Kampung Khatijah* in the process of being dismantled. Residents were busily working at tearing down their own homes as construction workers waited across the street. The evicted residents labored to clear a clean swipe through the maze of houses that had sat on that parcel of land for over sixty years. It was not only *Kampung Khatijah* that was disappearing. The elementary school immediately to the east of the settlement suddenly found itself without an eating hall, as the entire rear portion of the school had also been demolished.

In what remained of *Kampung Khatijah* itself, the former residents were out and about in the area where their homes used to stand. A few walls somehow remained standing. In an act of futile agency the residents

themselves were pulling down these walls as they collected the few possessions that remained in the rubble. One of the previously interior walls still
standing was covered with pictures of Tamil film stars from the 1960s torn
from Indian film magazines—a young man was at work pulling these
posters off of the wall and carefully folding them up.

The residents working in the rubble of their homes seemed willing to
talk, but were not quite sure what to say. Two young men, Siva and Abdul,
and Siva's father were willing to speak about the situation as they worked, but
their answers were short and hinted at an impatience as to why one would
bother to ask questions about what is going on. After some brief conversation
in Malay Siva's father excused himself and went back to working in the ruins
of his home. Abdul also drifted away, so I was left to question Siva regarding
the situation. Did people in *Kampung Khatijah* know that this demolition
was about to take place? "No." Did the workers just come in and tear the
houses down? "No, we wanted to do it ourselves." Are people angry? "Of
course they are! Wouldn't you be? Where will they go? I don't know." Did
people try to resist this? "Yes, but what can you do . . . ?" Siva's words, "*Ya,
tapi tak apa . . . ?*" can be literally rendered as "Yes, but who cares?" Or as he
summed matters up: "*tak boleh cakap*" (literally, "we cannot speak to them").

The conversation was over. Siva did not finish his sentence, but suddenly excused himself and quickly walked away from the site and down
into the cluster of homes that remained standing. Two police officers
slowly passed by. They seemed distracted and did not give us a second
look, but their presence was enough for Siva, and he was gone.

The police in this instance were merely administrators of an event
that had been vaguely anticipated and yet, upon its arrival, was unbelievable for residents of *Kampung Khatijah*. Those who could not be addressed here were not the police on the scene, but rather the state and its
agents who sent the police and construction crews to clear out the residents of the *kampung*. Interviews with the residents who remained in the
settlement and lawyers who had worked as intercessors between the state
and *kampung* residents revealed that Siva's characterization of the sud-
denness of the demolition was somewhat exaggerated. Although the specific time of removal was a surprise, the fact of the impending relocation
was known to the displaced residents, especially since most of them were
being offered some monetary compensation and a place in a development
of low-cost flats in Pantai Dalam, a neighborhood located a few miles

south of Brickfields. Strictly speaking, Siva's claim that residents had no idea that they were about to be relocated was factually incorrect.

Yet learning these facts through later interviews did not lead me to suspect that Siva was trying to mislead me with his answers. As with his father and Abdul, Siva appeared genuinely stunned and at a loss for words regarding what was taking place at the moment I spoke with him. While knowledge of the impending event may structure a particular mode of understanding the future and experiencing time in this urban space, this anticipation does not make the event itself any less disruptive. For the residents of *Kampung Khatijah*, at the moment of their displacement there was no way to imagine the future, with the experience of both state and local orders temporarily dissipated by the disappearance of their homes. Understood as the corporeal experience of finding his home had vanished, Siva's claim of "*tak boleh cakap*" related not just to the situation with the police and DBKL, but to the world generally. Siva told me the only thing he could truthfully relate; "We cannot speak." Although the Malaysian government has demonstrated ample willingness to censor critical expression in public domains directly, in this case authorities were not actively suppressing Siva's speech. Rather, faced with an event that made his world unbelievable, the ground for Siva's speech about his world and his life evaporated.

Swift, radical dislocations of this kind were not restricted to the experience of unregistered residents in Brickfields during the time of my research. With the continued construction of KL Sentral and the aggressive efforts to bring the KL Monorail into operation fully under way, even legal homes and businesses could find themselves suddenly displaced in the same manner as that experienced by *kampung* dwellers. Although most of the country enjoyed a long holiday during December of 2001 and January of 2002, construction workers in Brickfields were not so lucky, and the physical transformation of Brickfields continued unabated during the Hari Raya Puasa/Christmas/Chinese New Year celebrations. Given that KL Monorail was at that time projected to become operational in June of 2002 (it would not go into service until early 2003) work on the project continued around the clock during the normally sedate weeks of the holidays. This punishing schedule meant that buildings continued to be demolished during the holidays, as the construction crews moved on to knocking down legally established, permanent shop houses rather than just evicting unregistered residents. This was the fate of one popular South Indian restaurant, Sri Radha.[23] Although the narrow road running next to the restaurant had been closed and occupied by construction crews for several weeks, Sri Radha had continued to operate as normal, and it seemed that the restaurant would simply have to contend with the fact that the monorail was going to run right next door to it. As it turned out, this was a naïve thought; the restaurant and the building that housed it disappeared with shocking swiftness.

A short chronology of the eviction is illuminating. One Friday in early December 2001 the restaurant was open for business, operating normally. That evening there was no gossip in the restaurant regarding an impending move and there was no sign of distress or worry on the part of the restaurant owner or the staff. Casual conversation with everyone in the restaurant revealed nothing out of the ordinary. However, by the following Sunday morning the building was completely boarded up; a small handwritten sign directed customers down the street to a different restaurant owned by the same family, now "merged" with Sri Radha and operating in that location.[24] By Wednesday the two-story building that housed Sri Radha was completely demolished, with just a pile of bricks sitting on the former site of the restaurant. By the following Saturday this pile of rubble had been removed, with only the cement-slab foundation remaining. In summary, over the span of eight days the site had gone from housing a successful local restaurant to being simply an empty lot, annexed by the growing Monorail construction site.

As with the section of *Kampung Khatijah* cleared out a month earlier, the speed with which this disappearance took place was not unusual at this time in Brickfields. Nor was it surprising that the owners of Sri Radha had no idea until Saturday morning that they had to be out by the following day, as the proprietor confirmed later. Certainly, some broad plans had been in the works for a while and the possibility of closure was always present, especially with the construction crews preparing to erect the large concrete pillars for the monorail tracks right outside. The timing of the event, however, was uncertain until the very last moment. Luckily, in some vague anticipation of the destruction of Sri Radha, the family had opened another restaurant down the street and therefore had a place to relocate everything quickly and keep the overall business going. They did not set up the second restaurant for this express purpose, as they were looking to expand the business, not simply move it. As with Siva on the day of his removal, the restaurant owners regarded the manner in which they had to move as inconvenient, but expressed no overt anger or surprise in a later interview. They provided direct answers to my questions without the ability to form a wider narrative regarding what had happened.

For both the displaced residents of *Kampung Khatijah* and the owners and employees of Sri Radha, the previously stable spaces that they inhabited quite suddenly were transformed into spaces that could be felt "too much." The very real violence of removal is apparent here; however, one should not lose sight of the equally real violence to the senses and the imagination that these events inflicted on those directly affected by them. The literal formlessness of what used to be their dwellings lay at the heart of this violent experience. Although it may appear to resemble a more contemplative experience of something like the Kantian sublime (Kant 1914), the speed in which the liquidation of the space occurred does not allow for even the contemplation of the ruins necessary for such an experience. Reason did not surpass sense in these moments. Rather, the affect overwhelmed Brickfields residents, as shown by the fact that a narrative regarding the removals simply did not emerge from those subject to them. Whether in the midst of the event itself (*Kampung Khatijah*) or some time after the fact (Sri Radha), a narrative of the event was not forthcoming from my interlocutors.[25] How would one narrate an event that blocks the perception of past and future (of rules, order, and context) from the experience of the present? My answer is that those affected by the event cannot do so. In arguing this, I do not claim that these events produced *no* narratives. The narratives that did emerge, however, originated from witnesses rather than those whose homes and businesses disappeared. Those who found themselves directly involved in such events could only speak about their world later and often in indirect terms; these outcomes after the fact are the subject of Chapter 4. This form of witnessing was enfolded into neighbors' understanding of Brickfields as a place; it served to structure modes of anticipation by which these neighbors would imagine the possibility of their own disappearance, finding themselves caught in the space between threat and guarantee that arose out of the state's pursuance of its plans to constitute a new order in Brickfields.[26]

Neighbors

Events such as the removal of *Kampung Khatijah* residents and the sudden, forced move of Sri Radha restaurant are public, well known to everyone else in Brickfields. As such, the sudden, exceptional character of these events tended to structure understandings of the neighborhood and the experience of place for a wider public than those who were directly affected by them. The abstract anticipation of disappearance was grounded in the experience of others. For these onlookers, such events offered concrete examples of the space between the guarantee of the law and the threat of a state that seemed to operate outside of the formal regulatory aspects of that law.

The fact that the development efforts in Brickfields generally did not operate outside the law means that any analysis of the circumstances, by residents or scholars, cannot rely upon generalized concepts of domination and resistance in formulating a framework of understanding for the situation there. While scholars such as Abel (1982), Merry (1990), and Nader (1990, 2005) have engaged questions of dispute resolution and the workings of the law at the local level, the fact that a domination-resistance theme is often a principal assumption in their work makes it difficult to apply their insights to the Brickfields case. Though passionate advocates for the laudable idea that the law should ideally mean equal rights and treatment for all who are subject to it, most Brickfields residents themselves neither expected nor worked for this ideal in their own encounters with the law and state, and this fact calls for a different way of conceptualizing how the law is imagined by everyday people (Griffiths 1997; Hirsch 1998; Moore 2001). As Just (2001) and Bentley (1984) demonstrate, disputants in Southeast Asian courts often seek to manipulate the meanings of rules and evidence and the manner in which court officials themselves will selectively exercise established rules in order to produce desired outcomes in local settings.[27] While abstract notions of equality under the law often come into play in these encounters, both sides often exhibit a more creatively instrumental imagination of judicial processes that does not explicitly assume the law will be applied uniformly.

Although development projects in Malaysia often generated well-organized opposition movements, this was not the case in Brickfields. Rather, Brickfields residents often sought to mitigate the ambiguous experience of the law by more firmly indexing themselves as subjects within the law itself. These local strategies did not signal a fatalism or passivity in the face of the law, although the complexity of the local situation often meant that locating sites of control and possible action was extremely difficult; it often left Brickfields residents struggling to reconcile their feelings as to what was moral with their concrete experiences with the operations of the law and the state.

Zaina owned a small beauty parlor on the second floor of a shop house on Jalan Thambipillay, just a few doors down from the elevated tracks of the KL Monorail and directly across the street from *Kampung Khatijah*. Although a Malaysian Indian born and raised in Ipoh, Zaina was not South Indian; her family was originally from Pakistan. Zaina had operated her own business for two years, opening her own salon after working for a beauty parlor located in the Palm Court apartment complex for several years. She was single and maintained a close network of friends, including several that operated businesses out of the same building. Our interview took place in August 2002 and was conducted with Najwa, Zaina's childhood friend from Ipoh, sitting nearby and offering a mildly caustic parallel commentary as Zaina and I spoke.

Given the proximity of her shop to the KL Monorail site, the early focus of the conversation was the impact of the transformation of Brickfields on her business. Zaina began by describing the process as "painful."

I think that once they finish all of this, Brickfields will be much better. Still, it is really painful to see places that we have grown attached to destroyed. We used to all go and sit at the In-Town Pub [a club several doors down that was forced to relocate due to the KL Monorail project]—it was our place to relax and talk. Suddenly, they are just tearing the building down. I know that it's for the best, but I'm always torn. We really love these places and they just disappear. Well, In-Town Pub actually just moved down the street a little bit, but it isn't the same, you know? We don't really go there anymore . . . it just isn't the same.

At that time Zaina had managed to deal with the difficulties associated with the construction of the monorail, although she quietly emphasized the vulnerability of small shops to disruptions such as these. Unlike a retail store, Zaina's business depended on a small, consistent clientele. As Zaina described it, most of her clients were "proper North Indian ladies," who lived around Brickfields, though few actually lived in the neighborhood itself. Significantly, she also served many of the prostitutes based next door and across the street from her salon. "I was worried what my clients would think when I moved in here, with the red-light district so close and all," Zaina noted. "At first some were nervous, but they realized that there isn't any problem and now they come here without any reservation." Zaina secured her customers entirely on a word-of-mouth basis—so much so that she did not have a sign out front alerting potential customers to the presence of her salon. When I asked about the absence of a sign, Zaina replied "That [not having a sign] is OK, but I want my own sign, you know."

The desire to give her business a more permanent feel was understandable, as Zaina's space was little more than a modified rectangular room on the second floor of the shophouse, roughly eight feet by twenty feet. Customers entered the building through a nondescript door on the street and then had to negotiate a narrow staircase and turn left on the second floor landing in order to reach Zaina's salon. The salon had a glass entry door: upon entering one was immediately faced with a small reception desk. The middle of the room was open, with a few chairs and a small table piled with magazines positioned next to the wall for anyone who was waiting. The back portion of the room was where Zaina worked, separated from the rest of the room by a pink curtain.

Zaina did not have a formal lease to occupy this space. Her rental contract was strictly a "handshake" one, although it was generally agreed that nobody could make a move without giving thirty days notice. Zaina's landlord at this time sublet the entire floor from the registered building owner and had subdivided the space, meaning that Zaina's landlord was actually a middleperson in the transaction. When asked if the actual owner knew about this arrangement, Zaina responded by saying, "Yeah, I think she does. She runs the catering business downstairs and sees us all the time."

Most of the arrangements necessary for the operation of Zaina's salon did not possess the legal status vested in contracts, leases, and licenses. Although the owner of the building did not oppose the further division and subletting of the space, it was quite unclear if this division and use of space was formally allowed under the applicable zoning statutes. The ambiguous position of Zaina's business was further accentuated by the relative impermanence of her room and the fact that she was unable to post a sign on the street indicating the location of her salon; she continued to cite this fact throughout the interview as an indication of the tenuous position of her business at the time and a symbol of a status that she hoped her salon would achieve over time.

Zaina was ambitious and optimistic about her salon. When I asked her about the future, Zaina told me that she was planning to move in the next few months to a shop on Jalan Tun Sambanthan. She was somewhat ambivalent about making the move:

I'm trying to get a place next to the Gem Restaurant [a block away, on Jalan Tun Sambanthan]—we'll see. I hope to move in 2 or 3 months—I'm trying to expand and I want my own sign. I'm very attached to this place, though, so part of me doesn't want to move. I'm also very superstitious—maybe the luck won't follow me. I know its silly to think that way, but I do. I know that the clients will follow, but . . . well, I like this place. It has been good to me. It is my home, so I have a fifty-fifty feeling about it.

Zaina noted that the buildings on her side of the street would probably be demolished soon. "I don't think that will happen to the ones on the main road, though." Najwa interjected, "Actually they are going to tear down all the buildings over here—I've seen the plans. I know for sure they are going to knock down all the buildings around here." I then learned that Najwa had worked as a secretary for the KL Sentral Corporation. Thus, she had some credible inside knowledge of the plans. Zaina was startled by Najwa's statement, and she asked her friend "Are you sure? I don't think so . . . really? Are you sure?" She was then quiet for some time. Gathering herself, Zaina continued to speak:

Z: Well, who knows what will happen. I suppose that I'll just have to make the best of it.

RB: So, have you ever been told about the plans for KL Sentral? You know, what they are going to do as the station keeps developing. Or have they told anyone you know, like the people downstairs or next door over here?

Z: No, they never do that. It is always just a shock when they come. We have no information and suddenly they are here. I told you about the In-Town Pub—it really hurt. Taking away all of these old things is not nice.

Despite having just learned from a somewhat authoritative source that many of the buildings on this side of the area would be demolished, Zaina was still optimistic:

I think that all of this inconvenience is temporary. After the construction is finished, then maybe the parking situation will improve—traffic as well. [Pause] I suppose that they have to do all of this because of KL Sentral. Brickfields doesn't make a good impression on foreigners, so they have to clean it up, make it nicer and more modern. I think that once they do all of these things then the area will really take off and it will be much better. [Pause] I have a problem accepting it all. Like I said, I'm fifty-fifty. I really like all of the improvements, but I don't like it that so many of the old things are disappearing. I feel sad when this happens.

The trajectory of Zaina's narrative was more complex than it at first seemed. Beginning with a summary of her current situation, Zaina clearly articulated her ambition not only to expand her salon but also to link her business more firmly to the regulatory guarantees offered by the law. Specifically, her hope was to move to a space that was more permanently designed to house a "legitimate" business.[28] Although Zaina anticipated a feeling of nostalgia and unease regarding her imagined move and the physical transformation of the neighborhood (the "pain" of change), her desire for the marks of a lawful business, strongly evident in her desire for a proper sign announcing her location, was very real. The sense of a stable legal framework necessary for Zaina's future plans was momentarily shattered by her friend's casual remark that the space to which she hoped to relocate her business would also disappear. In the absence of direct information from the property developers and the state, Najwa's statement took on the status of authoritative knowledge.[29] For several moments after Najwa made this remark Zaina was literally speechless, shocked into the silence opened by the momentary impossibility of imagining a future at all. Although Zaina quickly recovered and was able to continue to talk about the transformation of the area, the tenor of the conversation had changed and she shifted her frame of reference from the specifics of her future to the generalities of the future of the neighborhood. Echoing how she began our conversation, Zaina again linked herself to the local situation through a description of affect, invoking her feelings regarding what was taking place rather than her plans for her business. She did not speak in specific terms about these plans again in the interview, nor did she again talk about the future of her business in subsequent contacts that I had with her.

The threat of not being recognized by the state was palpable in this exchange. While it would be overstating things to characterize Zaina's experience of her space during the moments of this exchange as trauma or shock in psychological terms, it was clear that the (inadvertent) erasure of her image of the future by her friend must be understood as affect. The turn that the interview then took supports this analysis as well, in that Zaina steered the conversation toward a discussion of the treatment of her immediate neighbors in the houses of prostitution and the threat under which these women lived. Picking up on Zaina's introduction of the prostitutes into the discussion, I asked her if she wanted to move due to her proximity to the brothels. She vigorously shook her head, saying "No, no—not that at all!" Najwa began to laugh:

> N: Why you so attached to this place? It's dirty and smelly—no one wants to come!
>
> Z: [Laughing] You are wrong! This place is fine. People are nice here. What wrong with you?
>
> N: Ya, OK . . . [Laughing] people are nice, but move, OK? Things will be better!
>
> Z [Turning to RB]: Well, this isn't a good environment for girls. The family ladies will still come, but they notice. It isn't so good because there are so many men just sitting around and they will stare and make comments sometimes. They certainly look . . . Now I'm known around here, though, so they don't really stare anymore or say anything. When I first opened men would make comments and sometimes they would even come up to the shop and ask for "facials." [N giggles—Z looks at her and smiles, mockingly waving her away] You know what I mean, right? They want more than a facial! [Z laughing hard] So I had to send a few of these fellows out of my shop. Now this doesn't happen. When people know you they will leave you alone. Sometimes we even help each other out.

Despite the fact that her "family lady" clients could be uncomfortable with the area and possibly take their business elsewhere as a result, Zaina strongly defended her neighbors. After scolding Najwa for interrupting, she continued:

I've grown attached to this place. Actually, I really like it. We all know each other up here and we look out for each other. Also, the people in the red-light district know us and there is no problem there. At this point a lot of the girls actually come up here for facials and other things. They need to look their best, you know. [N rolls her eyes and begins to laugh] Look! [Looking first at N and then me] We are good Muslim girls and all, but the way I see it we have a job to do and they have a job to do. Why am I going to look down on them for that? Everyone is doing their job, there is no problem. [N, who has briefly stopped laughing, begins giggling again—Z eyes her, smiling, then looks away with a mock-disgusted look on her face]

Zaina's concern for her neighbors extended beyond mere generalities. In a serious tone she recounted the humiliation the prostitutes suffered at the hands of the police. Even giggly Najwa stopped laughing as Zaina heatedly described the police raids that occasionally took place nearby.

[Angrily] The police have no respect for people! They do not have any respect for these girls at all! I have seen them handle them very roughly and sometimes they bring them out into the street naked. There is no need to treat them that way. Yes, they may be breaking the law, they may be illegals, but they don't have to do that. It's upsetting for everyone. [N looks away solemnly while Z is saying this] One time, not long after I moved in, I heard a lot of noise out on the stairs. I came out and saw a bunch of women, some of them not dressed very much, running towards the back—the bathroom is back there. [Points] So I looked around and then I went back and knocked on the door. "What are you doing in there?" I asked and they said "Oh, please don't give us away, the police are after us, please!" What could I do? So I came back to the front and looked around—didn't see any police. So I thought, "Oh, we could get in trouble too," so I went back and told them "Look, there are no police now and you need to go." Finally, they opened the door and went out—I started counting when they were coming out the door [N begins to giggle again] and I count one . . . two . . . three . . . all the way to six! [N is laughing hard again—Z is now smiling too] How did they get six people in that tiny bathroom? Anyway, I didn't like it that they were hiding back there, but I saw no reason to give them up to the police either.

Zaina forcefully denounced the humiliation that the women suffered under both their employers and the police. Although gently mocked by Najwa, Zaina articulated a sympathy and link to these women, noting that while their presence may actually hurt her business somewhat, they were still connected through proximity and the norms of hospitality that pass between neighbors. Najwa, who neither lived nor worked in Brickfields, was consistently skeptical of her friend throughout the interview, and "rationally" attempted to undermine the connection with the prostitutes that Zaina articulated. Zaina's insistence on an ethical connection as neighbors was striking, as her attachment was not based on religion, ethnicity, language, or common interests in an easily quantifiable sense. She did not greatly depend on the prostitutes as clients, yet a sense of neighborly connection was readily apparent.

In retrospect, the move to discuss the situation of her neighbors was significant and in my analysis directly related to the "break" that Zaina experienced due to Najwa's remarks regarding the disappearance of even the "legitimate" spaces on Jalan Tun Sambanthan. Deprived of a meaningful way to imagine the future in the face of an abstract exercise of legal power, Zaina turned to the situation of individuals whose lives are arguably more vulnerable to threat and disappearance. Unlike situations discussed by scholars such as Guano (2004) and Mitchell (2003) where, in the face of unstable urban configurations, social actors attempt to contain the uncertainty of the situation by abstractly mapping exclusionary spatial practices onto their own domains, Zaina restrains this threat by connecting her situation to that of a constantly imperiled group. Faced with this illegible, arbitrary threat, Zaina reaffirmed more informal, local ties; through these connections, she articulated her *experience* of being (possibly) subject to a power beyond the regulatory discourse of law indirectly, by expressing her anger over the treatment of prostitutes in Brickfields. In drawing the connections in this way, Zaina was not articulating a mode of resisting the regulatory power of the state; rather, she was expressing a desire for a more material sense of integration with an order that she anticipated being denied to her in the near future. The threat of failure haunting Zaina's efforts was personified by the situation of her neighbors, who found themselves consistently caught in the uncertain space between threat and guarantee that had come to shape the experiences of everyone in Brickfields.

Buildings That Move

It was impossible to spend any amount of time in Brickfields and not notice the overrepresentation of the blind in the area. For neighborhood residents the blind were simply one aspect of the overall fabric of the neighborhood. Occasionally, when traffic was too heavy for a blind pedestrian to cross, whoever was standing nearby would guide the waiting person or group across the street. Long-time residents would automatically slow their cars upon sighting someone tapping along the side of the road. Walking in the informal, narrow zone for pedestrians in the street between the parked cars and those zipping by, I would often find myself walking behind a group of blind friends, with the unmistakably sharp clicks of their canes lending an additional rhythm to the street. Although their progress was sometimes a little slower than mine, I had no thought of passing them, as this would have required stepping out into moving traffic. Where I was going would still be there, no matter when I eventually arrived.

Upon further reflection, it was clear that relative permanence and stability was not so assured as my expectation. The actions of blind pedestrians in Brickfields often pointed to the possibility of destinations disappearing before one arrived. Groups of blind pedestrians making their way through Brickfields would suddenly make a very simple move that indicated precisely this possibility. After many instances of walking behind or near groups of blind friends in Brickfields I noticed that at certain intervals the "click-clack-click" of their canes would cease. Still on the move, these walkers would wave their canes up into the space directly in front of and above them. It seemed at first to be a dangerous or counterproductive act at best. Why do the canes come up off the ground?

Francis, an official at the Malaysian Association for the Blind (MAB), explained that this move was an innovation of the walking techniques taught at the MAB. "Well, we don't train them to do it this way, but many people are modifying their training a little bit." He laughed, sensing my bewilderment:

You hear that construction going on outside? It's dangerous, especially for us. There is a lot of equipment and new construction—people don't know where things are. Even if they walked that way last week, it may be different this week. Some overhang, some heavy equipment that is off so they can't hear it. They don't trust their surroundings, so they make sure. It isn't just if the road or five foot way[30] is clear anymore—now there might be something in the air or something that just wasn't there yesterday. If it is silent and shouldn't be, they check.

I ask Francis if anyone had been seriously hurt due to the construction.

Luck-i-ly [Draws out word] . . . none so far. Some minor things—people falling into holes or hitting their heads on something, but nothing very serious. It is sad, ah . . . many have lived here for ten or fifteen years, but they don't know what they will find when they get out [into the neighborhood]. If they hear it [the construction] they avoid it, but cannot always hear-lah! Sometimes people coming here [to the MAB] get a little disoriented even though they have been walking here for years. The buildings are moving! [Laughs] Well, I don't really mean that . . . but the buildings seem to move.

Historically, a large concentration of blind or partially sighted residents have lived in Brickfields due to the fact that the MAB has been located in the neighborhood since 1951. The organization provides a variety of training programs and support for blind and partially sighted individuals, including occupational and educational programs, a clinic, a resource center, physical exercise facilities, and a Braille publishing and equipment unit (Malaysian Association for the Blind 2001, 7–8). The MAB is a national organization with satellite centers and programs throughout Malaysia. The Gurney Center in Brickfields serves as the national headquarters, attracting participants from throughout the country for its training programs. Many who arrive for training stay on in Brickfields after they have completed their program and most remain associated with the MAB in some way. Francis explained why many participants stay on:

> F: The blind like it here because you can get everything you need and generally people are quite nice and accepting of the blind. Also, it has been easier to start a business or get a place to live here until recently.
>
> RB: How many live here in Brickfields? I mean, do you know the approximate size of the blind population?
>
> F: Wah, I don't know . . . maybe 200 families with at least one blind or partially sighted member live here, although we haven't checked that. Huh! Perhaps we should do that-lah. I never thought of that before . . .
>
> RB: Is the community diverse? Brickfields has a reputation as an Indian neighborhood but . . .
>
> F: . . . Yes, yes, people from all three communities are here. Malays and Chinese too, doesn't matter. The blind really like Brickfields. They are really attached to the place. People are supportive—many people here give money or come out to the MAB for the reading program or other things. Great food here . . . it's easy to move around. Yeah, I would have to say that people really like it. Having many blind-owned businesses makes people feel nice. It is easier to have your own business here. The blind feel secure here.

RB: Brickfields has a reputation for being a kind of rough neighborhood. Is that ever a concern?

F: Yeah, people say that, but I don't agree. It's a good place. I lived here for years and really liked it. Most blind will tell you the same thing. Maybe it isn't a rich area, but it has always been a good community for us.

Between the institutional presence of the MAB and the relatively large number of families that live in the area, the blind have a significant presence in the day-to-day affairs of Brickfields. Despite this presence, however, the MAB and the community were not able to exercise a great deal of influence over the transformations taking place. Francis marked the MAB's frustration with recent events:

We don't really have any direct links with DBKL, so we don't know what's going on. We don't have very good communication with the government. Also, we have been trying to present our concerns during budget dialogue sessions—before they pass the final budget. For two years running we have tried and they always promise to get back to us but never do. So we have to do things informally. You know, a lot of ministers come out for events. When they do, we sometimes try to have a word with them, but just informally. The PM [prime minister] himself came out for our big reading program—the one where sighted people volunteer to read books on to tapes that the blind can listen to later. Anyway, the PM came out for this and while he was here we managed to talk to him a bit about what was going on. We have to do things like this.

Francis also noted that some party organizations have ongoing relationships with the MAB and that they try to use these channels to exert an informal influence over matters that affect the life of the Center. He specifically cited Puteri UMNO[31] as one such organization.

Others, not speaking on behalf of the institution, are much harsher in their assessment of the government's concern for the blind in Brickfields. Tsai, a blunt, chatty, partially sighted man who provides part-time professional services to the MAB, was much more caustic in his evaluation of the state's motivations:

T: DBKL, property developers . . . they never consult us. The government always comes and tells us "we know better than you"—that is always what they do. If you make too much noise they'll use the law against us. You know, we have been warned not to make too much noise.

RB: Really? Who said that?

> T: Aahh! [Continues, ignoring the question] You see, we Asians do not want to challenge authority, it's in our religion and in our culture. We have great respect for authorities. However, in Malaysia this respect for authority is used against us—used against people. They know that they can threaten us and we won't say much. Religion in government is not a good idea. They just take advantage of us.

Tsai's reluctance to reveal who did the "warning" was understandable. So was his deep anger about the process as it unfolded in Brickfields. I interviewed Tsai at the Gurney Center in July 2002. During the five months preceding our interview, intense construction on the KL Monorail project had been going on literally a few feet from the main gate of the center. The construction presented numerous problems for the MAB. Many of the MAB's activities took place in the afternoon. This was the time of the day that construction was halted and the relatively silent construction site[32] was a quiet menace for center participants who depended on sound to warn them of an unstable environment. It was impossible to enter the MAB at this time without first crossing the monorail construction site, making merely getting to the center extremely dangerous for the blind.

The gate and outer walls of the center sustained a great deal of damage due to the construction. "The contractor has promised to pay damages for all of that," Francis told me. "We'll see if they really do." Tsai, when I mentioned what I saw to him, came up with his own formula for the care that work of this kind requires:

> What needs to take place is that people need to follow the three Cs; Consultation, Cooperation, and Coexistence. All of these things have to be considered when building big projects like the ones in Brickfields. Of course this has not happened—they do not consider any of these things.

Francis was a bit more neutral about the developments, feeling that it was too early to tell what long-term impact the projects would have.

> F: The projects are incomplete, right? So we'll have to wait and see. Right now it is pretty dangerous for us, what with all of that equipment. There haven't been any serious accidents so far, but it is just a matter of time. You saw what they have done right in front here? It is hard for sighted people to get in here! So for the blind, it is really terrible. We have to walk through a construction site just to get in here.

RB: Has all of this led you to change any of your programs or how you train the blind to get around?

F: No, how would we do it? I'm not sure that we can account for these changes. I don't know what we would do. I'm just surprised that the tracks run so close to us. They are right outside! We had no idea that the tracks were going to be so close until they actually started putting them up.

As with most of my interlocutors, Francis was shocked when the project was suddenly under way. While most Brickfields residents were aware that "something" was going to happen, the timing and scale of what was actually taking place was a shock. Such events were always unexpected. Francis and the MAB struggled to imagine a future in the context of these transformations and attempted to intervene with the transportation companies on behalf of the community. These interventions had a negligible effect, as Francis made clear:

F: Well, the trains, when completed, will probably benefit the blind. It will be easier for them to get around the city by train. So maybe the inconvenience now will help us later. KL Monorail didn't talk to us beforehand about the layout of its stations, so I don't know if they will be very good for the blind or not. Putra [a different public transportation company] came to us years ago and asked our suggestions about station layout. Around '96 I think. Actually, they only did this because the blind were protesting their original plans, but they did come to see us and, when their stations were built, they incorporated most of our suggestions. Putra was supposed to build this line too, but they ran out of money during the crisis,[33] so suddenly its KL Monorail. They didn't contact us before they started, although we've had two or three meetings since construction began. I don't know what the result will be.

RB: What about access to KL Sentral? Have you talked to them about the difficulty of getting across the main road?

F: Well, they are supposed to build a pedestrian flyover, so when that happens then KL Sentral will be quite convenient for the blind. Now, however, it is impossible to get across the main road—really dangerous. I don't know . . . have you heard anything about the pedestrian bridge?

RB: I've heard rumors that they are going to build one, but I don't know.

F: Ah, yeah . . . well, these are national projects, so they have to go ahead. You can't stop development projects, right?

Tsai was sharply pessimistic in his assessment of what was happening. Unlike Francis, Tsai strongly felt that the development projects would destroy the blind community in Brickfields:

T: The blind will eventually have to move out . . . what do you call it? "Displacement." It is too expensive to live here. The fact that people do not have money will lead to illegal acts.

RB: What do you mean?

T: Well, they'll evade taxes or have to get involved in shady business deals. Things like this. They will have to because they want to keep their homes and businesses but won't be able to. I fear that the blind will start getting more involved in things like this. The government is doing this. The government teaches materialism and lust! They crave what they don't have and will do anything to get it, so we see that and we begin to crave the things we don't have and begin to do illegal things to get them. That's all the government has been showing us for years.

RB: But won't some of the project eventually make things better for the blind as well? Such as the trains . . . I mean, won't public trains make it easier for the blind to get around the city?

T: Sure, the blind will now be able to take a train to just about anywhere, but it is expensive. Before, perhaps we had to deal with the bus but we could afford it. Now, if we want to get across town, it is almost as expensive as a taxi! And we can't walk out of Brickfields now, so if you don't have the money to move you are really restricted. Before, at least you could walk to nearby places. So maybe the trains also make it harder to travel, wouldn't you say?

Tsai was quite willing to condemn the entire logic of the development process passionately. This was quite unusual to hear spoken so bluntly. Most Brickfields residents abstractly supported development projects such as KL Sentral and the monorail. It was the observable impact on their daily lives and lack of recognition in the process that gave most Brickfields residents pause. I pressed Tsai on his starkly negative view of the situation:

This is all for *e-lites*. [Draws out the word for emphasis] They will make a lot of money from all of this. They already have. Do we really need such grandiose projects? What about the simple things that everyone needs? It is not flashy but we need it and many people in Malaysia lack the simple things. Why do we need the

twin towers [Petronas Towers] or the biggest train station when people still lack
basic things?

Tsai may have been grandstanding for the interview, but it was obvious that he had put a lot of personal effort into understanding the "big picture" that was unfolding around him. Although he would generally deflect
specific questions about his quality of life in the neighborhood, Tsai was
quite willing to engage larger political issues such as city planning, government, corruption, and the rights of citizens. "Have you read Drucker?" he
asked me toward the end of the interview. "How about Schumacher? You
should read them if you are doing a project like this." The interview winding down, Tsai began to just talk, trying to hit every point he felt I needed
to know and had not asked about:

> T: How do you deal with mass rural to urban migration? This is what you
> are doing, right?"
>
> RB: Well, no not exactly . . .
>
> T: [Not waiting for an answer] Have you read Drucker? How about Schu-
> macher? You should read them if you are doing a project like this. When
> we talk about civil society we have to break it down. What is it? How do
> we build it? We have to take each term individually. "Civil," means . . .
> [Pause] citizen! Collective action. Therefore, we all have to be recognized
> as equal citizens! And "society." Society is a collection of people in a spe-
> cific place. We have to look at these things separately and then try to put
> them together to build a loving, caring . . . [Pause] caring community.
> City planners don't understand this. They don't even think about these
> terms. You know, people simply do not talk anymore. Rather than talking
> to their families they are in front of their computers now. Do young peo-
> ple talk to their families anymore? No, they would rather go to these chat
> rooms and make friends there. Then, they like their friends in the chat
> room more than their families, who they can see. Modernization makes
> strangers of people. Honestly, I think of modernization as a scourge. It's a
> sickness!

Although I had sought him out for an interview regarding the character of life in Brickfields for the blind and partially sighted, Tsai only
occasionally indulged this line of questioning. He was reluctant to speak
about his personal experience at all. For him, articulating his ideas regarding what is "really" wrong with Malaysian politics and Malaysian life was

the primary topic for the interview. Tsai's perception of immobility in the street was multiple, in that his experience as a pedestrian was merely a symptom of his perceived disappearance as a resident and a citizen. Like Zaina, he articulated a notion of what the proper order of development in Brickfields should be through recourse to talking about those whose lives are even more precarious than his. Rather than citing specific neighbors or events, however, Tsai sought recognition of his experience in the abstract understandings of urban life offered by the work of theorists. Because he lacked a more concrete local recognition of his experience, the buildings themselves seemed to move and disappear. The fact that the buildings in Brickfields were actually moving for the blind was an extreme example of the broader experience of change and disappearance articulated by many residents who could visually perceive what was going on around them.

Conclusion

This chapter opened by offering a theoretical framework by which one can begin to understand the local impact of large-scale development projects on the communities in which they are undertaken. By linking the domains of city planning and development, governance and the law, and the social worlds of residents, the ethnographic focus has been to show how modes of experience, association, and personhood emerged during the transformation of Brickfields. I have characterized the convergence of discipline, law, and bodies as a terrain of uncertainty between threat and guarantee.

Most Brickfields residents abstractly supported the techno-rational logic underpinning the modernization projects that the state pursued in their neighborhood. The source of conflict and indeterminacy that represented the threat was not the discourse of development in abstract terms, but their direct experience of the law in the pursuit of creating a more properly modern space. Blocked from knowing when or how the state would take possession of land and make buildings and residents "disappear," they felt it was the manner in which these initiatives were undertaken that violated local principles of justice and due process. The state's perceived refusal to recognize actors unless they had a formal role in the legal process highlighted the gap between legality and local principles of justice that made the actions of the state appear indeterminate and unjust, even through these actions were taken in accordance with the law.

In this way actions that were legal and that appeared to be ethical from the point of view of the state were actually productive of violence at the local level. This violence primarily took the form of a pervasive uncertainty that shaped the lives and actions of everyone who entered this space. Although those who lived and worked in Brickfields felt these effects most acutely, government officials and property developers were also subject to this uncertain space between threat and guarantee. Considering the extreme difficulty in concretely locating the cause or source of this violence, the world of the neighborhood itself was often experienced as unreal or unbelievable in a literal sense. This experience, therefore, produced *disbelief* rather than political resistance or legal action against the state and its agents. The unpredictability that characterized everyday life in the neighborhood and the seemingly arbitrary nature of change produced an environment where imagining the future often meant imagining how one could forge connections with the law, the state, neighbors, friends, and even the built environment itself despite the fact that any of these things could unexpectedly disappear. The efforts of Brickfields residents to believe in their world again are where we must now turn.

4

Strangers, Counterfeiters, and
Gangsters: Figures of Belonging and the
Problem of Belief

Introduction

> Our conversation the other day really disturbed me. It really bothered me. Somehow having to talk so much about Brickfields changed the place for me. Now I get up and walk out in the morning and I see a different place. The way we broke it down . . . I don't know. It suddenly seems very different. I think I'm going to have to move . . .
> —Chandra, Brickfields Resident, August 2002

How can talking about a place change it? Though Chandra was the only person who directly articulated the unease he felt after he had described Brickfields to me, I suspect that he was not alone in this discomfort. This ethnographic project was from its inception designed to derive some understanding of the experience of community and change in Brickfields. Yet for those who offered to speak about their experience of the community and the city, it turned out that the interviews were never neutral spaces of explanation or conversation. For Chandra, as I suspect for many others, the interviews produced narratives of Brickfields that upset the sometimes fragile imaginary orders that individuals had formulated in order to anchor their lives firmly in the life of the neighborhood. Much was at stake in these narratives, as it was precisely in this realm that neighborhood residents worked to imagine the space of Brickfields as a place where belonging, relatedness, community, and ethical life were possible.

As the previous chapter illustrates, the work of placemaking in the unstable context that existed in Brickfields was no easy task. The narratives articulated during my interviews were collaboratively produced, but the process of telling made the fragility of the neighborhood and the threats to the future come alive in concrete forms. In the context of the interview Chandra suffered a double violence; the violence of the recent transformation of the neighborhood on his understanding of life came to the surface, and the process of trying to piece together a credible image of Brickfields for the purpose of the interview only exacerbated this violence. Chandra and I had developed a close relationship that allowed him to tell me what others were probably feeling. By "making sense" in the direct, empirical manner that I sought during the interviews, Brickfields suddenly didn't feel right at all for my interlocutors.

This feeling should be taken very seriously. It is not enough for everyday life to simply be present and understood through authoritative institutional discourses; life must be thinkable and livable for individual subjects. In other words, one must be able to produce an image of the world that allows for a certain agency based on knowable relations between oneself and others within sensible horizons of possible meaning. Such images of livable configurations must engage authoritative institutional discourses, but are not necessarily the logical outcome of such discourses. If the authoritative judgments of the state, the law, or religious institutions do not produce vectors within everyday life that allow for action or agency on the part of individual subjects, such judgments can actually work to liquidate the sensible reality of the world for those caught in it (Deleuze 1994, 1997). For someone like Chandra, faced suddenly with the fact that everything he perceived to be real about his everyday world was excluded or denied by the authoritative "facts" generated by the very institutions that claimed to be the guarantors of social order and just living, it became impossible for him to *believe* in his world. My interview with Chandra inadvertently ruptured the essential link between perception and action that existed for him in his image of Brickfields; this in turn generated a crisis of belief for him.

When Brickfields residents spoke of their neighborhood, their narratives were shot through with ambivalence. On the one hand were themes of their belonging to a place where they could fashion their lives as Malaysians without necessarily needing to be ethnically or culturally

Malay. On the other hand they felt that the proximity to the majority Malay Muslim community was a political threat that hung over their lives, generating fear of discrimination, exclusion, and disappearance. As I have discussed in Chapter 2 and will take up again in more detail in Chapter 5, efforts on the part of the Malaysian state to make Islam a major source of its authority intensified this mood of threat and unease. The mental image of Brickfields as a vibrant but threatened margin was a key factor in defining residents' sense of place. It is not that my informants possessed a transcendent, utopian notion of community or of their religious of ethnic communities. Tamil Hindus in particular felt that the community in Brickfields was "backwards" and required the development projects of the state to become a fully modern participant in Malaysian public life. Thus, the characterization of Brickfields as a vibrant, necessary margin in the heart of Kuala Lumpur was a critical one in establishing the "legitimate" modality for belonging and agency in the neighborhood for local residents.

Henri Lefebvre argues in *The Production of Space* that social space is defined as "a locus, a medium, and a tool" for the perpetuation of social differentiation and inequality. Through the spatial reproduction of representations that normalize relations between subjects in particular places, a "consensus" regarding the identity and ownership of particular spaces is generated as an ideal. In Lefebvre's formulation this ideal discursively marks the relations of inclusion and exclusion that support the claims of certain groups while materially or symbolically evicting "others" who are not felt to belong (Lefebvre 1991, 32). In the context of aggressive spatial and demographic changes driven by the modernizing efforts of the state, members of the community seek to establish what Lefebvre has characterized as their "right to the city" through discursive and practical strategies of dwelling in the space and using it on their own terms. Such imaginations of the neighborhood serve to oppose the experience of being denied one's right to "place" through state practices that frame modes of habiting space that enable certain groups and alienate others (Lefebvre 1996, 2003). In my view Lefebvre's notion of "right" in this sense must be distinguished from the formal axioms of "human rights" or "rights of citizenship" that are largely invested in the authoritative discourses of the state or the *doxa* of religion. Unlike such notions of rights "granted" based on axiomatic criteria of identity, Lefebvre is specifically referring to an ethics of establishing spaces that are not only ordered and safe but also allow for action and a concrete sense of being able to create an ethical life. This capability to act is certainly dependent upon an ordered present but also requires the creation of spaces where individuals possess the means to imagine future life and action. In Brickfields, the problem for local residents was not just that their legal rights or physical persons were being literally violated in the present (although they sometimes were), but rather that the transformation of the space had shattered the link between present experience and the possibility of future action. Not able to believe in Brickfields as their place in the world, residents lacked resistance to the present (Deleuze and Guattari 1994) and, in Lefebvre's framework, were thus denied their right to the city.

In Brickfields ethnicity was most often the explicit mode of identification cited by residents as the basis for the social distinctions that shaped and sustained the social space of the neighborhood. Specifically, Brickfields was commonly understood to be an ethnic enclave for Malaysian Indians living in Kuala Lumpur, a characterization often circulated as a form of "common sense" knowledge regarding the nature of the neighborhood both within and outside of the area. This local understanding of ethnicity as the defining characteristic of the space resonates with anthropological literature regarding "ethnic cities" as spaces of political strategizing (Portes and Stepick 1993; Zhou 1992), manifestations of ethnic and occupational hierarchies (Brenner 1998; Margolis 1994), centers for immigrants (Markowitz 1993), and loci of marginalization and racial discrimination (Chen 1992; Fong 1994; Kwong 1987). While the notion of Kuala Lumpur as an "ethnic city" is strong in popular accounts,[1] the supposition that ethnicity operates as the basis for the organization of social space in the city has been criticized in the academic literature for unproblematically assuming, rather than empirically verifying, an ethnic basis for local social networks (Low 1999; Pessar 1995). Furthermore, the unproblematic use of ethnicity as the primary explanation for local social organization in Brickfields runs counter to the fact that each major ethnic group is well represented in the neighborhood; it assumes a social unity linked to ethnic identification that cannot be empirically established.[2]

Despite the demonstrated diversity of the neighborhood, Brickfields existed as a distinct place within the larger urban geography of Kuala Lumpur. Grasping the complex interplay of ethnic, socioeconomic, and religious factors that formed the basis of this distinctiveness requires a theory of urban space capable of grasping the complex interplay of differences without privileging one factor of difference over others (Hannerz 1980). Low (1999) identifies this approach within urban anthropology as the theorization of the "divided city" and argues that this approach attempts to place the urban itself at the center of its analysis, balancing tensions between notions of difference that produce complex urban forms of public life. While racism and ethnicity often remain key aspects in studies of the divided city (Keith and Cross 1993; Massey and Denton 1993; McDonogh 1993; Williams 1992), this approach also allows for a consideration of how religion (Abu-Lughod 1987; Levy 1990; Wacquant and Wilson 1989), crime (Caldeira 1996; Merry 1981, 1990), real estate and the alienation of land (Greenbaum 1993; Gregory 1992, 1998; Williams 1992), and work and economic relations (Guano 2004; Kondo 1990; Sacks 1997), also come into play in the making of "places" within urban environments. Although diverse in focus, researchers who engage the divided city all attempt to understand concepts of difference as related to a host of issues that produce complex modes of imagining place within the city. This complex understanding of urban placemaking is reflected in a handful of studies pertaining specifically to Malaysia (Nagata 1979; Goh 2001; Guinness 1992). Foremost among these shared concerns are the ways in which these practices of placemaking produce notions of "inside" and "outside" that are not always clearly marked, yet persist in the local imaginations of distinctive urban neighborhoods (Bestor 1989; Gupta and Ferguson 1997).

Drawing upon these understandings of place and the practices entailed in inhabiting local spaces, this chapter explores the inventive strategies through which Brickfields residents, faced with the possibility of displacement,[3] worked to constitute a sense of agency and create believable possibilities for establishing ethical lives by engaging a set of abstractly articulated figures of personhood. These figures, mental images that made it possible to experience Brickfields life as real for my interlocutors, were generated from a number of intersecting sites, including the Malaysian state, the popular media, and the discourses of self and community that circulated at the local neighborhood level. Two of the most commonly articulated figures at the neighborhood level were the *stranger* and the *counterfeiter*. Both strangers and counterfeiters gave a "face" to perceived aspects of everyday life that were felt to be real but otherwise difficult to identify. The elaboration of such figures often took the form of identifying "threats" to the neighborhood, but the ability to voice such identifications also had the effect of making the present livable for my interlocutors. In other words, while the mode of expression in relation to these figures was often negative, it reestablished the ground for *belief* in relation to the reality of everyday life in the community that the state and the law had shattered in its efforts to transform Brickfields. Such strategies generated ambiguously oppositional practices that, while rooted in modes of differentiation and exclusion through the generation of a normative cartography of belonging in Brickfields, only provisionally established who belonged where and why they belonged there.[4]

In contrast to these two local figures, the stereotyped figure of the *gangster* was the one most often associated with the neighborhood by outsiders. Although also a figure through which Brickfields residents sought to establish and understand relatedness, the gangster required local residents to engage how others characterized "them" and how these images of their "place" in turn structured that place and those who lived there. By considering the figures of strangers, counterfeiters, and gangsters in an ethnographic context this chapter seeks to, in the words of Gupta and Ferguson, "rethink difference *through* connection," and provide an understanding of Brickfields as a specific place within the topography of power that existed in Kuala Lumpur (Gupta and Ferguson 1997, 35).

The Stranger, the Counterfeiter, and the Gangster: Figures of Personhood in Brickfields

The use of the concept "figure" in this chapter has a specific meaning. Amelie Rorty has argued that modern notions of personhood are linked to cultural notions of "characters," "figures," "persons," "selves," "individuals," and "presences" (Rorty 1976). Regarding figures, Rorty explains:

Figures are defined by their place in an unfolding drama: they are not assigned roles because of their traits, but rather have the traits of their prototypes in myth or sacred script. Figures are characters writ large, becom[ing] figureheads . . . their roles and their traits emerge from their place in an ancient narrative. The narration, the plot, comes first: it requires a hero, a betrayer, a lover, a messenger, a confidant. (Rorty 1976, 302)

While such figures begin as abstract images in thought, they nonetheless take on a materiality that in turn works to define the individual subject in relation to others.[5] In this way, figures provide links between virtual notions of how everyday life "is" or "should be" and the experience of the actual. As I demonstrated in Chapter 3, links between these domains within legal, political, or state discourses had largely been severed in Brickfields, making it extremely difficult to locate oneself in the interstices between ideal and real in such a way that one could believe in one's capacity for action or the formation of a *life*. In wider public discourses, Brickfields has historically been the home of "Tamil outsiders" and "criminals," stereotypes whose characteristics were linked to broader narratives of race and culture. It is these figures that were, in turn, reworked by Brickfields residents themselves to index their place in relation to the state and to the city more forcefully.[6]

The figures detailed in this chapter, generated from images of thought, produced a way for Brickfields residents to grasp situations and events that concerned them in their everyday life. The fact that they were objects of belief and not factual in the empirical sense is beside the point when we consider the function of such figures. The "truth" of Brickfields was often divorced from prior dispositions and authoritative discourses regarding the area, emerging for residents only as a result of being violently impelled to reimagine the space. The necessity of "thinking Brickfields" in the face of this violence, rather than being safely anomalous or distant from "normal" experience, resembles the general violence that impels *all* creative human thought (Deleuze 2000). Individuals in Brickfields, trying to make sense of their lives concretely in a context where life was often experienced as sequences of serial accidents, were largely cast adrift and left to float in relation to the operations of the law and the state. Imagining themselves in relation to figures such as the stranger, the counterfeiter, or the gangster established a contingent link between perception and action that allowed for vectors of possible meaning that were largely absent or liquidated in institutional domains. From the empirical point of view of the city planner, the police officer, the political activist, or the social scientist, such figures were generally seen as the products of "illusions," "superstitions," or "errors." Yet in understanding how individuals could live within the fluidity of Brickfields, standards of fact and fiction in relation to these figures became a secondary concern in considering the meaning and horizons of possible action that such mental images concretely produced for neighborhood residents.

In a situation where one's sense of the real was so divorced from the authoritative discourses that sought to frame, order, and explain that reality, these figures functioned as graspable images of life and the world for Brickfields residents. They stood as objects of faith in a situation where the imagination of an ethical life that linked the individual subject to the possibility of acting in the world required the substitution of a model of belief for the authoritative model of knowledge produced by the state. Situations of this type have been observed in other locales, although most often substitutions of this kind have been understood as a form of cynicism in relation to life and the world (Navaro-Yashin 2002; Sloterdijk 1988). Certainly there is evidence for this conclusion, particularly in the discernable lack of faith in political action, the rule of law, and the idea (most often expressed in forms of nationalism) that one belongs to a larger community or a people that has been observed in places as diverse as Germany (Sloterdijk) and Turkey (Navaro-Yashin). In Brickfields, however, disbelief in relation to the state or the law did not automatically produce a cynical stance toward the world at large; rather, the image of specific figures who were not generated through authoritative discourses were nonetheless believed to be real and the possibility of knowable, believable, ethical life was often invested in one's relationship to such figures.

My argument regarding the figures of the outsider and the criminal that are the focus of this chapter are as follows. First, the notion of the "stranger" in Brickfields was loosely associated with the threat posed by the majority Malay community, particularly the Malaysian state, which was perceived to be a predominantly Malay institution. Imagining oneself in relation to the stranger was an attempt by Brickfields residents to subvert the popular understanding of Malaysian Indians as a shadowy minority population, and constituted a direct engagement with a law that recognizes a separate legal subjectivity for Malays.[7] Second, the local figure of the "counterfeiter" represented an engagement with the state that recognized the sovereignty of the state's law while enacting community understandings of justice and the Good that diverged from the law and made ethical life possible and real. Third, the popular stereotype of the "gangster" was inverted; Brickfields residents often regarded local criminal organizations as providers of an alternative form of security for the neighborhood that simultaneously engaged and circumvented the police. This understanding contrasted sharply with the more common belief that these organizations were by definition chaotic and dangerous.

Attempts to rework figures such as the stranger, the counterfeiter, and the criminal were concrete examples of how practices of marginalization faced by Brickfields residents were not always understood as forces to be overcome or resisted, but could also provide a tangible means by which understandings of self and community were often constituted at these margins. It is important to mark the "ambiguous" character of these practices as modes of differentiation related to conceptual types. Although these abstract figures were linked to broader discourses of race, religion, or the legal character of citizens, they neither fully conformed to, nor consistently opposed, these discursive categories. I understand this ambiguity as a space of creative engagement with the state, an engagement that allowed Brickfields residents to form an image of their world that they could, at least to some degree, believe in. This creative engagement is particularly evident in the narratives that follow in this chapter, as my interlocutors were often as concerned with anticipating and inhabiting the wider imagination of *themselves* as outsider figures in popular narratives as with simply rejecting or reversing these understandings locally.[8] Understanding these figures as an engagement from the margin underscores the fact that although notions of identity often derive their force from the imaginary of the state, individual subjects themselves engage the state through their own zones of experience (Das 2007; Das and Poole 2004). Although at variance with formal legal norms, the manner in which neighborhood residents engaged the figures of the outsider and the criminal were not simply attempts to take on the state in thinly disguised oppositional terms (Scott 1985, 1990). Instead, I suggest that the creative everyday practice of forming selves by fashioning imaginary others that is the subject of this chapter represents an inventive reworking of the possible relationships between self and outsider figures through attempts to locate an ordered regularity in everyday life.

These modes of imagining local relationships proved to be contingent and fragile configurations for my interlocutors. As detailed in the previous chapter, everyday life in Brickfields was often disrupted by a trajectory of change that was frequently felt to occur counter to local principles of justice and due process. Brickfields residents who found themselves in the space between the law and local principles of justice and ethics sensed the danger of "being made a stranger" within what was imagined to be "one's own space." Mitigating this danger meant carefully cultivating everyday practices that retained a sense of a *future* for community residents allowing for some agency to structure local social life. Thus, modes of local practice structuring relatedness and belonging were attempts to engage or rework the state's "promised" order, an order that seemed to local residents to liquidate the very basis for belief in the world that ethical life requires.

The Stranger: Personhood and Place in Brickfields

Despite the numbers provided by state demographers in the 2000 census, the belief that Brickfields was overwhelmingly "Indian" persisted. The area's overwhelming association with the Indian ethnic character was often cited as the source of its marginality and the primary obstacle to a desired form of order in the neighborhood. Devaraj, a professional who lives in Brickfields, negatively assessed the ethnic order of Brickfields as constituting both a target of racism from the outside and a source of "racial" inferiority deriving from the "character" of the community itself. While discussing the state's timing in initiating a development project, Devaraj stated that such changes were late in coming because "Indians live here." Muthu, a long-time Brickfields resident and operative for the political party Gerakan, stated the issue more clearly:

We are a black area! Just like blacks. [Pause] I don't mean to offend anyone here. I mean, I'm Indian too, you know, but it is true. They haven't cared about this area because we are Indians here. We are the blacks here.

Nagaraju, a local business owner, wanted to make the point in terms "that an American would understand" by calmly asserting, "All the niggers live in Brickfields. Does this offend you? [RB: No] We are niggers here, it is simple."

The expression of racism from the outside was seldom articulated without the "backwardness" of Indians also being cited as a rational explanation for the outside discrimination and for the marginality and instability of Brickfields. Expanding on his thoughts regarding the situation in Brickfields, Devaraj asserted that Indians themselves are also to blame for the situation because "they are not as entrepreneurial as the Chinese." According to Devaraj it was only after the state initiated large-scale development projects such as KL Sentral and the KL Monorail that Indian businessmen moved to develop the neighborhood. Even then, the manner in which these developments came into being was felt to be "strange." Devaraj cited the Villa Scott Condominium complex as an example, noting that the well-known Mr. Indran had owned the land for many years, but didn't develop it until recently. Then, once the building was completed, the owner reportedly refused to sell units in the condominium. "Only after the property market collapsed did he start selling off the individual units," Devaraj concluded. "I know that Mr. Indran was an educated, intelligent man, but I don't know why he did it that way." Devaraj did not express any respect at all for Mr. Indran's sons, who at the time of the interview were running the family business due to their father's death, saying that they are "really stupid—they don't have a head for this kind of thing and they are never around." Not having a "head" for business was an Indian trait for Devaraj and thus a central problem in Brickfields. In a later interview Devaraj revised his Indian-specific critique to include nearly all Malaysians, stating that Malaysians did not possess a "developed attitude" and remained mired in an outmoded past, unable to "really understand how to be modern." As was commonly articulated in such narratives, Malaysian Chinese were singled out as "different" in these terms, and Devaraj's sentiments regarding Malaysian Chinese, shared by many whom I interviewed, was that they "are very clever and entrepreneurial. Different than Malays and Chinese, who are not ready for globalization at all."

The complexity of how the qualities of being "an Indian" related to the imagination of self is evident, and a full exploration of these implications is beyond the scope of the argument here.[9] What is important is the centrality of an articulated Malaysian Indian ethnic identification in the course of understanding Brickfields as a unique space and as a distinct community. Despite the often articulated notion that the Brickfields Indian community was simultaneously a victim of outside racism and its own "racial" characteristics, only one interlocutor suggested that the solution was simply to erase the unique ethnic character of the area.

For the overwhelming majority, the notion of Brickfields as a specifically Indian space served to locate the individual's sense of place and community and oriented their narratives of what Brickfields actually "was" and "should be." My lengthy interview with long-time Brickfields resident Chandra illustrated this complex understanding of the Indian character of the area. While Chandra's vividly positive characterization of the "Indian" aspects of this sense of place and belonging was somewhat unusual, his overall emphasis on Brickfields as a uniquely Indian space was not.[10]

The fact that Chandra was so positive in his assessment of Brickfields as "Indian" is significant. Although Chandra was a creative artist who had received national acclaim for his work, he had specifically chosen to live in Brickfields in 1986, bucking the trend of emigration by moving to the neighborhood from nearby Petaling Jaya:

Well, I made the change for three reasons: security, convenience, and the Indian environment. I grew up in a very Tamil household. For me, coming to college was a real adjustment—just like the Malay *kampung* boys having to get used to different kinds of people, I also had to get used to much more diverse crowds. But I really love being in a place that is steeped in things Tamil. Growing up my mother used to cook all kinds of traditional Tamil dishes, especially for breakfast—*vadai*, *idiappam*, and so on. Then, when I went off to school and for many years after that I was stuck with toast, bread, and jam for breakfast. A prisoner's diet, you know! Still, it became my standard way to begin each day. Coming to Brickfields, it was like . . . well, I could get all of the Tamil dishes again and it wasn't like I had to look for a specialty shop. It is everywhere and I love that. I love hearing Tamil spoken freely and I love being able to just speak with others in Tamil without having to wonder "hey, do you speak Tamil?" Coming to Brickfields was like coming home, even though I had never actually lived here before. It is second nature to me. I feel really comfortable. Really, I love living in Brickfields.

It was clear to Chandra why Petaling Jaya wasn't right for him:

C: Living in Section 17 [of Petaling Jaya] wasn't that good. It wasn't good for a single person, especially because sometimes I am away for months at a time. So I just got tired of being robbed. You fix the window, they come in through the roof—you fix the roof, they come in through the back door— you fix the back door, they just break down the front. I really became sick of it and there was nothing the police could do. So, I moved to Brickfields for security. Sure, being in an apartment is not always the best thing—I had a house and a yard in PJ—but I don't have to worry about security issues that much.

RB: So you moved to Brickfields for greater security, despite the area's reputation for crime and being insecure?

C: Yes . . . ironically, it is true. But it has been safer for me and I don't think that the reputation is entirely accurate. Yes, there is crime and there are gangsters, but I haven't had problems with this. Also, Section 17 is probably the least Indian area in PJ—have you been there?

RB: Yes.

C: I really didn't like that. So I still find Brickfields to be a better place for me personally. I'm more comfortable here—I can hear the latest Tamil or Hindi pop songs blasting out of the local shops—I can go down to the temple on a festival day. [Laughs] You can take your pick around here in that way, right? When I moved here in 1986 there were thirty-three places of worship in this neighborhood—that includes churches, temples, and so on. I don't know what the number is now, but it is probably still around there.

The most obvious point of connection for Chandra is the Indian character of the neighborhood. Although not a native of Kuala Lumpur, he related living in Brickfields to the experience of his childhood growing up in a Tamil family in Ipoh. Everyday signifiers such as food, music, odors, and snatches of overheard conversations constitute the familiar for him. Chandra's description strongly referenced proximity as a key factor in why Brickfields is a better space for him to live compared to Petaling Jaya. *It wasn't good for a single person*, a reference to the notion that it is not good to be alone, to be anonymous, to be invisible. It was possible to know one's neighbors in Brickfields. Petaling Jaya, according to Chandra, did not easily afford such opportunities.

It was not supposed to be that way in Petaling Jaya. As originally envisioned in the 1950s, this "satellite city" was the way to a better future. Writing about Petaling Jaya not long after the suburb had been established, McGee and McTaggart wrote: "[Petaling Jaya] was first conceived of as a new town based on principles similar to those of the British new towns then in the course of construction;[11] by combining location of work, residence and recreation, it was hoped to develop a more modern and more agreeable form of urban living" (McGee and McTaggart, 1967).

As was the rule in British new towns, the spatial organization of the town sought to address each of the categories cited (work, residence, recreation) through strict, rational zoning codes and separation of land use. Therefore, while one could theoretically live, work, and relax without having to leave the town, one would not find coffee shops abutting homes or rows of food stalls lining football fields or streets. Reasserting urban planning goals that had been intended to govern growth in Kuala Lumpur since the beginning, Petaling Jaya promised happiness through order.

City residents responded to this promise and, given that land was quite cheaply available in the early days of the project, the population of the new town quickly swelled. Coupled with the fact that many resettlement projects that targeted unregistered residents sought to place them in low-cost housing within Petaling Jaya, it was not a problem to secure inhabitants for the new suburb. Many of these new residents were coming from Brickfields, as numerous interlocutors recounted housewives saving their "coffee money" toward down payments on land in Petaling Jaya. Strictly speaking, Chandra was incorrect in asserting that Petaling Jaya lacks an "Indian flavor," as Malaysian Indians, especially those from the Ceylonese[12] community, flocked to the new suburb. Although Malaysian Chinese are by far the most numerous group in Petaling Jaya today, the Indian community is statistically overrepresented there as well, relative to their overall numbers in Kuala Lumpur. Chandra was correct in his observation, however, that one would have little means of knowing about this Indian community based solely on the everyday life of the neighborhood.

The predominance of detached single-family suburban homes in Petaling Jaya contributes greatly to this invisibility. *"I had a house and a yard in PJ,"* Chandra noted. Yet this was *more* dangerous, not less, as his increased privacy simultaneously meant that he was more invisible to his neighbors. This specific problem may be mitigated somewhat, as Chandra surmised, if there is a family present rather than a single person, but this invisibility to neighbors remained. Contrary to the authoritative discourses regarding proper, healthy urban living that generated the satellite city, Chandra *felt* he was a stranger in Petaling Jaya. The fact that one finds a wealth of small ethnic shops in the designated commercial areas in the suburb made little difference to Chandra because they were out of sight, accessible only by car, and required a clear intention in mind to go there. One does not simply "happen upon" things in Petaling Jaya. The mitigation of the random was one of the central principles of the overall plan.

Chandra was not alone in his negative assessment of Petaling Jaya in comparison to Brickfields. I interviewed numerous Petaling Jaya residents who used to live in Brickfields and most expressed similar sentiments, although less directly than Chandra. The fact that I conducted most of these interviews in the coffee shops and food stalls in Brickfields and not in the restaurants and homes in their own neighborhood is significant.

The Petaling Jaya–Brickfields comparison offered here is a critical factor in understanding how Brickfields itself, as a distinctive area in the city, was conceptualized. This importance lies in the fact that the comparison was made all the time—by residents, but also in a very different way by city planners and agents of the state. Petaling Jaya–style development remained the contemporary ideal in many of these accounts, providing a model of development planning and successful urban space, even in cases where the interlocutor ultimately rejected the suburb as a good neighborhood to live in. While a place such as Brickfields could never be as thoroughly suburbanized as Petaling Jaya, this fact did not kill the state's dreams of imposing an analogous order over such older, "messy" spaces.

Chandra understood the continuing saliency of these desires for urban order very well. I asked him about the transformation of Brickfields:

> C: Well, my geographer point of view is that it is quite positive. Certainly, as I mentioned before, it is logical. Brickfields will connect KL to the rest of the country and the world and it makes sense to put something like KL Sentral here. Also, it will result in a lot of other development that will change the neighborhood and make it cleaner and more diverse. A lot of tourists will come in, others from around KL may visit, so I can see this happening.
>
> RB: Well, speak as a resident for a moment. In the context of the reasons you gave for moving here, how do you feel about these changes? For example, you said that you came here because it was a Tamil neighborhood. Do you think it will remain so? What do you think?
>
> C: Yes . . . from a personal standpoint I am quite sad about some of this. No, I do not think that Brickfields will remain an Indian neighborhood. There is no way that these families can afford to stay—the businesses as well. Most of them are really small businesses and I don't know how they could stay. So the projects are not for the local people. Sure, this makes me

sad. I do think that the temples and some of the restaurants will remain—good for tourists, you know. But it won't have the same kind of atmosphere that it does now.

RB: Do you think that making Brickfields less Indian is intentional?

C: Well [Long pause]—this gets into some politics. It's not just about Brickfields. I think that there has been an effort going on for a long time to break up non-Malay ethnic strongholds. Look at Sentul—same thing.[13] Maybe even more noticeable there. So Brickfields is affected by this too—and yet, Malays are also creating "Malay-only" spaces. Perhaps this isn't always so overt, but I look at Putrajaya . . . I look at Shah Alam . . . by default these are primarily Malay spaces and the attitude about this is very different.

Chandra later qualified his statement that Malays were intentionally trying to destroy neighborhoods like Brickfields:

C: I think that no matter what Brickfields will become less Indian because the community itself is changing. Fewer people speak and understand Tamil very well, and this is critical. Most of the ceremonies and stories in the temples are in Tamil and, without being able to understand the language, the meaning is lost. It is also a bit boring to go without knowing what is going on, so people stay away, especially young people. More and more young Tamils, especially those who have made a little money, cannot speak the language well and they tend to become more mainstream—less Indian. This has an impact in Brickfields because the . . . well, the Indian-ness of the neighborhood becomes less important to them and they move out. This has been going on for years. In many cases it was their parents that moved out to places like PJ, but perhaps the parents still maintained some ties to the area. The children don't really have a reason to do this—it isn't relevant to their lives. It won't completely disappear. You know, a lot of expatriates from India are now moving in here.

RB: Yes, I know.

C: They are generally professionals, but they come here because they can get things from home. Sure, most of them aren't Tamils—they are North Indians, I think—but it is still more familiar than most places in KL. So they will continue to move in and some middle-class Tamils will also stay. I think that some of the businesses will survive as well, although they will have to cater to tourists. Still, the Indian character of Brickfields is not just going to totally disappear.

Although somewhat idealized, Brickfields represented a space for Chandra that was simultaneously "home" and outside the norm, a margin to be retained rather than effaced. His account alternated between rationally explaining the "logical good" of the development projects and the quiet sadness of knowing that this will transform the characteristics of the area that he originally found attractive. The overt framework of Chandra's narrative was the loss of ethnic identity, but the loss of sociality associated with the predominant discourses of proper urban development remained a theme in his understanding of the transformation of the area as well.

Chandra's account of Brickfields at times seemed inconsistent. Yet, in broad terms, his account strongly resembled the understandings of Brickfields as a distinctive "place" that I heard over and over again during my conversations with residents. Central to this ambiguous discourse was a belief that the neighborhood was getting better and worse at the same time. The recognition that the broadly conceived city planning initiatives would make Brickfields cleaner, safer, and more attractive was often articulated precisely alongside the notion that the neighborhood was also getting dirtier, more crowded, and more chaotic. Some hope was often expressed that Brickfields would gain an identity as a tourist destination, although in doing so it was losing its identity as an Indian enclave, a critical factor that made Brickfields interesting, comfortable, and unique.[14]

The notion of Brickfields as a home for Malaysian Indians and an insecurity as to its continued existence as a familiar space emerged continually in the narratives of local residents. The anticipation of removal, upheaval, and disappearance was a dominant theme articulated as a characteristic of living or working in the neighborhood. These narrations of place and community were not, however, always overtly antagonistic toward the state or dismissive of the development projects that were under way. To the contrary, most residents welcomed the perceived "cleaning up" and "modernization" of the area. If anything, these changes were felt to be long overdue. What was threatening was not the fact of change, but that the character of these changes would forever disrupt or abolish the unique character of the neighborhood that made it possible for residents to not feel as though they were "strangers" in Brickfields. This felt sense of belonging contrasted with an experience of marginality within Malaysian society at large.

It is clear from Chandra's remarks that the fear many Brickfields residents felt regarding the figure of the stranger was primarily the fear of *being made a stranger oneself*. Although outsider others who enter the neighborhood and transform it through their presence (tourists, North Indian professionals) were also part of Chandra's narrative, he was clearly more concerned about how changing Brickfields "for the better" would also alter his own identity relative to the community. This was directly related to the gap between the Good as it is found in the law and in notions of local justice. The Good related to the state and development initiatives was dependent on the law and circulated in local discourses as something self-evident.[15] Local understandings of the Good and of justice, however, were articulated as concepts dependent upon higher principles of religious belief, established cultural practices, and community expectations regarding conduct between neighbors. Chandra addressed himself to both domains, but in trying to assimilate his mental image of Brickfields to a framework of causal facts and discursive knowledge, he clearly risked finding himself estranged from both and becoming a stranger. The figure of the stranger as a object of belief made it possible for Chandra to avoid the liquidation of "his" world and to continue to imagine himself as an ethical agent in Brickfields.

The overriding concern of "being made an stranger" was also evident in Mr. Rama's narration of his place in the neighborhood. Rather than articulating anger or fear, however, Mr. Rama contradicted the assumption that this imagination of the future is the only one possible for Brickfields residents who find themselves increasingly on the margin of inclusion or exclusion. The operator of a well-known vegetarian food stall, Mr. Rama had occupied his corner on the fringe of what remained of *Kampung Khatijah* for over thirty years, spending most of his adult life preparing late-night meals for neighbors and those who came from all over the city to experience his unique version of Indian cooking. In his telling he "has seen it all," surviving the gang-dominated period of the 1960s, earlier waves of spatial reorganization, and the changing fortunes of Brickfields residents through the 1970s and 1980s. Mr. Rama had to adapt to survive, and there had always been room for him to maneuver.

It was quite difficult to interview Mr. Rama, and my encounters with him consisted of me visiting his stall for a meal and attempting to talk with him while he served his customers.[16] Within minutes of sitting down

Mr. Rama would always ask, "Well, where are the questions today? Are you going to ask me questions?" The fragmentary conversations we did manage were telling, as this exchange illustrates:

> RB: What do you think of all of the changes that are going on in Brickfields? They are working just down from you here . . .
>
> Mr. R: I think it is great. Great! They are cleaning up the area, making it better, better for tourists, better for everyone. You know, this is where all the visitors to KL will come to the city. They come from the airport to the station. We are first, we have to look good.
>
> RB: So you feel that making Brickfields better for tourists is a good thing? Is it good for the people who live here also?
>
> Mr. R: Yes, yes, it is good. It will be cleaner, more shops. Maybe more expensive, I don't know. It will be better. I can be proud to say I'm from Brickfields. [Noting RB's raised eyebrow reaction] Yes, proud! Twenty years from now Brickfields will be an internationally recognized place. People will know about us and I can say I'm from here. What the government is doing is good, I say.
>
> RB: But what about you? Where do you see yourself during these twenty years? Are you going to be able to keep running your restaurant here?
>
> Mr. R: [Smiling, but looking away] Well, maybe I cannot stay. Maybe they won't allow me to stay, I don't know. I can't go anywhere else.
>
> RB: Why not?
>
> Mr. R: If I go anywhere else I'm a stranger . . . I do not want to be a stranger anywhere.
>
> RB: Is this fair? You just told me you have been here forty years . . .
>
> Mr. R: Maybe not . . . [Shrugs]

At this point Mr. Rama excused himself to return to cooking, and the conversation was temporarily halted. His mixed anticipation of the future was clear in this brief exchange, however, as he articulated the transformation of Brickfields as both the possible improvement of his "home" and his likely exclusion from this very experience of the place. The invocation of the "Tamil" or "Indian" character of Brickfields is only implied here, but given that Mr. Rama's stall *personified* the unique ethnic character of the neighborhood to many not only in Brickfields but throughout the city as a whole, his notion that he would be a "stranger" anywhere else indexes the character of his perceived belonging as related to this ethnic figure.

Simply remaining in Brickfields, however, did not abolish the specter of the stranger for Mr. Rama. As he indicated during our conversations, the danger was ultimately the fact that it was Mr. Rama himself and not the world around him that was becoming estranged. For Mr. Rama and many other Brickfields residents the expectation that one's long-term presence in a particular place would make a person familiar no longer applied. Location and personal histories were no longer stable, believable clues to identity. Certainly, it is questionable whether such factors were ever stable clues, but the fact that this indiscernability had become apparent generated a new fear of both "the Other" and "the I" equally at risk of becoming strangers in the unstable environment of Brickfields (Siegel 1997).

Local Institutions and the Stranger in Brickfields

The complex association between belonging to a place and ethnic identity was not always articulated as a problem of becoming a stranger due to removal. For some in Brickfields, the anticipated estrangement of the Brickfields Indian community was not about physical displacement but rather was tied to demographic shifts that would make it more difficult to see and know one's neighbors in the area itself. The presumed ability to "know" one's neighbors in this context was very often articulated through the cultural markers of ethnic identity summarized by Chandra earlier, especially those of language and religion.[17]

This set of markers linked otherwise seemingly separate communities within the figure of the Brickfields Indian. The articulation of belonging and the threat that the transformation of the neighborhood held for local Christian communities is one illustration of these links. Although a minority within Brickfields itself, predominantly Indian Christian churches were a visible, active sector of the community, with four large Christian churches (two Catholic, one Lutheran, one Methodist) located in the area. Linguistic and subethnic difference was a strong factor in determining the differences between these churches locally, although the open recognition of such differences did not in turn lead to any one of these distinct Christian communities being regarded as outsiders relative to Brickfields as a whole. Although on a national level Christianity is most strongly associated with Malaysian Chinese communities, in Brickfields being a Christian was as much a sign of one's belonging to the Indian community as being a Hindu. As with Hindu temples, Christian churches were materially linked to local practices through the use of Tamil or Malayalam in their services and outreach and the general retention of styles of dress, eating habits, and other markers of identity broadly associated with Malaysian Indians. In short, being a Christian was not automatically a mark associated with being a stranger.

As with other residents, this sense of relatedness was increasingly felt to be one of having to face outsiders within Brickfields. Reverend Abraham, the pastor of one local Christian church, articulated this understanding when describing the place of his church within the community in the context of the transformation of Brickfields. The sense of being "faced with strangers" was, in Reverend Abraham's case, strongly influenced by the fact that he personally grew up in Brickfields and, after many years of training and church work in India and throughout Malaysia, he returned to his "home" to pursue his ministerial activities.

> Rev. A: The church must be a resource for all neighborhood residents, not just church members. I strongly believe this, so all of these changes have made us change how we do our outreach. Recently we have started some new social programs aimed at addressing local problems.
>
> RB: What sort of programs?
>
> Rev. A: Well, a kindergarten, a tutoring program, a program for elderly Tamils around here, and an AIDS education program. They are all meant for the poor around here, so the actual work tends to overlap in all of them.
>
> RB: Are you doing specific Christian outreach in these programs?
>
> Rev. A.: Of course! Not to Muslims because that is illegal, but some of our motivation for establishing these programs is to promote Christianity and [the church's] message. I have to be clear, though. The main goal here is not just to convert people but community service.

Reverend Abraham's own motivation for trying to improve the entire community, rather than simply working for the expansion and benefit of the local Christian community, was strongly linked to the fact that he was born and raised in Brickfields. After leaving Brickfields to study at a seminary in India, he remained closely tied to the community. Although he spent five years undergoing training in India and had been posted in several Malaysian cities in the years since, Reverend Abraham's interest in the neighborhood remained strong. Reverend Abraham's thesis for the seminary considered the establishment and growth of his denomination in Malaysia and drew heavily upon the Brickfields church he would later lead.

As an institution firmly rooted in the local community and headed by an individual who had a personal stake in belonging to that community, the church undertook its work practically, through an openness predicated on familiarity and trust between neighbors. According to Reverend Abraham, the church's "open compound" served as a metaphor for its place in Brickfields. The basis for this openness, however, had become increasingly hard to sustain:

Well, all of these changes are making it harder for us. Recently a lot of con artists have come in wanting help and then turned around and robbed us. We just lost an expensive PA system . . . burgled! For the first time, we have hired security guards for the compound. We may also do some other things, I don't know. The main problem here is that we are ministering to, or otherwise trying to help, people who we don't know. This is very difficult for us. Most of our activities are small and for anyone, which means that we would know them. They would live or work nearby normally. We can't turn away, but now there are risks in being open.

The notion of "risk" here was intimately tied to the increased presence of strangers in Brickfields. While Reverend Abraham later admitted that the church has been the occasional victim of burglary or deceit by members of the community seeking assistance, he insisted that the character of such acts had changed in recent years. The risk was not just that of being robbed or tricked but of falling victim to such acts perpetrated by strangers. Like Mr. Rama, who exhibited a complex fear of being cast out into a world of strangers, Reverend Abraham articulated a fear of being made a stranger without having gone anywhere at all. In this context, the authoritative framework of Christian faith that explicitly guided Reverend Abraham's understanding of ethical life was not enough to prevent his belief in the world itself from being shaken; as with others in Brickfields, the figure of the stranger came to characterize the reverend's mental image of life in the neighborhood and his place in it.

Understanding social imaginaries of "home" and "belonging" haunted by the specter of threatening outsiders is a common epistemological problem in anthropological work. This theme has become particularly relevant in ethnographic work regarding cities, as urban spaces often constitute the defamiliarized nonlocal, simultaneously expanding and eroding the spatial contours of inside and outside (Holston and Appadurai 1996). Attempts by Brickfields residents to concretely map an increasingly shifting terrain of space and community through the citation of figures such as the stranger link their experience of change and the urban to a more general experience of transformation and modernity marked throughout the world (Comaroff and Comaroff 1997; Ferguson 1999; Ghannam 2002; Guano 2004). In this specific context, this imaginary provides a shared understanding of Brickfields that provides an orderly narrative of the present rooted in the *habitus* of the community and continues to make common local practice possible in the face of increasingly dislocating changes due to the state's efforts to reorganize the neighborhood (Bourdieu 1980; Gaonkar 2002; Lefebvre 1991, 2003).

The figure of the stranger emerged in the narratives of many Brickfields residents as a mode of establishing knowable boundaries that would, in turn, more solidly link subjective notions of place and self to the space of the neighborhood itself. Although this aspect of local social imaginaries was discursive and ideological, this did not make the stranger any less a material presence in the daily life of the neighborhood (Handler 1986; Hannerz 1992; Holston and Appadurai 1996). Significantly, imaginations of home and outsider served to index Brickfields as a knowable margin, despite its geographic centrality within the Kuala Lumpur metropolitan area, with this margin serving as both a point of orientation and a place of belonging for those who felt excluded or out of place within the mainstream "center" of Malaysian society (Das and Poole 2004). Chandra's preference for the "marginality" of Brickfields over the mainstream order of Petaling Jaya was a case in point. Furthermore, while this marginality emerged in ambiguous ways, such as Mr. Rama's overt enthusiasm regarding the long-overdue recognition of Brickfields despite the fact that he anticipated his own estrangement in the process, it was concretely imagined. In the context of the fluid physical and demographic situation in Brickfields, even a solid marginality was preferable to the exceptional.

The Counterfeiter: The Imagination of Place
and the Multiplicity of "the Good"

Although organized criminal gangs retained a central role in the everyday life of Brickfields, this mode of activity was directly undertaken by only a small number of residents. The most common practical experience of Brickfields as a "criminal" space took the form of a wide range of activities that are loosely understood as types of "petty corruption." Nearly every such form of activity had an essential purpose for those engaged in the practice. This purpose was primarily the falsification of the evidentiary narrative of a particular business transaction between individual parties or between individuals and agents of the state. Following James Siegel's work regarding similar practices in Indonesia, I will refer to this category of practice as a form of counterfeiting (Siegel 1998).

This mode of counterfeiting was that of producing various forms of documentary evidence that represented certain transactions as being in accord with the law, even though additional amounts of money or favors had been exchanged for advantageous treatment regarding eligibility, time of procedure, or actual exemption from other formal rule-based factors. Although I could not verify this empirically, it was clear from strong and consistent anecdotal evidence (including my own direct experience as a temporary Brickfields resident) that it was impossible for anyone living in Brickfields to avoid engaging in these practices at certain times. Obtaining a driver's license, a commercial business license, a passport, title to one's home or car; making arrangements for work or repair to one's home; securing residency permits; holding a social or political meeting; gaining admittance to a school or college; all these and a wide range of other activities where the desires or needs of individuals took the form of a contract or matter formally regulated by the law were directly cited by my interlocutors as transactions that required them to engage in a multileveled mode of negotiation and falsification in order to accomplish the task at hand or acquire the goods or permissions sought within the transaction.[18]

Most often such dealings were direct, spontaneous, and took the form of a quick cash payment to a secretary, bureaucrat, or guard in order to gain entry or favor in the course of dealing with an institution of some sort. These "tea-money" transactions were not the primary form in which counterfeiting was practiced in Brickfields, although they are related to the notion being articulated here. Rather, the practice of collectively negotiating alternative narratives regarding specific business and governmental transactions in order to anchor them more firmly in the required time of the law was the form of counterfeiting activity that served to structure relationships of order and belonging in the increasingly fluid physical and social space of Brickfields. Such practices were not merely resistances to the law, but took the form of reactions against the ambiguous, exceptional aspects of the execution of the law and the corresponding lack of belief in a world dominated by the "rule of law" that faced area residents on a daily basis. In this sense, these practices served to *reterritorialize* Brickfields and its residents within the law (Gupta 1997). This reterritorialization was no simple matter, however, as ethical judgment in everyday life was displaced from moral imperatives conflating the Good with the law. Relative to this general situation, counterfeiting practices in Brickfields constituted an odd form of hope that the law was as solid and unexceptional as it represented itself to be *without* wholly investing the possibility of ethical life in legal systems of judgment. "Fake" evidentiary narratives were produced locally as a meaningful way of engaging the law and ordering events and transactions more to the advantage of the individuals involved, clearly marking local social relationships in the process. The fact that such narratives recognized the empirical reality of the institutions of the law without granting such institutions an ethical centrality meant that the state and the specific organs of the law loomed over local counterfeiting of this type, requiring an investment in making "better," believable counterfeits that would pass simultaneously as real in legal domains and ethical in local spheres.[19]

Most academic literature devoted to transactions of this type focuses entirely on the impact that these practices have on development in macroeconomic terms. In the wake of the Asian economic crisis of 1998 a number of scholars have revisited the concept of "rent seeking,"[20] with a particular emphasis on the impact that patron-client exchanges and corruption have on economic efficiency and growth (Gomez and Jomo 1999; Khan and Jomo 2000). While this literature challenges the assumptions of earlier theorists who presumed that developmental success is predicated on the absence of rent-seeking activities (Myrdal 1968), most of these works limit the scope of their inquiry to the market and the economy, without attending to the complex relationship such activities have to the law itself.

In particular, the assumption that "corrupt" or "patron-client" exchanges must be understood as supplemental to the legal contracts between economic actors effaces the socially constitutive role of counterfeiting practices at the local level.[21]

Counterfeiting at the local level is generally understood as an act of bad faith or, at best, as an error in moral judgment and an example of a specific *misrecognition* of the Good. The evidence presented in the following section troubles this dogmatic notion of the law's relation to local ethics. As Deleuze reminds us, everyday ethics often evades such systems of judgment, even as it must empirically engage the institutions of the law and the state (Deleuze 1991b, 1997). Although economic gain was always a central factor in these relationships, they were simultaneously complex forms of contract that creatively engaged both concrete legal rules and local principles of relatedness and justice. The ability to form these relationships and achieve forms of association through counterfeiting practices was therefore often understood as a sign of positive engagement, a "success story." Such efforts seldom opened its practitioner to charges of "actually" being fake, a liar, or a hypocrite. Rather, the ability to create some order, connection, and authority for oneself through modes of falsification was a mark of skill. In the secondhand narratives of counterfeiting of this sort told to me, the stories were offered as a means of recognition and, at times, admiration. Interestingly, the notion that such actions were undertaken in bad faith was almost exclusively reserved for specific representatives of the law (such as police or government ministers) who engaged in them. In local terms, counterfeiting served not as an oppositional judgment of the law as a whole or as conscious resistance to the law but rather as an empirical demonstration of the law's separateness from ethical life and the Good.

Unlike the generally negative figure of the stranger, the figure of the counterfeiter was associated with admiration and a relative lack of rancor,[22] centered on a recognition that this figure often implied a mastery of the self in a fluid social context and a mastery of the tools necessary to produce "valid" copies. In these cases the "tools" were the means of fabricating invoices, receipts, contracts, and other documents that would circulate as valid forms of evidence under the law while the counterfeiter was also able to address local notions of the Good and the hope that ethical life was, in spite of everything, possible.[23]

Counterfeiting, Contracts, and Local Sociality

Gaining firsthand ethnographic experience of the processes of counterfeiting was difficult.[24] One direct interaction with a local printing business in Brickfields, however, illustrated these points more concretely. Mrs. Ramachandran[25] owned a printing business with her husband in Brickfields, not far from the new site provided for two small Hindu temples that were relocated in March 2002 (see Chapter 5).[26] Although they were able to fulfill a wide range of print orders, the shop's specialty was wedding invitations aimed at a predominantly Indian clientele.

Mrs. Ramachandran told me that most of her orders were for Indian weddings and they preferred to focus their efforts on printing for the Tamil community:

We have everything needed to quickly print up brochures and pamphlets in Tamil. Yet we don't get much of this business anymore. So we try to generate business in different ways. You know, the temples that just moved in across the street, when they need something done we'll do it for free and just make sure that we have our logo and telephone number on the paper somewhere. It helps, brings in a little more work, but not very much. I just don't see much printing in Tamil going on anymore.

Mrs. Ramachandran related this to me in a weary, sad tone of voice. It appeared that she had more at stake in the decline of printing in Tamil than simply a loss of revenue. The receding importance of the "personal touch" and the diminishing returns in running a business that serves the Tamil-speaking community seemed to gnaw at Mrs. Ramachandran as she answered my questions. She emphatically told me that "personal contacts are *everything* in this business," but she gave the impression that a commitment to the local community was no longer sufficient to ensure success.

It was clear that some of Mrs. Ramachandran's personal contacts were still proving to be somewhat lucrative, albeit they were not with individual customers. The nature of these business dealings complicated Mrs. Ramachandran's articulated detachment and her seemingly straightforward "business is business" demeanor. When I arrived at the shop one evening at 7:00 p.m. to conduct our interview I found that Mrs. Ramachandran was still dealing with some customers. Having already postponed the interview several times, Mrs. Ramachandran apologized and asked if I would like to wait. Offered a chair a few feet away from Mrs. Ramachandran's desk, I took my seat and waited. For the next hour I was present during the negotiation of an order to produce preprinted test booklets for a local college. In the course of the negotiation the techniques of closing a deal and maintaining a personal tie with a customer were apparent.

The main "protagonists" in this transaction were Mrs. Ramachandran and her husband, with her secretary and one of the shop assistants occasionally called in for advice or to perform a task. The representatives for the school were a Malay couple and a young man who could have been the older man's brother or assistant. The locus of the action was around the small desk at the front of the shop. The couple representing the college and Mrs. Ramachandran's husband were walking around, appearing and disappearing throughout the transaction. The female representative from the college spent most of her time standing behind the secretary's desk in front of me distractedly flipping through a women's magazine, occasionally looking over the shoulder of Mrs. Ramachandran's secretary as she typed up the latest invoice for the order. As the terms of the deal changed several times throughout the negotiations, numerous invoices were produced, occasionally causing confusion as to which one was the "current" record. The younger man from the college sat smiling and not saying anything save for a few offhand remarks and jokes that worked to lighten the mood when things became a little tense. The male negotiator from the college would alternately sit in the chair in front of Mrs. Ramachandran's desk and fidget, stand up and pace around, or walk out of the shop entirely, only to return a few seconds later. While I detected no overt disagreements between the two parties during the entire episode, the tone of the negotiations was occasionally aggressive.

The negotiations transpired in Malay, although when Mrs. Ramachandran wanted to discuss a point with her husband they spoke in Tamil. They did not remove themselves while doing this, but instead turned to each other and spoke in front of the customers. At first the discussion between the two parties concerned the type of paper to be used, with the college negotiator insisting that Ramachandran Printers use the paper that he had brought with him. During this time Mrs. Ramachandran produced first one check and, a few minutes later, another check, apparently buying the paper from the customers. Photocopies of these checks were also made and handed to the male negotiator, who then would hand them to his female counterpart. After she scrutinized them for several seconds, he would take the checks back, shuffling them into the other papers he was holding. Occasionally he would rifle through his file for the checks and again display them to his female partner. She in turn would walk over to the desk where the negotiations were taking place, casually glance again at the checks, and then quickly return to the secretary's desk and her magazine. This back-and-forth continued during the entire negotiation.

Once the issue of paper had been settled, the discussion turned to the print job itself. A long, somewhat heated discussion ensued regarding the terms of the contract, with the price per unit articulated as a clear point of contention. After a half hour of proposals and counterproposals, the price per unit was settled (12 sen per piece) and Mrs. Ramachandran's secretary started producing invoices, letters, and other documents reflecting what had just been agreed upon. During this time, Mrs. Ramachandran produced several RM 50 notes from her cashbox beneath the desk and handed them to the male negotiator from the college. Later, as the papers were still being drawn up, Mrs. Ramachandran produced several more notes and again handed them across the desk to the college representative. In both cases the man pocketed this money and then jumped up to pace, briefly exiting and then returning to the shop. It appeared that she handed him about RM 500 in total, although this is an estimate based on my attempts at discreet observation during the transaction. Once the papers and invoices were ready, everyone signed where required and official stamps were affixed to the relevant documents. The female college representative abruptly closed her magazine and took a more active interest in this part of the process, overseeing every action carefully. After photocopies were made, a great deal of confusion arose regarding which contract was the correct one. It did not help that several older invoices and drafts had gotten mixed in with the current documents.[27] Finally, after all was sorted out, the three members of the university delegation got up and exited the shop for good. No goodbyes or pleasantries were exchanged, although nobody seemed particularly angry either. The younger man from the college made a few more smiling jokes on the way out, with Mrs. Ramachandran playfully engaging him in Malay. Then, it became quiet and Mrs. Ramachandran and I began the formal interview.

A summary of what transpired is this: This transaction was a complex arrangement whereby the customers provided (and were paid for) the paper for the printing job. However, based on the amount of unrecorded cash that was being paid out above the purchase of the paper by Mrs. Ramachandran, it is clear that there were additional kickbacks also paid out to the customers. Then, as the records must all match, it took a great deal of time to record what was "officially" negotiated while simultaneously keeping track of what "really" transpired. I noticed that Mrs. Ramachandran did not make any ledger or "cash out" notes when she distributed the cash payments. Given that the contract was drawn up on behalf of the college, great pains were taken to ensure that the documents provided a consistent narrative of the transaction. This appeared to be the female representative's responsibility during the proceedings. The negotiation itself had a performative character. At various times both parties would adjourn to discuss matters, but they would not actually remove themselves from the room. Rather, they would suddenly just start discussing things among themselves as if the others were not actually there. For Mrs. Ramachandran and her husband this was understandable because they spoke in Tamil, but the Malay customers would also confer in the same manner. When the male leader of the college delegation would suddenly exit the shop, he would go alone and no side talk would occur in his absence.

Everyone on both sides spoke in general terms to each other, but neither side offered direct answers to queries. Instead, proposals or questions were met with further questions and counterproposals. Eventually the matter was settled, but much in the conversation seemed "understood" and therefore went without being verbalized in the exchange. Essentially, it seemed to be a deal where the negotiators skimmed approximately 20 percent off the top of the settled amount (hence the exchange of cash) and closed the deal. Furthermore, the negotiators sold the paper, most likely originating from the college directly, to Ramachandran Printers at a higher price than its original cost. The university representative took the difference in cash. As Ramachandran Printers was clearly going to make several thousand ringgit in the deal, Mrs. Ramachandran did not balk at paying out the necessary cash or keeping portions of the transaction out of the written record.

Although it may appear that only Mrs. Ramachandran and the senior member of the college delegation were the primary agents in forging the contract, in fact every person in the room had a well-defined role to play in the transaction. Mr. Ramachandran, the secretary, and the female college representative all worked to keep track of what was taking place on multiple registers throughout the entire negotiation. As the formal legal rules regarding contracts and the local principles of doing business often diverged, it was essential for witnesses to oversee the final outcomes. The inadvertent mixing of these registers could mean the production of a flawed formal narrative (making its counterfeit status apparent) or the exchange of too much or too little cash on the informal "across the desk" register. The young "joker" from the university also had a critical role to play, as the very real danger of having to account for notions of "the Good" that often opposed each other weighed heavily on the interaction. During moments that were particularly tense, the young man's injection of a joke or nonsense comment highlighted the darkly ironic situation of having to simultaneously "follow" the law and break it in order to reasonably satisfy multiple understandings of the Good that framed the proceedings. The laughter he generated on all sides allowed a potentially dangerous and somewhat absurd process to continue.[28]

It was astonishing to me that Mrs. Ramachandran would allow me to witness this transaction. She had rescheduled our interview several times before and she could have certainly asked me to come back. Having some idea of what had just taken place, starting the interview as if nothing had happened was awkward. "That seems like a pretty important job," I began, hoping to find a way to follow it up. Mrs. Ramachandran rubbed her temples and waved me off. "Its nothing . . . now, what did you want to ask me?"[29] Further inquiries regarding this specific transaction were summarily rebuffed. Clearly Mrs. Ramachandran did not wish to talk about the transaction that I had just witnessed, despite the fact that she certainly knew that I would understand most of it.

In very general terms,[30] I confirmed the mechanics of the deal with Tan Piow, the owner of a small local bookshop who had himself edited and published literary journals (although he had never worked directly with Mrs. Ramachandran). I explained what I thought the details of the transaction were and he nodded emphatically:

> T: Ya, ya . . . that's exactly how they do it! I know, because I've had to do
> it myself. It's amazing what these fuckers will do sometimes! At least these

were books for [the college], so they'll actually get printed. Sometimes these deals are struck and the books or catalogues or whatever are never even printed! Or, maybe they'll order a print run of 1000 and only really print 100. When you ask for the book, they say "don' have—*habis*" [finished].

RB: What about the paper? If they order up a thousand, then they bought the paper too, right?

T: That's probably where this guy got the paper he brought. Might have been for some other project where it was left over. So he takes it, already paid for, and sells it to the printer again. No, wait . . . they made out an invoice for the paper, right?

RB: Right, I think so. I didn't look over their shoulder or anything, but that's what they were talking about.

T: Maybe not, then . . . but sometimes it works out that way too.

RB: Is this the normal way to do this?

T: Ya, I think so. Once they have established something, then they can cook up all kinds of things together.

"Once they have established something." In other words, once they know each other. While deals of this kind are quite common in Malaysia, it is still certainly regarded as corruption and can backfire. The deal that I witnessed strongly implied a longstanding relationship between the two parties, although Mrs. Ramachandran refused to confirm or deny this. The entire transaction seemed choreographed, with the pacing and occasional walkouts of the main negotiator contrasting with the calm, detached air of Mrs. Ramachandran and her husband. Everyone seemed to know what to expect.

This calm security regarding the face-to-face deal contrasted sharply with Mrs. Ramachandran's assessment of the future of her business in Brickfields. Although the transformation of the neighborhood had ramifications for Ramachandran Printers, Mrs. Ramachandran felt that the primary change regarded the built environment itself rather than her customer base. She did not know if the building they occupied would remain intact much longer and, if not, what would replace it:

RB: Do you know if there are plans to tear down this row and build something else?

Mrs. R: [Laughing] No! We never know what is going to happen.

RB: Have there ever been any public discussions or newspaper articles or anything that gives you some information about this?

Mrs. R: Are you kidding? We are always the last to know anything! Look at those temples over there [pointing across the street]. We came in to work one day and they were building the temples. I figured that something was going on when I saw them clearing away the rubbish, but we were never informed.

RB: Does that bother you?

Mrs. R: No, not really. When you do business in Malaysia you just have to be ready to change. Something will always come up, so just be ready to react.

RB: Do you think the government or the developers should be more involved in letting people know . . .

Mrs. R: No, its just another thing to deal with, you know? You have to pay tax, you have to get a license . . . that's it! I don't want to deal with them any more than I have to.

RB: If they want to tear down this building, what will you do?

Mrs. R: [Flatly] Then we'll move.

According to Mrs. Ramachandran, the state was merely one more variable in the insecure world of business in Malaysia. As with many other business owners and residents in Brickfields, she regarded her future in the area with wary anticipation. The possibility of the sudden liquidation of her place in Brickfields was evident in her understanding of the future. Her downplaying of the importance of the law and the state in structuring a narrative of futurity through the material social relationships of doing business was somewhat misleading. As her transaction with the local college illustrates, the solidity of the law was important to both Mrs. Ramachandran's sense of stability in Brickfields and the material practices by which she secured this stability, if for no other reason than to succeed in skirting the known procedures and limits of the law through producing counterfeit narratives of legality. In this sense, these documents both required and exceeded their literal relationship to the law and to the possible "meaning" offered by the documents themselves (Derrida 1988).

Working against the promised regularity of the law, Mrs. Ramachandran was able to simultaneously form and solidify material social relationships and develop her printing business by strategically tacking back and forth between registers of legal reproduction (her literal business) and techniques of producing believable counterfeits. The fact that Mrs. Ramachandran was professionally a printer only serves to clearly demonstrate the doubleness of forms of counterfeiting that most Brickfields residents engage in at certain times. In this scenario, it was not the possibility of her documentary replicas being recognized as false that was the most dangerous threat to her place in Brickfields; such recognition would point to a strategic error rather than a moral one. The danger in such situations was the prospect that the law would *intrude* in ethical life in such a way that the very possibilities of sociality that arise out of such modes of fabricating evidence would be liquidated. The error of the counterfeiter is that one's copies may not be believable and may fail; the error of the law is that in its sui generis assumption that ethical life follows legal aptitude, it produces a world that everyday subjects cannot believe in.

The Gangster: The Materiality of a Dangerous Romantic Figure in Brickfields

The figures of the stranger and the counterfeiter represented attempts on the part of Brickfields residents to make sense of themselves and the neighborhood space that they inhabited. Although these imagined figures represented engagements with the city, the public at large, and the state, they were not "types" imposed from the outside or characters that dominated wider perceptions of Brickfields residents to those outside of the area. Standing between the experience of everyday life by Brickfields residents and the ideal legal subjectivities promoted by the Malaysian state, these figures were literally, in Rorty's terms, *prototypes*. This is not the case with the gangster, the third figure that I will discuss. The Brickfields gangster was a well-articulated figure in popular accounts, often serving as a shorthand "character type" in accounts of the neighborhood generated by journalists, state officials, and city residents who lived outside the neighborhood. The image of the gangster was a potent, literal *stereotype*, often locating Brickfields and its Tamil and Chinese residents at the center of a discourse of backwardness and danger that demanded remedy. The fact that the vast majority of Brickfields residents were not in any way connected to the criminal gangs that operated there did not diminish the importance of the figure for the community. Unlike locally generated strangers and counterfeiters, however, engagements with the figure of the gangster were characterized by attempts to imagine Brickfields as a place through an anticipation of how Malaysians generally characterized the area and its residents. The power of the gangster for outsiders is clear, in that the common circulation of this figure generated a folklore regarding local criminality that in turn shaped policy, the manner in which the law was executed, and the overall "place" of Brickfields in the city. For Brickfields residents, the power of the gangster was just as strong, however; imagining the neighborhood as "home" required residents to think about how others thought about them, which in turn shaped the possibilities available for Brickfields residents to imagine themselves. Unlike the stranger and the counterfeiter, Brickfields residents took this entirely unbelievable stereotyped figure and reworked it in a manner that reflected the empirical realities of the neighborhood itself in an attempt to locate a believable local world.

"They are ruthless and menacing," began an article (*Malay Mail*, July 28, 2002) regarding the problem of Indian gangsterism and attempts to apprehend "hardcore" Indian criminals. Under the headline "Hardcore gangsters to be banished," the *Malay Mail* reporter provided a single-sentence outline of the "common sense reality" of Indian criminality in Kuala Lumpur. This notion was so firmly rooted in widespread beliefs regarding the nature of organized crime in the city that the police formulated specific operational plans to deal with it. At the time this particular article was written the program was "Ops Copperhead," initiated "to tackle the problem of Indian gangsterism in Selangor and Kuala Lumpur." Ops Copperhead netted forty "hardcore" gangsters, all Indians. Specific offenses by those arrested were not detailed in the article, nor was the place to where twelve of the worst were to be banished. Ops Copperhead was rooted more in common sense understandings of crime rather than in addressing specific instances of criminal behavior; a clue to this was given by the reporter when he clarified that the forty men were arrested due to the threat of *future* criminal activity. "Using preventative legislation which allows for banishment and detention without trial, authorities believe these undesirable elements should be isolated, as they have proven to be a threat to society," he explained. Evidence of this threat in the form of specific crimes was not, however, offered by the reporter. Rather, it was simply taken for granted that the accused were violent criminals and that they must be removed.

Ops Copperhead is not cited here to argue for the guilt or innocence of the specific men detained due to its execution. Rather, this operation and the publicity regarding the arrests clearly illustrated strong associative links commonly made between organized crime, the nature of the criminal, and the space that produces such figures. The areas of the city felt to be "appropriate" as targets for the operation were all regarded as predominantly Indian neighborhoods. Ops Copperhead, with its legitimacy rooted in the provisions of the Internal Security Act rather than in the enforcement of the criminal codes, was specifically designed to prevent crime through apprehending dangerous individuals who inhabit dangerous spaces, and in this way was clearly driven by the concerns of the state.

The associative link between Indian bodies, Indian spaces, and criminal activity was not one that was regularly applied to Malay or Chinese communities, even though the criminal underworld of Kuala Lumpur is wildly diverse. The spectacularly violent robberies of the predominantly Malay "Gang of Thirteen Thieves," led by the infamous Mat Komando (Ahmad Mohd Arshad), did not lead to preventative arrests or public calls to eradicate "Malay gangsterism." Although Mat Komando and his colleagues were feared and aggressively hunted by the police at the same time that they were executing Ops Copperhead, the exceptional specificity of the Gang of Thirteen's actions was emphasized in official and popular accounts.

The figure of the Indian gangster was apparent in popular accounts of the activities of the Oxy Gang as well. "OXY GANG GOES 'JOINT VENTURE,'" screamed the headline on page 3 of the *Malay Mail* for August 5, 2002. Compared to the headline-grabbing shootouts instigated by Mat Komando at roughly the same time, the relatively sedate specialty of the Oxy Gang (break-ins using oxyacetylene torches) hardly seemed worthy of such lurid attention. Although ostensibly the arrest of the gang was the event being reported, the "terrifying" significance of their operation was the fact that the predominantly Chinese gang had, in the six months prior to its arrest, formed partnerships with established Indian gangs in order to carry out its criminal work. Police discovery of these links was deemed "surprising" by the *Malay Mail*[31] and established the robberies of the Oxy Gang as something more sinister than previously believed. Without the "Indian connection" the arrest of this relatively small, nonviolent gang of robbers would not have been particularly newsworthy. However,

its partnerships with Indian gangsters made the Oxy Gang more dangerous and significant, in that Chinese gangsters were represented as having
tapped into a powerful criminal world that was exceeding its own limits.
Chinese "triads," while vivid figures in historical accounts of Kuala
Lumpur (Comber 1959; Gullick 2000; Middlebrook and Gullick 1989), were
generally believed to be a thing of the past. The tone of popular accounts
suggests that the contemporary partnerships were more dangerous than
the robberies themselves.

The trope of Indian gangsterism was so strong in popular accounts
of crime that nearly any illegal or violent act was attributed to its perni-
cious influence. Popular columnist Akbar Ali, writing in the *Sun* on November 11, 2001, in support of preventative operations such as Ops
Copperhead (albeit before the execution of that specific initiative), illustrated the possible discursive connections between being Indian and being
"criminal" when he cited the unrelated murders of three Malaysian
Indians—a garbage collector on Jalan Ipoh, a young girl living on Old
Klang Road (both locations within greater Kuala Lumpur), and a child
drowned in the state of Johor—as evidence of a predisposition toward
violence and the mark of probable illegal behavior by Malaysian Indians.
Ostensibly chastising the police regarding their "after the fact" ineffective-
ness (i.e., the police generally wait until after a killing before arresting
someone for murder), Ali stated that these factually unrelated cases "bring
to light the different cultural and racial characteristics of violence which
must be addressed accordingly by the police so that they can be more
effective in saving lives or preventing violence." Later on, he emphasized
this point, writing that "each race has to be handled in a way appropriate
to them. The police should therefore be more knowledgeable about the
peculiarities of violence among Indians." Ali does not, however, cite any
peculiarities common to all Malays or Chinese that police should be aware
of. The logic Ali articulated in his column was not merely evidence of an
individual predilection toward racial discrimination or a private quirk on
his part. Rather, he restated an authoritative "common sense" understanding of the link between criminality and being Indian, suggesting that any
violent or illegal act was evidence of gangster ties. Under this logic, vandalism in a hostel by students at the predominantly Indian polytechnic
Tafe College[32] was immediately "linked" to the influence of gangsters (see
"Gangster link in Tafe College rampage?" *Malay Mail,* July 12, 2002).

The fact that any violent or criminal act involving Malaysian Indians was so easily coded as evidence of broader community dysfunction is significant when understood alongside the fact that specific urban spaces were similarly associated with this particular ethnic group. Brickfields was almost universally regarded outside of the neighborhood as a criminal, dangerous space through this chain of associations. The fact that very few residents and business owners in Brickfields held any direct connection with the criminal gangs that were based there did not mitigate the material impact any association with criminality had on the neighborhood. Rather, the increasingly regular mode of organization that *actually* characterized the operations of the gangs came to represent, in contrast to the popular perception, a mode of alternative order that marked the everyday life of Brickfields. Although this order was less directly concerned with control of neighborhood space than in years past, the presence of the gangs remained a factor in how residents dealt with the fluidity of the situation in the area. The continued presence of the gangs shaped individual relations with the state, the law, and the city, with the gangs themselves at times delivering the local modes of order one would generally associate with more "legitimate" forms of sovereign power.

Local Order and Social Life: Brickfields Gangs and the Community

In contrast to the wider "shock" regarding the links between previously small, discrete criminal groups, the transformation of Brickfields gangs from primarily local collections of young men interested in controlling the space of neighborhood *kampungs*[33] to networked organizations involved in a variety of criminal pursuits was common knowledge to local residents. In relation to the recent "gangsterism" issue that had been making headlines, Raymond, a local activist who was personally familiar with the structure and operations of organized criminal groups in Brickfields, felt that the character of gangs had changed quite a bit in recent times. "It never used to be about drugs and guns. It was always much more local and small-time. Today, though, organized gangs offer a kind of 'career option' for many youths. They don't really have a lot of choices, and the gangs are good money for someone with little education and no other sources of income." Although excessive consumption of alcohol had long been a problem in Brickfields, Raymond noted that illegal drugs had become a serious issue in recent times. "In those days you wouldn't see gang members on drugs. There was some idea that it would be shameful to do that, and the gang leaders would be the first to whack you for it. Now, all the gangs are interested in is drugs. Raymond detailed specific sites in Brickfields where it was possible to buy drugs from street dealers.[34] He also suspected that the police had some role in regulating these spaces, although he offered no specific proof regarding the details of any specific arrangement.

While it was clear that the formerly local gangs of Brickfields have formed closer links to regional criminal organizations and become potentially more violent and dangerous as a result, links with hierarchical organizations whose interests extended beyond the confines of the neighborhood have transformed, rather than obliterated, the modes of spatial order that the gangs have traditionally been concerned with. In Brickfields itself, the primary activity of controlling space through various types of "protection rackets" had given way to a need for merely keeping the space relatively orderly as a cover for larger operations and in order to escape the attention of the police. This mode of order retained certain links to the gangs of years past, in that individuals who were active in the gangs of the 1950s and 1960s remained in the neighborhood and served as both a loose surveillance network and a link between average citizens and the current gangs. The experience of Tan Piow, a local businessperson who was being victimized for protection money by an individual known to be involved with these organizations, illustrated how this network often worked in Brickfields. Tan Piow, through his long association with the neighborhood both as a resident and as the owner of a business, understood the basic outlines of the network. Thus, rather than going to the police to put an end to the extortion, he contacted the current gangs through a "retired" member of a now-defunct gang who retained some contact with the groups that had replaced his own.

In relating his story to me, Tan Piow remarked that an older Chinese man who at the time of the interview sold fruits on the corner near Tan Piow's shop was once one of the leaders of the local gang network.[35] This was during the 1970s and 1980s when the gangs were being transformed from primarily local gangs concerned with controlling the neighborhood space to the larger networked gangs that Raymond described earlier. The old gangs were mostly run by Indians (specifically Tamils) but now only the street workers and enforcers were Indians; leadership was primarily Chinese. This man was the boss around Brickfields for many years, but several years ago he publicly renounced his gang activities and became involved in the activities of a local Buddhist temple. This declaration was sufficient to keep active gang members at a distance and prevented rivals from "legitimately" settling old scores with the man. Tan Piow believed that he renounced gang life because he was getting into much more serious criminal activity and that he would probably have ended up dead or in prison for life had he continued.

Despite the old man's renunciation, he still maintained informal ties with currently active gang members and would sometimes act as an intermediary for local residents or business owners to settle disputes or other problems that would concern the gang leadership. Tan Piow called upon him for help because a couple of years previously a young Chinese man began extorting RM 50 monthly payments from him.

The gangs are not interested in petty extortion in Brickfields any more, so I wanted to see if this joker was actually working for the gang. I went to the old man and found out that this idiot had been kicked out because he was using all the drugs, not selling them. They didn't want any money from me! He just needed quick cash for his habit, you know. So he went around threatening people and since they used to do this, who would argue? When they found out, the gang went around to find him and when they found him, they beat the shit out of him. He was using their name to get drugs and that almost got him killed! Now I have a guarantee from them that I will never have to pay protection. None of this is direct . . . the old man told me that too.

Tan Piow noted that extortion of small businesses and stalls was still common in other parts of the city, with Chinatown being his prime example.

Twenty years ago I know that the gang that controls Petaling Street demanded daily payments of fifty ringgit from all of the stalls and businesses around there. Can you imagine? Do you know how many individual payments that is? I don't know the rate nowadays, but I know that they still do it. Probably around 100 ringgit every night.

The instability of the Brickfields community and the fact that the area was squarely under the gaze of the state due to the development plans for the neighborhood made such carefully maintained protection schemes impractical. Rather, with the general shift toward wider-reaching coordinated activities with other illegal organizations, the local focus on order no longer had an extractive aim, but rather one of maintaining some cover for the operations of the gangs themselves.

As a local business owner with ties to Brickfields spanning over fifty years, Tan Piow knew the local structure of criminal gangs very well;[36] when it was more direct or efficacious to do so, he would turn to them to mediate issues with neighbors or solve local problems of disorder rather than to the police. In expanding on how he handled the incident with the freelancing drug addict, Tan Piow carefully detailed the relationships between (1) the houses of prostitution that operated in Brickfields, (2) the organizations primarily operating in tandem with larger "national" organizations, (3) ostensibly legal establishments that operated as "fronts" for each of these groups, and (4) everyday residents who had no formal ties to any of these other groups. Most of these interconnected ties were maintained through careful surveillance of the space, indirect forms of mediation, and when such interventions failed, the very real threat of violence. Woven into Tan Piow's narrative were other examples of how everyday residents who were not part of this network (the vast majority) had to negotiate with or call upon the criminal organizations at certain times to settle disputes or solve problems. These contacts were never undertaken out of a feeling that the gangs were benevolent or fair, but rather out of necessity and oftentimes fear.[37] While the ideal situation was to avoid direct contact with both the gangs and the police, there were times when this would be impossible, and residents would have to plan carefully and choose wisely to best address the issue at hand.

Knowledge of this network often represented both a mode of belonging that was denied to relative newcomers and an avenue to actually address certain specific problems (such as the drug addict demanding money) in a manner that was both less expensive and more efficacious than going to the police. Taking such problems to the police was commonly regarded as an unwanted engagement, entailing similar "side" negotiations that could ultimately involve more money changing hands without any real sense that the issue would be rectified. While everyday residents and local business owners always approached even the most indirect contacts with local gangs cautiously, and often consciously understood the state of affairs through the racialized discourse of the "Indian gangster" as articulated by the state and the local media, this gangster was often a representative of an alternative source of order rather than simply a material manifestation of the disorder of Brickfields. More often than not, by the reckoning of local residents the gangster "kept" the promise of the law's unexceptional regularity "better" than the police or the state itself and inhabited a more solidly believable local world than the abstractly moral universe of the state, the law, or the police.

Conclusion

Brickfields residents drew on a variety of ways of thinking about their lives and about the neighborhood as a distinct place. The figures of the stranger, the counterfeiter, and the gangster were important conceptual personae in the context of an individual's daily involvements with others. These figures should not be regarded as total or all-encompassing makers of meaning in Brickfields, however, since their invocation and circulation always occurred in a untidy world of multiple contexts and registers of being and acting. In the flow of everyday life, subjects constantly moved between these figures, registers, and relationships, displaying multiple and sometimes seemingly contradictory orientations to the law and to others in the neighborhood. The limit of the analytic framework regarding important figures of identity is that it temporarily extracts these figures from the flows in which they materially circulated. For the purpose of forming an understanding of these figures and how they materially circulated and shaped relations between Brickfields residents and between residents and the state, this conceptual mode of abstraction was unavoidable and necessary in order to demonstrate the relationship between belief, the necessary images of the world, and the everyday life that emerges out of such relationships.

Tanya Luhrmann has written that "there is no unitary, simple, coherent, entity which is selfhood; there are persons purposefully acting according to various notions of their selves" (Luhrmann 1996, 209). Her statement succinctly underscores the anthropologists' attempts to engage theories of the self and agency concepts through the lens of ethnography.[38] The contribution that this ethnographically derived understanding of Brickfields offers turns on two issues: (1) the often unstated or subliminal role of abstract figures of subjectivity in forming an understanding of one's self and place in relation to others, and (2) a concern with how the imagination of the law itself comes to shape both the figures that circulate in discourses of self and place and the material relations that emerge out of such engagements. When faced with difference in their daily lives, Brickfields residents thought about themselves in relation to several abstract figures in order to index themselves and their place in the neighborhood. Contrary to accounts of Malaysian urban spaces that singularly privilege ethnic figures (Jesudason 1989; Provencher 1971) or class figures (Goh 1979; McGee 1967; Ong 1987), I argue that the fluidity of everyday life in the neighborhood precluded consistent, singular affinity with any one category of identity.[39] As Rorty points out, different figures of personhood often work beneath the surface and reflect the complex social terrain that individuals must negotiate (Rorty 1976). While these engagements did constitute a form of agency for Brickfields residents, this agency was an ambiguous one; my interlocutors were often as concerned with imagining how outsiders imagined them as with engaging in more unambiguous strategies of self-definition and characterization.

The ability to imagine the possibility of a life within Brickfields was an essential task for residents faced with change that came upon them suddenly. My interlocutors often struggled with linking their perceptions of the neighborhood with coherent meaning and the possibility of action within this domain. The figures detailed in this chapter existed as mental images that provided this link and consequently allowed residents to believe in their worlds. This belief was often marked by fear and negative perceptions of others; however, despite the often pessimistic register within which figures such as the stranger, the counterfeiter, or the gangster were expressed within, they nonetheless stood as vehicles for Brickfields residents to arrange their spaces of possibility and possible action.

I have argued that this possibility is linked to Henri Lefebvre's notion of the "right to the city" (Lefebvre 1996, 2003). Not being dependent on concepts of human rights that are wholly invested in the formal discourses of the state or of religion for its force, Lefebvre's framework highlights the ethics of establishing spaces at the everyday level that allow for action and a concrete sense of being able to create an ethical life. Unlike most understandings of ethical living that conflate the law with the Good and agency with politics or resistance, Lefebvre's notion of the right to the city does not unselfconsciously link to the authoritative discourse of the state or the law; it allows us to understand the varied responses to the perception that state interventions in the everyday life of Brickfields was unethical without resorting to easy terms such as "apathy" or "failure" when this local judgment does not in turn result in radicalization or resistance to the state. Subject to forces and events that often shattered the link between present experience and the possibility of future action within the law, we must move cautiously in judging how Brickfields residents concretely responded to such phenomena.

The practice of creatively thinking Brickfields through figures that originated as abstract images in thought was a concrete, material response to the transformation of the neighborhood. Following Deleuze's understanding of the relationship between thought, image, and the real, I argue that these figures provided links between virtual notions of how everyday life "is" or "should be" and the experience of everyday life and served as vehicles that allowed residents to locate themselves in the interstices between ideal and real and *believe* in one's capacity for action and the active creation of *a life* (Deleuze 2001). That fact that these figures were objects of belief and not fact in the empirical sense cannot lead us to the conclusion that these understandings were entirely rooted in the imaginary or in "fictional" modes of apprehending the world. Rather, Brickfields as a concrete, believable place emerged only through such mental images.

The fear of either encountering or becoming a stranger in Brickfields altered local notions of belonging that were predicated on the legal and social site of the *bumiputera*, the Malay "son of the soil." While being Malaysian Chinese or Indian was more widely understood to be the status of a "outsider within," in Brickfields the meanings ascribed to the material practices of these communities (especially that of the Tamil community) was that of belonging, with the Malay majority itself held to be the threatening stranger. Chandra's articulation of belonging through the affect (sights, sounds, smells, etc.) associated with the cultural space of Brickfields ran counter to abstractly understood notions of "who" was familiar in Malaysia. His rejection of Petaling Jaya, precisely *because* it successfully materialized the mode of orderly urban living promoted by the state, spoke to the terms of attraction and familiarity that an explicit margin can offer. The fragility of Chandra's belonging is apparent, however, in that even a careful discussion of the empirical situation in the neighborhood could unexpectedly estrange him from it. The specter of disappearance haunted his regret in having consented to be interviewed by me, as it did Mr. Rama's imagination of his place in the future of Brickfields. Although Mr. Rama did not overtly reject the state's understanding of proper urban order (in fact, he voiced clear support for it), without the material relations of this community in place *as a margin* he could not concretely envision himself as anything but a stranger in this new order.

In the "get tough on crime" atmosphere in Kuala Lumpur during the years 2000–2002, the violent gangster and the corrupt counterfeiter were two of the most reviled social figures on the urban landscape. With them as symbols of disorder, it was not much of a leap to regard Brickfields, popularly regarded as one of the most corrupt and criminal areas in the entire country, as hopelessly disordered and in need of radical, severe action for the purpose of rectifying the situation. Columnist Akbar Ali's sentiments regarding "Indian criminality" were widely held and often linked directly to Brickfields. Practical understandings of the gangs as possible sources of order simultaneously confirmed this believed connection between crime and place and destabilized the idea that the law was actually any different. The widespread recognition of modes of counterfeiting such as the one I witnessed in Mrs. Ramachandran's print shop clearly illustrated that corruption of this kind was *not* automatically an indication of open resistance to the state. As Foucault has argued, the force of the law relies precisely on the instances of exception from it that emerge in everyday social practice (Foucault 1991, 2003). At times, the state and the counterfeiter become *rivals* for the control of this exceptional force (Siegel 1998).

This "rivalry" was not absolute in Malaysia. As I will illustrate in the next chapter, the Malaysian state also addressed itself to the fact that normative understandings of the Good, rooted in western legal traditions, suppress references to higher principles of morality that exist outside of the law. The Malaysian state had attempted to reintroduce principles of the Good above the law through its recent engagements with Islam, and had explicitly pursued strategies to formulate modes of governance that are both properly modern and properly Islamic. Siegel marks a related process in Indonesia, where the presence of ghosts and the materiality of supernatural worlds provides a framework that shapes and limits the meaning of the law for the state and its citizens (Siegel 1998; see also Coronil 1997; Taussig 1997). In Malaysia, the material power of Islam and the divine has also been invoked in recent times to frame the relations between the state, the law, and individual subjects and mark out a notion of the Good that is valid by virtue of more than simply its own form. These notions were not wholly invested in techno-rational forms of reason, but rather explicitly depended upon belief as an open aspect of proper and ethical Malaysian life. As the next chapter shall demonstrate, this overt introduction of belief (largely coded as Islamic belief) as an aspect of formal governmentality in Malaysia produced unexpected consequences that exceeded the control of the state and other formal institutions in Malaysian society.

Ambivalent Encounters in the City: Islam, Hinduism, and Urban Governmentality

Introduction

Two seemingly opposed processes frame most understandings of global politics and modern public life in the early years of the twenty-first century. The first is the emergence of notions of proper governance and public life defined by ideals of secularism, democracy, and capitalist free-market economies throughout the world. The second is the "resurgence" of ethnic and religious issues in public affairs. These simultaneous events, most often understood as binaries linked by the actual and virtual networks of "globalization," are commonly understood to be a "paradox" of modern life. Within this imagination of the condition of global politics, the problem of the "Islamic resurgence" and the issue of Islamic states is often cited as a particularly vexing and potentially dangerous phenomenon that threatens the human rights, freedom, and at times the literal safety of individuals living in these societies (Fukuyama 1992; Huntington 1996; Lewis 2003).

This framework has been questioned by a host of scholars in recent times. In this body of work binaries that unproblematically equate secular governance with the possibility of recognizing religious difference are called into question, and the widely held belief that states that explicitly recognize Islam as a core aspect of governance are, by definition, intolerant and oppressive is challenged. Although many of these writings complicate dualistic understandings of Islamic governance and societies (Deeb 2006; Devji 2005; Euben 1999; Hirshkind 2006; Varzi 2006; Verkaaik 2004), most continue to privilege the West as the primary point of reference when discussing diversity *within* contemporary Islamic societies; the particular understandings of modernity articulated from within these states is often unexplored (Anderson 1983; Hefner 2000; Peacock 1978). In this chapter I shift the basis of this engagement away from these binaries and ask the following questions: How does the governmentality of the Malaysian state shape the everyday practices of a predominantly Malaysian Tamil Hindu urban community? How does this non-Muslim community imagine its place and future within a polity that seeks to formally institute Islamic practice as a concrete source for techniques of governance and to articulate its own sovereignty in Islamic terms? What are the specific effects and outcomes of explicitly introducing *belief* into the realm of modern governance? I will address these questions and the translocal nature of urban governance in Malaysia through a detailed ethnographic account of the larger questions of belief, governance, and the operation of local forms of ethics in the creation of community in the religiously and ethnically mixed neighborhood of Brickfields.

This chapter considers interventions made by the Malaysian state and civic actors regarding several unregistered Hindu temples in Brickfields during the years 2000–2002. These specific events are contextualized by a discussion of how the widely debated issue of Islam's role in governance in Malaysia provided certain avenues of engagement and agency for these temples through their interactions with agents of the state and indirectly affiliated proxies such as educational and Hindu religious organizations. Rather than arguing that the Malaysian state's efforts to make Islam a central basis for governance constituted a mode of exclusion or indifference toward these temples, I will show that the state articulated a clear interest in the "proper" practice of Hinduism and the formation of a public life that, while not denying difference, was in accord with its wider notions of modernity. In seeking to allow for belief in public life rather than quarantining faith within private domains, these efforts by the Malaysian government produced unforeseen consequences both in terms of how non-Muslim faiths were present in the public sphere and in relation to how belief was lived at the everyday level. As I demonstrated in the previous chapter, belief in general terms was an essential aspect in the formation of a life within sensible realms of possibility and meaning (Deleuze 1994, 2001); this chapter extends this argument to show how belief operated as an important aspect of public life that, in its introduction as an allowable basis for ethical life and practice, often exceeded the formal boundaries of authoritative discourse regarding proper or "true" belief articulated by the state or religions institutions.

It is crucial to note that the Malaysian state's efforts to locate Islam as a primary moral basis for rule did not entail the rejection of techno-rational modes of governance, nor did it require the radical overturning of laws and institutions associated with secular governance. In fact, with its concern for properly identifying and regulating religious practice, efforts to morally ground the law and the practices of the state in Islam *required* an active mode of engagement with secularist understandings of proper governance.[1] Just as Brickfields residents struggled with competing notions of morality, justice, and the Good in locating themselves within the neighborhood, the state also sought to "become modern" while simultaneously recognizing the existence of a divine sovereignty outside itself. Thus, rather than rejecting the laws and institutions of the postcolonial nation in favor of the *Shari'a* (a path advocated by many *dakwah* reformers and the PAS), the Malaysian state pursued a program of Islamic reform that sought to embed an Islamic morality within domains commonly understood to belong entirely to the secular realm. Although contrary to the findings of many Muslim jurists historically (Hefner 2005), the idea that not only should there be no distinction between Islam and politics, but also that the fusion of these domains is a requirement modeled on the life of the Prophet and his successors, constituted an passionate debate in Malaysia.

At its core, the debate over the introduction of Islamic concepts in governance centered on the question of how Islam could legitimately function as authoritative within larger discourses of governmentality. Although non-Muslim communities were uniformly suspicious of the state's efforts, misgivings regarding the idea that an orthodox version of Islam was appropriate to modern governance in a religiously and ethnically diverse country were also quietly present in the minds of many Malays. This issue was often acutely difficult for "everyday Malays," in that while most would openly support the notion that "Islam" was an appropriate source of legitimacy and practical techniques for the government, the orthodox governmental discourse of Islam often cast their own specific beliefs regarding the nature of the Divine and the world and the proper place and actions of humans in the world into question (Peletz 2002, 2005).

It would be a mistake, however, to understand either the tactics of the state or the disquiet of the people in purely linguistic or symbolic terms. In his long engagement with similar questions of belief and discipline, Talal Asad has asserted that issues of authoritative discourses related to religion and ethical life generally cannot be limited to these domains, but rather that the authority of such discourses refers to a complex internal structure that engages a multitude of material domains (Asad 1993, 2006). Certainly the discourses of the state and authoritative institutions occupy a central place in the production of proper belief and living, but our understanding of the possibilities produced by such operations of power must also account for what Asad terms "the somatic processes that authoritatively bind persons to one another, of discourse as a physical process" (Asad 2006). For Asad, everyday practice, ethics, and belief together constitute vectors of living not only through authoritative institutional discourses but also through the experiential sense of the world of the individual subjects of the discourses. Understanding how individuals are able to produce a unitary image of *their* world that can be believed and is essential for the production of ethical life and selves out of the vast diversity and movement of the world requires a consideration of all of these factors (Deleuze 1994). In Chapters 3 and 4 I argued that the link between institutional power and the world this power produced was often shattered for individual Brickfields residents due to the specific strategies of urban development and reform deployed. Following Asad's insights, this chapter explores how the fact that belief itself had come to be an important explicit factor in the constitution of subjects and spaces of living in Malaysia produced unexpected outcomes and possibilities for residents of all religious faiths in reestablishing links between authoritative institutional discourses and everyday living that allowed for engagement with, and belief in, the world generally.

This is not to say that belief does not factor into more explicit notions of secular governance (Connolly 1999); however, the role of belief in the Malaysian case must be distinguished from notions of "privatized" religion and belief (Asad 2003). Unlike classical secular notions on which religious belief and sentiment are properly expressed in strictly circumscribed private domains, belief as it was often articulated in

Malaysia was explicitly a public concern. This public role, particularly in relation to Islam's role in governance and public life, well exceeded the limited role of acting as a "moral conscience" whose only legitimate mode of authority is that of rational debate and persuasion (Taylor 1998). As I will demonstrate presently, Islam, and belief generally, was ambiguously accorded a space in the public sphere on its own terms, and at times was cited as the source of the sovereignty of the state and the law itself.

A transition in the role of belief in the overall argument of this work must also be marked. In the previous chapters I outlined a process whereby the everyday sensory worlds of Brickfields were increasingly destabilized and perceived to be disorderly and unbelievable by neighborhood residents. In response, individuals would formulate modes of living and imagining their world that were rooted in the specific operation of being able to believe one's own senses. This operation, while clearly an engagement with public domains, was most often a private one. This chapter marks a transition to the outcome of such efforts in the context of how the Malaysian state itself has attempted to refigure the place and meaning of belief generally in public life. Faced with exclusion from formal domains of the state, the law, and capital, this shifting terrain of belief as an essential aspect of public life has provided unexpected outcomes and opportunities for engagement with the state that, in a classically secular understanding of proper public life, would be limited to political, legal, and economic domains of public action.

My argument is that the Malaysian state's particular understanding of its own Islamic modernity and the diversity found within the wider Muslim community engendered the possibilities of articulating a spiritual public life that produced possibilities, if only partial, for non-Muslim modes of religious practice to shape the everyday life of Brickfields. In a wider sense, this suggests that the national subject in Malaysia must be conceptualized in terms of everyday practice and overlapping imaginaries of order, both material and divine, that exist alongside formal domains of law and governmentality. As one would expect, the state's explicit engagement with Islam sought to shape horizons of available meaning through faith by advancing a reformed notion of the world that more strictly conformed to understandings of nature, the human, and the Divine as articulated within orthodox notions derived from within mainstream Sunni Islam. Rather than understanding this power as a totalizing, determining factor, however, this chapter demonstrates that the power to shape and limit these horizons oscillated between the individual's imagination of the world and the practical conditions that helped constitute, shape, and allow expression for such imaginations of the self and the world outside (Asad 2006).

The Tamil Hindu community of Brickfields itself shaped its practices in a continuous engagement with the state, most literally experienced in the material transformation brought about in the neighborhood by the imperative of development. The weight in my analysis is on the way in which the diasporic Tamil Hindu community imagined itself as *Malaysian.* This orientation represents a significant departure from the emphasis in diasporic studies on the place of origin as providing the primary term of analysis with which diasporic experience is understood. It is assumed in most accounts of diaspora that loss is implicit in the material experience of dispersion. Yet such a view misses the opportunity to understand how this process is mapped on to an experiment in cohabitation that shapes identities by creating local communities that imagine a future in mutual investment in each other. Experiences of pain and loss are not absent in this experiment, but they also offer ways of thinking about newness and diversity in the everyday that go beyond the current views in diaspora and postcolonial studies (Axel 1996, 2001).[2]

The issue of homeland and origins is important in the Malaysian Tamil imagination of self and identity, but I seek to understand how non-Muslim communities are actively created *as Malaysians.* Rather than imagining themselves to be peripheral to a larger Tamil or Hindu community, I argue that Malaysian Tamils in Brickfields actively sought to fashion notions of self and community that directly addressed both the Malaysian state and the Tamil diaspora. Efforts to claim a place in Malaysian public life were often related to strategies of religious reform deployed by the state in its attempt to modify Malay Islamic religious practice. Many traditional Malay practices declared to be un-Islamic by the state bore a resemblance to rituals targeted by Malaysian Hindu religious reformers in their own attempts to reform Tamil religious life. The Malaysian state's understanding of its own modernity and its attempt to produce properly modern subjects across religious communities provided an important link for both Muslim and Hindu communities, in that they were subject to similar reforms and were often able to use this recognition by the state to make their own claims within Malaysian public life.

The remainder of this chapter is organized as follows: First, I provide a discussion of the trajectory of Hindu reform movements and changes in local Hindu religious practices in relation to changes taking place in the larger Muslim community; then I provide a detailed ethnographic analysis of three unregistered Hindu temples that were able, through discourses of Hindu spirituality and understandings of community order, to gain recognition from the Malaysian state and its functionaries in debates over the immediate physical transformation of the urban space of Brickfields; finally, I consider the limits of the possible recognition of minority religious groups in Brickfields through an analysis of sites where the intersubjective diversity of particular actors exceeded the recognizable limits of legitimate religious practice in the eyes of the state and the broader community.

Islam and the Malaysian State

The month of September 2001 is now remembered by Malaysians as a milestone in which events occurred that transformed the notions of politics, citizenship, and nation that frame and define the rhythm of everyday life for ordinary people in the country. It is not the infamous "9/11" attacks in the United States that definitively mark this particular month for Malaysians; rather, it is the "9/29" announcement by then–Prime Minister Dr. Mahathir Mohamad at the Gerakan Thirtieth National Delegates Conference that Malaysia was "already" an Islamic state. This announcement set off an emotional debate regarding the "true" nature of the Malaysian state and the place of the law in everyday life, with most of these public discussions focused on the potential expansion of the domain of Islamic *Shari'a* law. Mahathir's opponents forcefully argued that the law was on their side, citing a long juridical history affirming the secular character of the Malaysian state. The federal constitution, buttressed by the Reid Constitution Report 1957, the Government White Paper on Constitutional Proposals, the Cobbold Commission Report 1963, and the famous court precedent *Che Omar bin Che Soh v. Public Prosecutor* ([1988] 2 M.L.J. 12) were all cited as events in the long debate over the place of religion in governance that forcefully rejected the idea that Malaysia could ever be anything but a secular state. Democratic Action Party president Lim Kit Siang, a long-time opponent of the *Barisan Nasional* and the idea of an Islamic state, made the following statement regarding Mahathir's announcement:

It jettison[ed] the fundamental constitutional principle and nation-building cornerstone in the 44-year 1957 Merdeka "social contract" agreed by our forefathers from the major communities that Malaysia is a democratic, secular, multi-religious, tolerant and progressive nation with Islam as the official religion but is not an Islamic state. (Lim 2002, 1)

Lim's statement summarizes the general argument against the Islamic state that emerged from its secularist opponents; not only would an Islamic state be undemocratic, monoreligious and backward, it would also be against the law. Linking the intensified activities of the Special Branch[3] in apprehending "terrorists" in the wake of 9/11 with the perceived illegality of the 9/29 announcement, the opposition began to organize resistance to these moves under the slogan "No to 911, No to 929, Yes to 1957."[4]

The debate at the time over Mahathir's announcement highlighted a number of important political and social issues regarding the nature of the Malaysian state and the modes of governance proper to it. By framing the prime minister's statement solely within a juridical framework, much of the outcry over his announcement misunderstood the modality of the statement itself. First, Mahathir was not signaling a dramatic shift in policy; as many scholars have shown, formulating modes of governance that are in accord with Islam had been a central aspect of Mahathir's administration from the very beginning of his tenure as prime minister (Hilley 2001; Khoo 1995; Martinez 2001; Milne and Mauzy 1999; Peletz 2002). The emphasis on the "already" in his pronouncement lends it the character of a clarification of the present rather than a signal of a shift oriented toward the future. Thus, Mahathir was not suggesting an entirely new direction for the Malaysian state; rather, he was articulating what he understood to be the "true" force of the law and the state itself, a force that at times stood in opposition to the defined legal instruments the state had at its disposal to govern. In short, Mahathir was openly articulating the state of exception upon which the state he headed maintained its rule. Unlike the Islamic state in Iran that has produced a formal constitution based on the *Qur'an* and the *Shari'a*, the Malaysian government has not attempted to solidify its proclamation by replacing the secular constitution with one that is openly grounded in Islamic tenets.

This fact sits in striking contrast to the PAS's position on the Islamic state. In contrast to Mahathir's contested approach to Islamic governance, PAS advocated an explicit replacement of many Malaysian civil codes with *hudud* laws[5] and has worked to implement this strategy in Kelantan and Terengganu, where they controlled the state governments.[6] As with the federal government's efforts to promote Islam, PAS's effort to enact *hudud* legislation remained an unsettled, complex, and contested issue in 2002 (Mohammad 1995, 2000; Peletz 2005). Stalemated by the fact that the federal government refused to validate *hudud* legislation passed by PAS-controlled state governments, the party went so far as to threaten to build separate jails, train and maintain separate volunteer police forces, and enact *hudud* laws without the approval of the federal government if necessary (Peletz 2005). Although often cited as evidence of inconsistency regarding the status of Islam in governance, the federal government's aggressive opposition to PAS's version of an Islamic state, undertaken simultaneously with its claims of Islam as a basis for rule, is consistent with its longer-term efforts to infuse (rather than replace) largely secular civil institutions with an Islamic morality.

I argue that the Malaysian state's moves to formulate particular modes of governance in accord with Islam while overtly rejecting the outright replacement of Western-derived secular institutions were possible because the Malaysian state was not a purely rational-bureaucratic entity; rather, its forms of governmentality, as literalized in the everyday practices of formulating what it deemed to be a proper urban order in Brickfields, oscillated between a techno-rational mode of regulation and an apparent supernatural limit to that regulative power. The moral basis of rule in Malaysia was thus complicated by the fact that, in explicitly introducing the power of the divine as a justifiable basis of governance and belief as a legitimate aspect in the cultivation of a properly Malaysian self, the sovereign power of the state was in turn marked by the fact that this power was linked to a higher Good that stood outside of the law.

Religious Reform in Malaysia

Prime Minister Mahathir's announcement that Malaysia was already an Islamic state in September 2001 was not particularly surprising, despite the firestorm of indignation the announcement provoked from political opponents.[7] Throughout the twentieth century, and particularly since the advent of the *dakwah* movement in the late 1970s, the issue of the Islamic state had been a source of debate and conflict in Malaysia (Kessler 1978; Nagata 1984). Khoo captures the tenor of what he terms "the Islamic resurgence" when he writes:

At a basic level the resurgence seemed to express a gathering sense among Muslims in Malaysia that Islam ought to be accorded a larger role in the personal lives of Muslims and in the conduct of public affairs. Where the former was concerned, there was a feeling that Islam had to be more than a matter of personal conviction or individual observance and that, unlike other religions, it had to be fully practised as *ad-din* or a "way of life." (Khoo 1995, 162)

Since taking office in 1981 Mahathir had been responding to this "gathering sense" by articulating a version of "modernist" Islam that valued capitalist economic development, technological innovation, and educational achievement, fusing Euro-normative notions of proper citizenship and progress with his own somewhat idiosyncratic views on Islamic jurisprudence and history (Martinez 2001; see also Mahathir 1986). Although not always directly articulated, a key aspect of this vision of governance was a more public role for Islam in both formal and informal spheres (Hilley 2001; Khoo 1995; Peletz 2002).

One might be tempted to assume that such reforms would automatically be antagonistic toward non-Muslim communities. Although there was a clear policy of discrimination against non-Muslim communities ("*bumiputera*" or "Malay privilege"), the state's insistence on a public life partially defined by spiritual matters had not led to the radical exclusion of non-Muslim communities from Malaysian public life. Rather, diverse attempts by both government officials and *dakwah* activists to articulate a more rigorous, logical, and correct form of Islam in Malaysia were also loosely guiding reform efforts in Malaysian Hindu communities. Under certain circumstances, a common concern with molding proper spiritual subjects actually provided the means by which Malaysian Hindus could assert their place in Malaysian public life. Although these Hindu reform efforts formally lacked the force of law that characterized similarly oriented initiatives directed toward Malays (Peletz 1997, 2002), there were numerous efforts under way, in the words of one interlocutor, to "promote the correct practice of Hinduism." As with attempts to transform everyday

Islamic practice through a promotion of a rationalized interpretation of the *Qur'an* and the delegitimization of *adat* and local observance among Malays, reform initiatives targeting Hindus were strongly rooted in a more textually based, Sanskritic understanding of what it meant to be a proper Hindu. Articulated by the middle class and spearheaded by several larger Hindu temples patronized by this group, most of these efforts focused on two major issues: the reform of existing "village" temples that strongly retained elements of what used to constitute local practice in South India, and the "proper" education of Hindu youth.

In Brickfields it was rare to observe middle-class devotees visiting a Munisvaran or Mariamman temple.[8] Educated Hindus were ambivalent about these temples, consistently stating that while they were not "against" them, their deviation from *agamic* Hindu practice was a source of concern and embarrassment. They were concerned that the popular practices in the temples, such as spectacles of mortification of the body and animal sacrifice that were highly publicized in the Malaysian press, strongly influenced the way that Hindus were perceived in the broader Malaysian imagination. This fact led a number of middle-class Hindus I interviewed to express anger and resentment over the continued existence of these temples. Ackerman and Lee indicate why this embarrassment would lead to deeper resentment when they write: "If Malaysian Hinduism is characterized by a relative lack of textual authority, the sources of change are more likely to be found in the laity and non-Sanskritic priests. These people are the major practitioners of the faith, actively involved in defining and redefining the boundaries of Hinduism for themselves and others" (Ackerman and Lee 1988, 91–92). Hindu reformers in Malaysia seem well aware of this fact and increasingly aim to reverse the equation by stepping up their efforts to educate local Hindus regarding the "incorrectness" of their own beliefs and practices.

Sri Murugan Centre: Hindu Reform and Modernity

Specific efforts to reform the Hindu community were often loosely tied to organs of the state. The understanding of proper Hinduism promoted by such organizations explicitly replicated many of the assumptions regarding the relationship between correct spirituality and correct citizenship that the Malaysian state had been promoting in reference to the Malay Muslim community for many years. The Sri Murugan Centre (SMC) was one clear example of the ties, both practical and moral, that many reformist Hindu groups had with the state. The SMC was a Hindu-centered program that combined the veneration of Murugan with a more specific, "practical" motivational skills course. The program primarily targeted secondary school students, although occasionally undergraduate college students also participated. The stated objectives of the program were to (1) provide educational guidance for Hindu children, (2) inculcate family and religious values, (3) motivate students to acquire self-esteem and learn the value of hard work, (4) inspire students to be high achievers, and (5) integrate Indian students generally into the mainstream of Malaysian society. The SMC was a national organization, although the Brickfields branch on the grounds of the Sri Vivekanenda School was one of the more active sites. The SMC maintained close ties with top government officials, such as then–Deputy Prime Minister Dato' Seri Abdullah Badawi[9] and the Public Works Minister, Dato' Seri Sami Vellu, who was also the president of the Malaysian Indian Congress (MIC) and the highest-ranking Malaysian Indian in the cabinet. The head of the SMC, Dr. Thambirajah, was a well-known lawyer in Kuala Lumpur who had previously held high positions within the MIC and who had sat on the Advisory Board of the Dewan Bandaraya Kuala Lumpur for nearly a decade.

Notions of modernity and the forms of spiritual life proper to modern subjects articulated by the SMC were quite similar to those expressed by the state for Muslims. In broad terms, the SMC articulated its mission as part of a larger project of formulating a specifically Malaysian version of being modern and envisioned the organization and its members as having an active part in the process of "nation-building": "We believe Asian societies face problems peculiar to our own society and solutions must be our own. Western technologies can be transplanted but not all educational methods . . . We hope to contribute to nation-building, national growth, unity and harmony" (Sri Murugan Centre 2001). Despite the specific call for an alternative approach to the problems that are deemed "peculiar" to Malaysia, the core principles articulated by the organization remained firmly rooted in notions of the sovereignty of the individual and the necessity for modern subjects to cultivate a specific form of techno-moral reason:

The founders, volunteers and students of SMC have adopted these 3 core principles:

1) All are created equal

2) All have been bestowed with the same intelligence

3) Faith in religion is crucial to succeed in education

A student who understands and internalizes these principles will free himself from the clutches of feudal attitudes and espouse confidence, optimism and a positive self-image. (Sri Murugan Centre 2001)

The specific character of these "feudal attitudes" is left unsaid, but its recourse to a humanistic language of rights, freedom, and equality typically associated with secularism is striking. Yet point three of this statement and the brief declaration that follows subsequently locate the moral force of the work of the organization in a religious framework, mirroring the understanding of the spiritual and the formation of proper Malay subjects articulated by the Malaysian state. Interestingly, faith is explicitly introduced as a basis for the formation of an ethical public self, and then quickly linked to its "proper place" in relation to the authoritative discourses of the state regarding "success." Although not excluded from the public sphere or quarantined in the private as "cultural," the SMC's principles clearly link legitimate belief to the orthodoxies of the state. Thus, it is not enough to believe; one must believe *properly* and *effectively*. The idea that education could creatively marry Enlightenment notions of the subject with particular religious beliefs and practices was not new either to Tamil Hindus (Irschick 1969, 1994; Kelly 1991; Ramaswamy 1997; Willford 2006a) or to Muslim Malays (Bowen 1993; Ibrahim 1994; Milner 1995; Riddell 2001; Roff 1994; Wan Mohd 1998). In Malaysia, *bhakti* devotionalism itself has long been a means by which upper-class Tamils have sought to reform the everyday religious practices in homes and temples. Organizations such as the Pan-Malayan Dravidian Association, inspired by the Dravida Kazhagam in Tamil Nadu, have been active in Malaya/Malaysia[10] since the 1930s and have sought such reforms as allowing all castes entry to temples and the abolition of devotional practices deemed "primitive," including animal sacrifice, fire walking, and rites of possession (Collins 1997, 101). These early efforts focused on the home and temple, although the emphasis on educating properly "modern" subjects was also a concern for these movements. In these early cases the schools tended to remain "out of bounds" because involvement in educational affairs would have brought the reformers more directly under the dominion of the British colonial government, and later the post-Merdeka Muslim-dominated state (Arasaratnam 1970, 172–174). What was unique about the SMC and its imagination of its own mission and the proper education of the students the organization serves was that it actively formulated its idea of the "proper *Hindu* student" in an ambiguous collaboration with the Malaysian state. Thus, in addition to the uplift of everyday temple devotees, the domain of the school itself became the focus of their reform efforts.[11] Combined with an emphasis on promoting a "proper" form of *bhakti* devotionalism, the SMC imagined a more comprehensive notion of transformation than the reform organizations that came before it.

The activities of the SMC spanned an array of activities, but its main purpose was to prepare students for their college exams. To achieve this, Datuk Dr. Thambirajah devised a "two-fold path" that combined Murugan *bhakti* with long-term exam preparation. Participating students committed to the program a year in advance of their exams, and the stages of the SMC process were timed according to the national Form 5 exam schedule. Most program activities were aimed at developing study skills, giving tutoring and additional instruction, and teaching test-taking strategies. It was also this set of activities that led a number of the SMC's critics to claim that the organization was merely a "tuitions program" and that the spiritual training offered alongside these courses served as a "disguise." Dr. Thambirajah explicitly denied that the SMC was only a tutoring program masquerading as a religious organization (in public speeches he often exclaimed, "We are not just a study center! We are much more than a study center!" in English, Tamil, and occasionally Malay). Yet his own explanation of what the SMC did, articulated in an interview with the author on January 24, 2002, was ambiguous:

I actually am no expert in Hindu theology! There is power there, though, so it doesn't matter. I think that the transformative power of religion can be harnessed to motivate students in worldly matters. Western motivational techniques don't work with Indians . . . they aren't moved by such pitches. However, they believe in Murugan, they already are familiar with Him, so we can reach them through Murugan worship, Murugan *bhakti*. Murugan protects everyday people, the lower classes, and He can remove obstacles and help people overcome adversity. We want to uplift the youth and this is how we can do it.

Dr. Thambirajah both confirmed and denied his critics here. On the one hand, he was clearly articulating a vision of "what will work," noting that Western motivational techniques have little appeal and thus the SMC deployed a different strategy in drawing students into its programs. At the same time, Dr. Thambirajah spoke of Murugan's power as something real (rather than the *imagination* of Murugan as something to exploit), referring back to the power of the deity to protect devotees and help them overcome adversity. His explanation casts Murugan *bhakti* as doubly instrumental in the sense that the deity can both help students become properly modern Malaysian subjects and simultaneously address spiritual needs that are not primarily governed by the instrumental rationality associated with secularism. The problem of belief for Dr. Thambirajah was not one of finding ways to suppress the role of belief in the lives of SMC participants, but rather how to bring the everyday beliefs of organization members into line with the allowable frameworks of belief as articulated by the Malaysian state generally. This complex notion of agency and becoming was reflected in the SMC's spiritual activities.

The ongoing preparation for the national exams in academic terms ran alongside a series of rituals and ceremonies dedicated to Murugan, such as the formal taking of vows, periods of meditation and prayer, and fasting. This process culminated with the "sacrifice" period (*Kalvi Thyagam*). These ceremonies were performed at Batu Caves, where participating youth make offerings and pray directly to Murugan at the temple inside the cave that is also the location of the annual Thaipusam festival in Kuala Lumpur. As with most of SMC's activities, the *Kalvi Thyagam* combined techniques of Murugan *bhakti* with a modernist sensibility regarding individual empowerment, achievement, and progress, providing a model for proper spiritual and educational growth for temples and Tamil medium schools alike.

The mode of Hindu religiosity the SMC offered marked both a distinctive Hindu religious identity and a more general sense of belonging along national and spiritual lines. Discursive links between proper citizenship and properly *agamic* Hindu practice were evident in SMC literature and events, although as Dr. Thambirajah made clear, the organization was not afraid to innovate Hindu practices for its own ends. The necessity to mark and model a proper Hindu spirituality, separate from Islam yet not radically in conflict with the state, was an important strategy for distinguishing the Malaysian Indian community as properly spiritual subjects of the Malaysian state. Events such as *Kalvi Thyagam* were quite important in this regard, especially in light of the fact that the dominant notion of Hindu spirituality in Malaysian public life is the barely controlled ecstasy of Thaipusam,[12] a festival that resists recuperation by the more generally modernist imagination of religion articulated by the predominantly Muslim Malaysian state. *Kalvi Thyagam* domesticated those practices that are a source of embarrassment for reform-minded Hindus and Muslims alike, a correspondence that lay at the heart of the SMC's success. Thus, the invocation of Murugan in the *Kalvi Thyagam* linked to the symbolic character that Collins ascribes to Thaipusam in that vow fulfillment neither radically distances participants from the spiritual and material goals of the Muslim-dominated nation nor compromises an imagined notion of "Hindu-ness" or "Tamil-ness" that participants must inhabit, embody, and return to. Collins frames Thaipusam in symbolic and psychological terms, arguing that Murugan *bhakti* constitutes both an indirect protest against the Malaysian state and an expression of the psychic pain experienced as Tamils in a Malay-dominated society (Collins 1997, 13–15). The SMC's notion of Murugan *bhakti* does resonate to a limited degree with the idea that ritual vow fulfillment of this kind can *symbolically* express a more egalitarian social order that more decisively links Malaysian Hindus to the state's articulated notion of proper subjectivity. However, this primarily psychological understanding of Murugan *bhakti* does not account for the fact that even belief of this kind concretely seeks to engage authoritative discourse of the state that are predicated on the notion that a proper Malaysian subject is also a spiritual subject. Therefore, to understand Murugan *bhakti* primarily as resistance or as an overt index of difference is to miss the explicit links between belief, subjectivity, and governance that the state itself had introduced into Malaysian public life.

Religious Reform and Local Practice

As with the *dakwah* reformers in the Malay community, there was a great distance between the abstract ideals articulated by larger groups such as the SMC and religious practices at local levels. This distance was evident when I interviewed Srinivasan,[13] the editor of a respected popular magazine devoted to the propagation of a "proper" Hindu message. Srinivasan had long been involved with initiatives intended to reform local Hindu religious practices, especially those of the Munisvaran and Mariamman temples. He believed that the magazine and his organizing through the numerous reformist Hindu organizations he was involved with, including the Hindu Religion Propagation Committee (through Sri Kandaswamy Temple), and the Malaysian Hindu Sangam, were the most efficacious means to articulate his message regarding proper Hindu ritual to ordinary people.

Srinivasan described himself as a teacher. During our interview he made it clear that one must regard Hinduism as a body of knowledge to be learned and mastered rather than simply followed. For him, the local practices of the Munisvaran and Mariamman temples reflected a mistaken interpretation of Hindu belief and a clear reluctance to change due to what he terms "culture":

There are two streams of practice in Hinduism, the philosophical stream and the cultural stream. The philosophical stream is based on holy texts, like the Upanishads. You know what that is? [RB: Yes] People who are more educated believe in this way. This is the correct way. The cultural stream is tradition, what people have just been doing, whether they think about it or not. They don't really know the texts. People who do this, who just do the rituals without knowing why, do not really understand the religion. You know, things have been improving in Malaysia, but it is hard. I have personally undertaken a lot of work to try to help people understand their religion and to practice it correctly.

I asked Srinivasan how his ideas were received in the local temples, and he answered, "Not so well." He made it clear that he regarded the pedagogic discipline found in these local temples to be lacking:

S: The temple priests are part of what I just mentioned, the cultural stream. They are not really trained at all . . . I mean, they know how to say the prayers and do the rituals, but they don't really have a deep understanding of the religion. So I think that these temples aren't the best place to teach people about the correct way to worship. Unlike you Christians [gestures toward RB] we Hindus do not really have sermons or teachings as part of our prayers. That is right, isn't it? You have a pastor who gets up and teaches you something every Sunday, right? But in Hinduism this doesn't happen . . . the priests just conduct the ceremonies, nothing more.

RB: So you don't focus your efforts on the little temples, like the ones here in Brickfields?

S: No, no . . . I do work with them, but they don't really respond. Well, many of the people that go to those temples respond, but it can be difficult. Older people are much more resistant and attached to the cultural stream. I must say that even my own mother is still very attached to some of the old practices . . . she is quite insistent that animal sacrifices and so on are really part of Hinduism and I haven't been able to change her.

RB: Really? Has that created difficulties for you? I mean, has it created problems between you and your mother?

S: Nothing like that. She listens to me, but I'm still her son, she's still my mother. I can't force her to stop. Besides . . . she truly believes she is doing something wrong if she doesn't do some of those things, you know. Insulting the gods or bringing bad luck. If I get angry with her, what's the point?

Srinivasan did not exhibit the overt resentment shown by some of my other interlocutors regarding the local practices of area Hindus. However, he did articulate a vision of a rationalized religious practice that was, in its aspirations, not far from the imagined ritual correctness espoused by *dakwah* activists and government institutions charged with formally regulating Islamic practice. Local observance was "cultural," not supported by the foundational texts of the religion, and must be addressed through education. Srinivasan linked these local religious practices to a Tamil rural culture "that doesn't even exist in India anymore," indicating a widespread belief among Hindu reformers regarding the atavistic character of local temple practices in Malaysia. However, Srinivasan could not address these "incorrect" practices in a purely abstract mode, since his own mother insisted through her own religious practices upon the material veracity of what he labeled "the cultural stream." Having recognized belief generally as an important aspect in the cultivation of ethical selves, Srinivasan could not in an absolute sense deny his mother's specific beliefs on the grounds that they were irrational or empirically wrong. Lacking recourse to the empirical system of judgment available within more explicitly secular modes of reasoning, Srinivasan was forced to negotiate with his mother and her own beliefs in the context of everyday living without being able to deny her motives or morality.

Efforts to clarify, reform, and regularize local Hindu religious practice in Malaysia were crucial factors in the formation of intelligible Hindu subjects. Given that the state showed a clear investment in the formation of such subjects but had not explicitly attempted to regulate religious belief and practice in the same manner as it had with local Muslim communities, efforts along these lines generated by the communities themselves came to have a crucial, albeit indirect, role in how the state could "see" local Hindus. The activities of the SMC, Srinivasan and his magazine, and other local reform movements bore the signature[14] of the state, in that these organizations anticipated and shaped their reception based on the more formal system of regulation in place for Malaysian Muslims. The legal codes, procedures, *fatwas*, and judgments of the *Shari'a* courts did not directly apply to non-Muslim communities; yet this complex terrain of religious discourse exceeded its explicit context and found its way into the everyday practices of Hindus in Brickfields through the efforts of local religious and community leaders to regularize the activities of temples and individual subjects. These efforts worked to shape the margins that were recognized by the state and created a mode of limited agency for those individuals and Hindu religious institutions that had managed to gain some measure of recognition. For those who were located outside of this margin, the agency that came with this recognition was often elusive.

The State and the Power of Temple Deities: A Wheel Falls on a Man's Head

On August 16, 2002, an accident occurred during a test run of one of KL Monorail's trains. The following day the *Star* reported:

NEWSMAN HURT BY FALLING WHEEL

kuala lumpur: A senior journalist from national news agency *Bernama* suffered serious injuries to his head and body when a back-up wheel from a monorail on a test run in Jalan Sultan Ismail landed on him in a freak accident here.

David Chelliah, 41, attached to the agency's economic desk, was crossing the road after an assignment at Shangri-la Hotel to a car park nearby when the mishap occurred.

The wheel, measuring 34cm in diameter, fell off the vehicle from the tracks 15m above at 2:30pm yesterday.

Each car of the two-car monorail have 24 safety wheels secured by six fasteners. Initial findings revealed that the remaining 23 safety wheels were intact.

MTrans Holdings Sdn Bhd communications general manager Soh Yeh Bee said the firm was investigating the incident.

"We have not determined how this highly improbable event could have occurred and how all six fasteners of the wheel could have come off."

This event was a public relations disaster for the KL Monorail Corporation. Already several years behind schedule, the monorail project was revived in early 2002, with the system projected to open at the end of October. This incident would set the opening back for nine more months. The fact that the wheel injured a senior editor of the national news agency Bernama and the spectacular nature of the incident only served to intensify public speculation regarding what "really happened" during the test. Numerous possible causes were advanced, including carelessness on the part of monorail workers and sabotage. As the following extract demonstrates, no specific cause for the accident could be identified despite strenuous efforts to establish one. In the absence of any other known causes, the most persistent popular explanation cited supernatural grounds as an explanation. As the *Malay Mail* reported on August 28, 2002:

FIRM AWAITS RETURN OF MONORAIL TRAIN TO FACTORY

Monorail Malaysia Technology Sdn Bhd, the manufacturer of KL Monorail's trains, is hoping the train from which a safety wheel fell onto a man on Aug 16 would be allowed to return to its Rawang factory.

A meeting with the Department of Railways, police and Department of Occupational Safety and Health later today will determine if the train could be transported back to Rawang.

Monorail's director of systems, Alan Trelfa, said they need to strip the train to find out why the wheel went off, hitting Bernama senior journalist David Chelliah.

Until now, none of the six 20mm screws have been found.

Trelfa stressed that such an incident had never happened in any of the test rides or the rigorous tests conducted at the factory.

Monorail's chief manufacturing officer C.C. Lim was equally baffled how the screws went missing as the trains move forward and backward.

"Even if the screws had loosen [*sic*] while moving, they would tighten once the coach moves to the opposite direction," he said, adding that even if a screw is held to the wheel, it would not be easily detached.

Lim said because of the incident, the KL Monorail launch would have to be postponed.

The screws simply disappeared. The wheel then fell and injured one of the most prominent journalists in Malaysia. For many, this event was not regarded as an accident. Rather, the violently ironic wrath of a god or ghost was often cited as the cause. Hearing these rumors in local coffee shops was unsurprising; to hear remarkably similar explanations from KL Monorail officials themselves, however, was striking.

In early September I met with a public relations officer at the KL Monorail headquarters in Brickfields. Ong[15] was charmingly efficient and took me up to her office to have the interview there. The tone of the encounter was set in the small talk that passed between us as we made our way to her office. I mentioned the horrible incident involving David Chelliah and the bad press they have been receiving over the accident, omitting the supernatural "street" explanations that I had been hearing. Ong sadly offered her own interpretation of what had happened:

> O: Oh, what happened to that poor man was horrible! We all feel really bad about it. Thankfully, he'll be OK, but my goodness . . . we must have really done something wrong. We have to get together with the temple priests and find out what is happening.

> RB: With the priests? Are you serious? So you think that a ghost or something knocked the wheel down on him?

> O: Well, I don't know [Embarrassed]. Maybe. How else can you explain this? There is no logical explanation. The wheel shouldn't come off like that. I don't even think that the engineers can make it come off like that. No screws at all! And it hits a famous journalist? What a disaster!

> RB: Actually, I was going to ask you about this. I know that KL Monorail has been working very closely with the temples here in Brickfields and trying to move them around with some sensitivity to what they believe the gods of the temple require, and so on . . . I wanted to ask about this strategy . . . is it a strategy, or . . .

> O: Sure, it is a strategy. I mean, we have to work with the people who are affected by the construction. We can't just do it without working with them as much as we can, so . . .

> RB: But you are saying that the company's response is to consult with the temples. A legitimate way to address why the wheel actually fell.

> O: Of course! We have to. You never know. Not that I believe in this [Laughs] . . . but you never know.

This was not KL Monorail's public position regarding the accident. Formal press releases and public statements never mentioned the contacts the company had with various temples, both Hindu and Buddhist, in Brickfields during the construction of the line. These contacts were well known locally, however, and according to Ong KL Monorail regarded the temples very seriously and understood the success or failure of the company's plans as related in part to the spiritual interpretations that local temples articulated to it.

Attributing the cause of this accident to divine forces would seem to be precisely the mode of understanding that religious reform efforts in Malaysia were attempting to "correct." However, the fact that the event was widely understood in these terms by Muslims, Hindus, and Buddhists alike is an indication of why the state and its proxies would negotiate with unregistered Hindu temples in Brickfields. These negotiations indicate that neither religious reformers nor the state were immune to the claims of these temples in relation to the spiritual frameworks of understanding that they articulated. Rather than deploying legal techniques to address the issue of how to move the temples away from the KL Monorail site, the state engaged the spiritual discourses of the temples in order to determine the proper arrangements. The law and discourses of modern urban planning remained important throughout this process. However, techniques of divination and other ritual practices that fell outside of reform definitions of proper religious worship were common *across* religious communities in Malaysia and shaped the form of recognition offered by representatives of the state to these temples.[16]

The Law, Housing Rights, and Unregistered Residents in Brickfields

In the previous two chapters we saw the blurred boundaries between the legal and the illegal in relation to housing rights and the impact of state-initiated urban development projects on the everyday lives of ethnic and religious minorities in Brickfields. Many of the small Hindu temples in Brickfields formally violated the law in two major respects. First, under the National Land Code 1965, these temples did not hold legal title to their land, nor did they have the permission of the landowner (in most cases the government itself) to occupy their land in the form of a legally binding lease. As we saw earlier, the supremacy of the state authority[17] in matters of the proper alienation of land is formally incontestable. Even the long occupancy of land confers no actual rights to those occupying it unless they possess title to the land in question. Judicial review in matters of possessory rights has upheld this stringent view of the supremacy of registry under the Torrens system (see *Mahni v. Ali & Anor.* [1965] 1 M.L.J. 234, *Teh Bee v. K. Maruthamuthu* [1977] 2 M.L.J. 7). The law makes no exceptions or provisions for religious institutions that have occupied a parcel of land for long periods of time, although the state authority can legally make certain exclusions "under Malay custom or *adat*,"[18] which could in theory be extended to apply to the affairs of individual mosques (National Land Code of 1965, Section 340[2]).[19] This codified exception to the primacy of title is not formally extended to non-Muslim temples, shrines, or churches.

Second, most small temples in Brickfields were not formally registered as religious organizations under the Societies Act of 1966. Non-Muslim places of worship are traditionally recognized by the state through registration under this act, which covers "any club, company, partnership, or association of seven or more persons whatever its nature or object, whether temporary or permanent" (Harding 1996). Certain companies, partnerships, business associations, trade unions, and societies of an educational nature must register under separate acts such as the Trade Unions Act of 1959, the Industrial Relations Act of 1967, and the University and Colleges Act of 1971. While registration under the Societies Act affords certain rights under the law, the Registrar and the Office of the Prime Minister possess wide powers to refuse or cancel this registration if the organization is found to threaten security, public order, or morality. Specific definitions of security, order, or morality are not given by the act. Most long-standing non-Muslim religious institutions were granted legal recognition under the colonial-era Societies Act of 1894, but it has become increasingly difficult for newer religious groups in Malaysia to gain formal standing as legal organizations, because of the consistent refusal of the state to register Christian, Buddhist, and Hindu groups that are only now trying to establish themselves in Malaysia (Harding 1996, 198–203; see also Ackerman and Lee 1988).

Not every unregistered temple in Brickfields, however, was understood by the state as an enemy to morality and order. The intensive urban development schemes put into motion during the past decade did not automatically lead to the demolition of many of these temples, even though a number of them sat directly on land needed for the construction of the new regional train station (KL Sentral) and two local mass transit train systems (Putra LRT and KL Monorail). This cannot be said, however, of the thousands of unregistered residences in the neighborhood; nearly every one of these homes was demolished and the occupants were relocated to the fringes of metropolitan Kuala Lumpur. How was it that the long-standing *kampung* communities in Brickfields were summarily dispatched to the edge of town while the local temples that served them remained generally intact, still within the neighborhood, albeit reconstituted on a nearby site?[20]

By my own count, Brickfields had ten functioning Hindu temples in September 2002. Seven of these temples were not registered with the local authorities and had neither title nor lease to the land that they were occupying. The tenuous status of these temples had been exacerbated historically by the fact that most unregistered temples in Brickfields engage in practices that many educated Hindus find incorrect, embarrassing, and generally backwards. In these temples it was not uncommon to find such practices as animal sacrifice, spirit possession, and various rites of devotion that included extreme acts of bodily mortification. Therefore, many Hindus in Kuala Lumpur have historically shunned these temples, leaving them to fend for themselves when it came to dealing with municipal authorities and local landowners. The public statements of the Malaysian Hindu Sangam (MHS) exemplify this understanding of local temples as embarrassing and at variance with the "real" practices of Hinduism. As reported in the *Sun* on October 3, 1998, the MHS publicly urged devotees to "not waste their time and hard earned money on superstitious beliefs." The MHS was particularly disturbed by the fact that they "slaughter goats and chickens and ask worshippers to suck their blood, and encourage them to consume alcohol."

How is it then that while residents living in these areas were summarily displaced, several of these temples were able to resist eviction and successfully legalize their status in the neighborhood? My research suggests that there is an important tension between the idea of the temple as a non-Muslim religious space and the notion that *all* religious spaces have powers that are derived from broad notions of spirituality. It is the latter notion that has come to inform the state's explicit introduction of the spiritual into the realm of proper governance. Using the state's investment in regulating "proper" religious practice across communities as an opening, these temples were able to present themselves in a legitimate and intelligible fashion to the state and therefore were able to remain in Brickfields.

Murugan and Hanuman Temples

The experience of three local temples illustrates the tension between a state seeking to order its urban space and populations based on the discrete diversity of public subjects, and the materiality of a spiritual domain beyond the reach of such an imagined order.[21] Two of these temples, one dedicated to Murugan and one to Hanuman,[22] had existed in Brickfields for decades. The third temple was dedicated to Krishna and, having been allocated a site in the neighborhood only ten years before, was a relative newcomer to the area. Unlike the other two temples, the Krishna temple was relocated once before and was previously sited in a nearby area.

The temples devoted to Murugan and Hanuman, while unsuccessful in totally blocking efforts to move them off the land they occupied in Brickfields, were nonetheless able to negotiate agreements with the Dewan Bandaraya Kuala Lumpur (City Hall) and the KL Monorail Corporation that allowed them both to remain in the neighborhood. As part of this arrangement DBKL purchased a plot of land that both temples then jointly occupied. The Murugan temple was previously located across the street from the Palm Court condominium complex. The Hanuman temple occupied a site about a quarter of a mile away from this site, on the banks of the Klang River. Until early 2001 this temple sat amidst the residents of *Kampung Cina*, a separate cluster of unregistered homes that lined the riverbank. These residents were relocated out of Brickfields in spring 2001, although the temple remained.

Despite the fact that construction on the monorail had begun in Brickfields, these two temples remained standing. Intensive negotiations took place between the temple committees, government officials, and representatives from KL Monorail during the early months of 2002. Although these discussions were devoted to issues such as compensation and the timing of the temple removals, it was clear that the framework governing the negotiations was the impact the proposed removals would have on the spiritual life of the temples and the neighborhood.

Agents of the state went further than simply listening to the concerns of the temples during these negotiations. In the face of their impending displacement, the temples undertook a number of astrological ceremonies (*vanasastiram*) to divine the proper manner in which the efforts to build the KL Monorail could be accommodated by the temples and the deities themselves. While it was neither widely reported nor maintained by individuals with an inside knowledge of the process that KL Monorail representatives were present during these divination ceremonies, sources from the corporation and individuals involved with the temples claimed that officials were often aware of these rites of divination and related ceremonies of restitution to the deities and were receptive to what the deities communicated through these ceremonies.[23] It was never specified which mode of divination was used in the negotiations, although a number of techniques are commonly practiced to discern information regarding the disposition of the deities and the future, including the interpretation of astrological considerations and sacrificial rites intended to both honor the deity and obtain direct spiritual guidance.[24]

Time was the overriding consideration for both sides in these interactions. KL Monorail was primarily interested in removing the temples as quickly as possible, especially since the project had been revived after having been suspended for nearly two years. For the temples, the primary concern was that any attempt to move or alter the temple be made with a proper understanding of what time would be auspicious for such moves (*nalla neram*) and what manner of restitution (*parikaram*) must be made to the deity due to the disturbance generated by the move. The different understandings of time that each side exhibited, however, were not mutually exclusive. The temples knew that to oppose the time of the project unbendingly would most likely reduce or eliminate their ability to extract a reasonable settlement from the developers; for KL Monorail and the state, the consequence of disregarding the demands of the deities and their time was uncertainty and very likely physical danger.[25]

The proliferation of accidents on the monorail worksite, including the near-fatal injuries suffered by the editor from Bernama during the testing of one of the trains,[26] was subsequently cited by officials at KL Monorail as evidence that they had not properly heeded the time of the deities in the execution of their plans to reorder Brickfields. It was the editor's accident, wholly unexplainable due to defective equipment or human error, which caused the opening of the monorail to be delayed for nearly nine months.

The one nonnegotiable demand articulated by each temple was that another structure be built as soon as possible, relatively close to the old sites. The rationale for this was that the current sites were already consecrated and considered sacred spaces. Thus each location will always contain the *sakthi* (power) of the god even after the demolition of the temple buildings. Although the deity will, with proper prayers and invocations, inhabit the new site, this *sakthi* is not simply transferable; therefore the temple must be reconstructed near its original site. Removal of the statues and sacred objects must take place at the correct time astrologically, and must be done with all of the necessary rituals paying homage to, and asking forgiveness from, the deity of the temple. As Eck (1998) explains, the building of a Hindu temple represents a reconstruction of the sacred order of things as a microcosm, with the power of deity manifested in the work of constructing and maintaining the temple itself as well as through ritual objects and practices.[27]

Many unregistered Hindu temples were being demolished in Selangor during this time without consideration of the spiritual consequences of such an act.[28] Thus, the success that these temples in Brickfields had in addressing the state and its representatives as legitimate members of the local public life is significant. State agents moved very cautiously in dealing with these particular temples. Deadlines were extended, alternative plans discussed and negotiated, and ultimately DBKL purchased a plot of land at the north end of the neighborhood and granted both temples permission to occupy sections of this land and construct new buildings there. Although exact figures were not made public, members of local temple committees claimed that each temple was given a lump-sum payment of approximately RM 100,000 (approximately $27,000) to construct new temple buildings and conduct the elaborate ceremonies necessary to move the deities and consecrate the new space.[29] After much delay, both temples were moved in late February 2002.

Krishna Temple

The situation of the Krishna temple was similar to those of the Murugan and Hanuman temples, although the outcome of its negotiations with the state was different. This temple was not located directly in the path of the train line. Rather, it sat on the site of a planned leisure park. Therefore, the urgency of moving this temple was not as strong in 2001–2002. Yet, once the plan to move the Murugan and Hanuman temples to another site was settled, it became clear that KL Monorail and local government officials felt that moving the Krishna temple to the same site would solve an impending problem for them. The temple did not agree, however, raising objections based on spiritual considerations. The major points of contention were two: (1) the temple priest judged that the proposed new site was not suitable for a third temple, and (2) the astrological considerations showed that the time was not advantageous for moving the temple. Also, the Krishna temple had only occupied its current site for a little over a decade. Because certain rites of consecration take place throughout the first twelve years of a temple's existence, this temple was barely considered fully functional by devotees. To disrupt this process yet again by moving could prove to be disastrous. Thus, despite some internal dissent on this point among temple committee members (one member stated "I don't know why they are waiting! The temple will just have to move eventually anyway"), the position of this temple was that it should not be moved at all. Although the temple committee did not reject the monorail plan outright, it raised serious objections to moving and flatly refused to relocate until the astrological configurations were more suitable. Thus, KL Monorail formulated a new plan for the temple, incorporating the temple into the plan for the *Jalan-Jalan* Leisure Park. The blueprints for the park provided to me in September 2002 by KL Monorail officials indicated that the temple, rather than being moved, would ultimately become part of the "entertainment" planned for visitors.

Ambiguous Legitimacy

Each of these temples was successful in negotiating with the state and with large-scale business concerns such as KL Monorail, whereas the communities they served were not. A normative understanding of politics and the public sphere would lead us to suspect that the demolition of the temples would have generated outrage in the community and that local officials simply wished to avoid such a confrontation. This explanation, however, is not borne out by the facts of this situation, in that the communities these temples served had already been relocated. Furthermore, many middle-class Hindus who remain in Brickfields have little sympathy for these temples and would have supported their removal, since they find the specific religious practices of these temples to be backwards and at variance with what they characterize to be the "true" beliefs and practices of Hinduism. These small temples were able to communicate better with the agents of a state that is primarily concerned with the correctness of Islamic practice than with elite Hindus. Therefore, each temple could to some small degree exploit the state's overall concern for properly moral modernity and the stated commitment to allow non-Muslims some degree of freedom to practice their religion. Ironically, the temples could also benefit from the fact that the functionaries of a predominantly Muslim state, while directly interested in assigning a proper "place" to non-Muslim religious observances, were not in a position to make judgments as to how "Hindu" the practices followed in these temples really are. Because the temples appeared in the general public sphere as being legitimately Hindu (in spite of severe criticisms within the Malaysian Hindu community) and simultaneously articulated a general notion of the supernatural world that resonated across discursive boundaries between religious faiths, unexpected links between belief and governance that were made possible by the state's *own* discourses of the role of the spiritual and the divine in everyday life came explicitly into play. While non-Hindus would deny that they were "believers" if asked directly, this disavowal was accompanied by concrete practices that seemed to recognize these overtly disavowed beliefs.

Clearly these "successful" temples were able to exploit certain tensions in the discourses of religion and public life in Malaysia. Although in theory most state functionaries did not subscribe to any specific belief in the power of Hindu deities at the level of everyday life, they had the shadowy feeling that moving the temples would have a material impact on the well-being of the neighborhood. This subtext was never fully articulated, yet never fully denied. So state agents, unable to predict the outcome of removing the temples, indirectly relied upon temple priests and astrologers to guide them in the process. Each temple was aware of this, with one person at the Hanuman temple saying to me that "Hanuman is a powerful god, but also unpredictable. The Malays know this and most are afraid to even enter the temple because Hanuman may be able to influence them." This individual attributed their ultimate success in delaying the process[30] directly to the power of Hanuman and the fact that Malays, despite being Muslims, are familiar with the god's power and fear it.

Thus, though the state articulated a basis for rule that combined the techno-rational modernity of the "secular" West with Islam, its accommodation of spiritual concepts generated outside of Islam opened a wider space for the non-Muslim divine. This fact is important for our understanding of how these unregistered Hindu temples were able to engage state actors during the transformation of Brickfields. In this context, much as the residents experienced the arbitrary implementation of the Land Code and Acquisition Act as events where the order of the state is experienced as momentarily absent, the state and its agents in these cases believed themselves to be subject to an exceptional power that could disrupt their own imagination of order in the neighborhood. The fact that the question of time itself was central to the interactions between the state and the temples is indicative of how state functionaries anticipated that the arbitrary liquidation of these small temples would have exceptional consequences beyond the limits of rational planning and the exercise of sheer sovereign force. Events such as the accident involving the editor from Bernama only served to confirm this possibility. Thus, in the very act of regulating non-Islamic practices, the state invested the temples with new powers in the production of the altered space of Brickfields.

In these instances the power of the state did not render these temples outside the law. Rather, an ambiguous space was created within the law that afforded these temples an enhanced legitimacy in the eyes of state functionaries. As the demolition of similar temples in rural areas demonstrates, this recognition retains the uneven, exceptional character of power as it often appears in urban Kuala Lumpur. In order to formulate a broader understanding of this uneven application of the law, we must interrogate how these temples in Brickfields came to be recognized in relation to the state's efforts to reform Islamic religious practices and formulate modes of governance that are understood to be in accord with Islam. As the state tried to make the Malaysian state "more Islamic" it also brought about unintended transformations in the religious practices of non-Muslim communities and Malaysian political life.

The Limits of Acceptable Belief and Public Ritual: *Seng Hong Tokong*

The *Seng Hong Tokong* sat adjacent to a temple devoted to Krishna on the banks of the Klang River.[31] It was easy to miss this temple, given that it was situated well away from Jalan Berhala, nestled behind a crumbling apartment building directly behind the large Palm Court complex. The presence of the Krishna temple[32] next door was obvious, with eye-catching statues of the deity mounted on the roof of the open building and a lit sign. Next to the Krishna temple was a fenced-off area where residents in the apartment building parked their cars and motorcycles. Only someone really "in the know" would recognize that behind the red metal gate protecting the vehicles was where the *Tokong* sat—even if one looked directly through the gate, the *Tokong* could not be seen. Since the gate was normally padlocked, it was impossible to explore what lay behind it unless someone unlocked and opened the gate. Only after being granted entry to the little yard did one view the small shed that housed the deities and ritual implements of the *Tokong*.

Most Brickfields residents regarded the *Tokong* as an odd artifact. Many residents denied that the temple existed as all, as illustrated by a conversation with a neighbor not 500 feet away from the *Tokong*. This man asserted that there was no such temple despite the fact that the compound was within sight. When I pointed out the *Tokong's* gate to him he replied, "*That* is not a temple—that one over there [pointing in the opposite direction, up Jalan Berhala and generally in the direction of Buddhist Maha Vihara, the headquarters of "mainstream" Theravada Buddhism in Malaysia and Singapore] is a temple!"

Talking with individuals who visited the *Tokong* did not clarify the status of the temple. After finding the temple empty and locked several times, I found it open one day. A man was retrieving his motorcycle while a young boy visited with him. The older man introduced himself as Muniandy, and the boy shyly said "David."[33] I asked them if they knew anything about the *Tokong*. "Yeah, we come here," David cheerfully answered.[34]

> RB: What kind of temple is it? Some people tell me it is a Hindu temple, some say Buddhist . . .
>
> D: Yes, it is.
>
> RB: [Puzzled] It is what?
>
> D: It is a Hindu temple. It is a Buddhist temple. Chinese people come and so do Indians. I go with my grandfather . . . he is up there [points to a veranda five stories up—an older gentleman clad in a dhoti is quietly watching our conversation].
>
> RB: Ah, OK . . . so are you a Hindu or a Buddhist?
>
> D: I'm a Christian!
>
> RB: Really? Oh, I should have known because of your name . . .
>
> D: Well, I'm a Hindu also.
>
> RB: What?
>
> D: Well, I come here when I visit my grandfather, I go to other temples with my mother . . . sometimes I go to church . . . [35]
>
> RB: I see. So you don't choose . . .
>
> M: [Interjecting] Why choose? We are all the same.
>
> RB: All religions are the same?
>
> M: Well, they all come from the same place. We may be Buddhist or Hindu, but we are all similar . . .
>
> D: [Excited] I'm a Hindu-Christian! I'm not a Muslim, though . . .
>
> M: Muslims come here though. They shouldn't, because of the government, you know, but some do.
>
> RB: [To David] Why aren't you a Muslim too?
>
> D: [Looking down] I don't know . . . I don't like them so I won't be a Muslim.

Neither Muniandy nor David claimed to belong exclusively to one faith during the time that I knew them. Their reluctance to identify with a single faith was common among members of the *Tokong*. The caretakers of the temple, Tan and Murugasu, whom I came to know during the next several months, would similarly refuse to choose one faith over the rest.

Although David's rejection of the label "Muslim" was not expressed as directly by the adults, I never did hear the claim from anyone at the *Tokong* that they were Muslim. This ecumenical attitude toward recognized religious categories was reinforced by what the *Tokong* itself consisted of. Outside and to the left of the building and at the base of two trees growing were two altars, one dedicated to Kali and the other to the Buddha. Inside the temple was a third altar depicting several Chinese folk deities.[36]

Aside from the daily prayers of worshippers, the *Seng Hong Tokong* was active during the Wesak festival, Thaipusam, and the Festival of the Hungry Ghosts. In keeping with its "village" orientation, the rituals at the temples involved spirit possession, walking on hot coals, and the fulfillment of vows through mortification of the body with small spears and hooks. The Wesak rituals were particularly public because temple worshippers annually staged a procession through Brickfields.[37] During this procession entranced devotees menacingly walked through the neighborhood, cracking bullwhips, cutting themselves with knives and razors, and thrusting large spears through their cheeks, arms, and backs. One local business owner (somewhat) jokingly summed up residents' feelings about the procession by saying, "Fucking hell, man! They are dangerous. It makes the hair stand up on my neck when they come around. I do enjoy the bullwhips, though."[38] This mixture of fear and desire was evident in the actions of local street vendors who would have a quick look at what was going on and then literally flee the scene. Many Muslims believed that this procession was satanic and particularly feared it, a perception reinforced by the fact that the *Tokong* devotees themselves believed that they were channeling evil spirits and carried a chair during the procession for "the Dark Lord" to sit in.

Commemorating the Festival of the Hungry Ghosts did not involve a procession, but also included rituals of possession, and culminated in the dramatic burning of a large paper ship intended to carry the roaming, hungry ghosts back to the underworld, thus freeing the earthly realm of their presence. Devotees called the hungry ghosts out of the Klang River and made sure that they boarded the ship to the afterlife. *Tokong* members reported that they could literally see the ghosts emerge out of the water and board the ship.[39] Like the Wesak Day rituals, these events were quite public and known to area residents.

The issue here was not the intensity of the proceedings at the *Tokong*. Rather, the limit transgressed by this temple was the fact that the shared practices between nominally Hindu and Buddhist residents became too apparent in their articulated discourses of identity and religion. The most transgressive aspect of the temple was that it was home to both Tamils and Chinese, with worshipers who variously identified as "Hindu," "Christian," "Buddhist," or some combination of these groups all involved in the life of this place of worship. Thus, while authoritative discourses regarding proper religious belief remained very important for the *Seng Hong Tokong*, these discourses did not automatically dictate belief for members of the temple.

Outside of the temple compound, the *Seng Hong Tokong* was finding it increasingly hard to breathe in 2002. KL Monorail required the compound for the planned *Jalan-Jalan* Leisure Park and, unlike the other temples mentioned, state functionaries did not fear the power of this temple. In August 2002 the *Star* published an article regarding plans for the construction of the entertainment complex, although its schematic drawing of the projected park simply left the *Tokong* area blank. Armed with the article and the plan provided to me by KL Monorail, I asked Tan and Murugasu if they knew about the *Jalan-Jalan* Leisure Park. "*Ya, sudah baca ni*" [Yeah, I've read this], Tan answered, pointing to the *Star* article. "They haven't told us about this, so I don't know," Murugasu added. "They can't just get rid of us, though." Tan, now speaking in English, added, "Who would rid us of ghosts?"[40]

Tan's question was a legitimate one. It implied that there was no room for either ghosts or their earthly attendants in the modern world. Yet we should not infer from their lack of interest in the well-being of the *Tokong* that members of techno-rational institutions do not believe in ghosts and the power of gods not their own. Given the *Tokong*'s explicit concern with locating, placating, and removing disturbing sprits from the realm of human time, it can be argued that their modes of anticipating the exceptionality of the spiritual world more closely matched the nervous anticipation articulated by certain agents of the state. The issue with the *Seng Hong Tokong*, however, was its uncategorizability within accepted normative standards of identity as recognized by the state. Without being clearly marked as part of one religious tradition to the disqualification of all others, the *Tokong* was excluded from avenues of public discourse available to Munisvaran and Maryi-amman temples whose ritual practices materially resembled those of this particular temple.

Memory and Individual Devotional Practice

The importance of clearly identifying with a religious group that was recognizable to the state also emerged in Ramalingam's[41] situation. In his case, it was the continued practical beliefs of an individual that went un-recognized, despite his persistent effort to attend to the local deities found in Brickfields. Ramalingam was practicing a mode of devotion that was not recognized by the Mariamman temple that it was originally linked to, by continuing to worship at a site voluntarily vacated by the temple some twenty years previously. He persisted despite the opposition of the temple, which still existed in Brickfields in 2002, and despite threats of arrest for trespassing on the original site.

Ramalingam was not who I expected him to be. The stories I heard of a young man scaling the high fence around Palm Court in order to make offerings at the foot of the tree which marked the original temple site had led me to expect that Ramalingam was an assertive, confident man who did not fear arrest and could withstand the occasional assaults of the Palm Court security staff. The shy, small man who met me at a small South Indian restaurant[42] did not strike me as a rebel or a religious radical.

Ramalingam was puzzled as to why someone would be interested in talking to him at all. He did not imagine his efforts to worship at the original temple site as particularly unusual or out of the ordinary. "I am just the one that does it," he quietly said in Tamil.[43] By occasionally joining Ramalingam when he made his offerings, I later learned that this statement was not entirely accurate. A young woman often joined him inside the compound and many older Brickfields residents came by with offerings, handing them to Ramalingam through the fence. Rama-lingam characterized himself as an instrument for the making of such offerings.

The site itself was a small courtyard immediately inside the Palm Court complex, near the corner of Jalan Sultan Abdul Samad and Jalan Berhala. The courtyard itself was accessible from the street through a gate that leads into the fenced-off space—one could enter without going through the main gate but entry from inside the Palm Court complex itself was not possible, as there was no gate leading into the grounds themselves. The gate was normally padlocked. The original temple was moved to a new building on Jalan Berhala, across the street from Palm Court on the north side of the complex and within sight of the courtyard. The property developer who built Palm Court erected this courtyard as a memorial to the temple that once stood there. The original temple was demolished in 1982 and the courtyard was completed in 1984.

Ramalingam was twenty-three years old when I interviewed him. Thus, he was only three years old when the original temple was demolished. "Do you remember the original temple?" I asked. "Yes, I have a few memories of it," he replied. "I used to wander over to it from my house in *Kampung Khatijah* [across the street, due west]." Did his parents worship at the temple? "No, they seldom did. They sometimes would go, but preferred to go to some other temples." Did he offer prayers there even though he was very young? "Oh, no!" Ramalingam laughed. "I would just wander over and play there. I didn't really know about praying at that time." I asked, "How did you come to pray here now, well after the original temple has disappeared?"

This question was translated for Ramalingam and he became quite serious, thinking it over carefully. "It is a holy place," he answered seriously after a few moments. "The power of the place is still there, even if the temple is gone." In his teens he became more convinced of the power of the site and felt drawn to go there and make offerings under the tree. Ramalingam did not cite a specific incident that led him to believe this, however. He retrieved a small Ganesha statue from the new temple and positioned it under the tree. I asked Ramalingam if he had permission from the temple to take the statue. He smiled and looked away, but did not answer the question. This statue gained the attention of the Palm Court authorities. When Ramalingam came by to make his offerings the guards attempted to stop him, often physically ejecting him from the courtyard. They left the Ganesha statue in place, however, as according to Ramalingam, "Malays are afraid to disturb our gods." A small sign written in English, Tamil, and Malay was then erected in the courtyard, explaining that praying at this site was prohibited and providing directions to the new temple site. Ramalingam was undeterred by these events and continued to visit the site on a daily basis in order to make prayers and offerings. Finally, Palm Court authorities padlocked the gate to the courtyard.

Ramalingam continued to enter the space, however. At first he would scale the fence. Later he obtained a bolt cutter and would remove the padlock from the gate. This cycle continued for some time, with new padlocks appearing only to be cut off by Ramalingam. Finally, Ramalingam bought his own padlock. He could then discreetly enter the courtyard while maintaining the appearance that he was no longer disturbing the site. In his telling, it took the Palm Court authorities some time to figure out that he had replaced their lock and was still praying at the site.

Ramalingam characterized the space as "miraculous." "About five years ago Ganesha began to accept my offerings of milk. I was the first around here. After that, many who came by and made an offering of milk also had their offerings accepted. It was a miracle."[44] Ramalingam also cites more direct miracles granted to him by Ganesha. During the economic downturn in 1998 everyone in Ramalingam's family was unemployed. Desperate for a job, Ramalingam turned to Ganesha and undertook an intense regimen of prayer and fasting, praying that Ganesha would answer his prayers for a job. After about ten days, the prayer was answered according to Ramalingam. While making his offering in the courtyard a friend of his came by and told him that DBKL was hiring some workers and a friend of the family who already worked for DBKL was asking for Ramalingam to apply. He applied, got the job, and has worked for DBKL ever since. "Ganesha brought that job to me," he said. Ramalingam noted that his position, with its RM 1,500 per month starting salary, immediately pulled his family out of their financial quandary. "I didn't finish Form 5,"[45] Ramalingam noted. "How else could I get a job like this except through the intervention of Ganesha?"

By the time Ganesha began accepting milk at the site Palm Court authorities had begun to turn a blind eye to Ramalingam's activities. As a compromise, Palm Court "officially" agreed to allow Ramalingam to make offerings in the courtyard, with the understanding that others who wanted to make such offerings would have to give them to Ramalingam and say their prayers outside the gate. This was the arrangement that was in place when I interviewed him, and Ramalingam continued to visit the site nearly every day to make his offerings during the time that I knew him.

I asked Ramalingam if he was bitter about the way that he has been treated. "No, not really. I was angry when they began padlocking the gate, but I'm not angry about that anymore." Did he resent that fact that the temple was torn down in the first place? "I don't understand why they couldn't have just kept the temple, but it doesn't really concern me. We are still able to pray here." For Ramalingam his insistence on the sacred character of the original site of the temple structures indicated an ordered relationship between the spiritual, the space of Brickfields, and himself. His understanding of these relationships was marked by the refusal of the human time of "progress" at the expense of the deity, despite the fact that the temple was moved "correctly." Ramalingam's case further complicated the relationship between the experience of order and its materiality, in that the past that structures his sense of duration in Brickfields was neither entirely one of his own experience nor that articulated by the temple itself. It was significant that Ramalingam's family, who had direct experience worshipping at the original temple, did not understand the significance of the space in the same manner. For them, the migration of the temple was expedient and, undertaken in the proper way, perfectly acceptable for both the deity and devotees alike. Ramalingam, faced with his disappearance from Brickfields, articulated an understanding of the past's relation to the present in a mode of time that was not interlaced with the human order but distinct from it. While able to forge a contingent peace with the agents who materially controlled both the land and the spiritual orientation of the temple, Ramalingam nonetheless found that he could not escape a human order that would soon liquidate his place in Brickfields.

Conclusion

This goal of this chapter has been to rethink issues of religion, the power of the state, and their relations to belief and public life in Malaysia. Specifically, I have explored three critical issues related to how these broad issues are concretely manifested in Brickfields. First, I have situated recent intersections of state practice and its efforts to reform along what it imagines as properly Islamic lines with concurrent efforts by non-Muslim communities to transform their own religious practices and engage the framework of public life that the state's own imagination of the spiritual defines. Second, by focusing on specific goals and actors, I have shown how these parallel initiatives have played out in Brickfields during a time of dramatic spatial and social change generated by these broader national efforts to modernize. Finally, in linking the recent events taking place in Brickfields to these broader imaginaries of religion, belief, and order I have sought to open larger questions regarding competing forms of life that are negotiated in ritual spaces generally regarded as "private" by normative standards of political theory. I suggest that an understanding of order and time as articulated through the material transformation of these sites offers empirical evidence for an articulation of theoretical models of governance and modernity that reframes the issue of religiosity in public life.

Most paradigms that seek to address these issues mark secular rationalism as the standard by which the relative "modernity" of a given state is understood. Modes of governance that explicitly exclude the spiritual are characterized as the elusive "now" in a teleology of progress that shuns alternative modes of governmentality that afford the divine a material place in the world. Yet, as Asad, Chakrabarty, Connolly, and others insist, such styles of governance are not a thing of the past and thus require an analytic engagement that does not take the normative presuppositions outlined in the beginning of this chapter as its baseline assumptions regarding the character of modern states (Asad 2003; Chakrabarty 2000; Connolly 1999; Hancock 2002). It is my argument that the Malaysian case clearly illustrates this point.

Due in part to the efforts of organizations such as the Sri Murugan Centre and individual activists such as Srinivasan many local Mariamman and Munisvaran temples in urban Malaysia have adopted some degree of recognizable Sanskritic Hindu practice. The three Brickfields temples analyzed in this chapter are no exception. Although many of their ritual practices resembled those of the *Tokong*, these three temples associated themselves to some degree with a notion of "proper" Hinduism that was also recognizable to the state as "proper spirituality." The reality that most middle-class Hindus were suspicious of these adaptations, feeling them to be misunderstood or insincere, had a decisive impact on these temples. The fact remained, however, that they shared certain marks of intelligibility with their mainstream counterparts. Ironically, the state was more willing to recognize the legitimacy of these temples than many Hindu reformers, and this fact was decisive in each temple's attempt to mark out a recognized space in the public life of Brickfields. The politics of spirituality that provided the Sri Murugan Centre and Srinivasan a recognized stake in Malaysian public life also served to mark these individual temples as valid players in the local space of Brickfields, despite their formally illegal status regarding their occupation of government land.

Yet this recognition also sustains a more ambiguous set of relations between seemingly discrete subjects, as demonstrated by KL Monorail's attempts to manage overlapping imaginations of the divine world. The state's recognition of non-Muslim groups allows not only for a form of association between these populations but also opens up the possibility that subjects from one group will find themselves literally subject to the power of another's gods. Such blurring between non-Muslim groups is less of a concern for the state here, but the fact that it becomes possible for Malays themselves not only to believe that Hindu deities will harm them but also to act on this fear publicly indicates that the excesses of the everyday in relation to subject categories such and "Muslim" or "Hindu" remain a central aspect of public life in Malaysia. Thus, the explicit introduction of ritual and the spiritual to public life opens the door to unstable and unforeseen connections across seemingly discrete communities, worlds, and times, manifested through the arenas of public order and religious devotion that are explicitly linked to the domains of law and citizenship.

The situation of the Hindu temples in Brickfields described above also compels us to reformulate our understanding of South Asian diasporic communities, because the issues of subject formation and relations between a minority Indian community and the Malaysian state do not sit easily within the commonly articulated framework of diaspora described in the opening section of this chapter. The common presumption that diaspora is a totality where displaced subjects remain *wholly* defined by place of origin clearly cannot be automatically applied to the Malaysian case. As I have described throughout this chapter, the very idea of belonging and *homeland* for Tamils in Brickfields has been transformed not only through a continued imagination of origins and proper religious practice as it exists in South India, but also through direct, sustained engagements with the Malaysian state and its efforts to transform everyday Islamic religious practices, public life, and the urban terrain of Kuala Lumpur.

Conclusion

Between 2000 and 2002 the state and local communities struggled in urban Kuala Lumpur over the right to imagine and enact ideals of public space in the city. More specifically, this struggle was waged over the *right to the city* itself. Therefore, this book began with questions regarding the ideals of space and public life as articulated by the Malaysian state and by local communities in Brickfields, and the possibilities of believing that such spaces were domains in which one could act to create an ethical life in relation to neighbors, family, the state, and the Divine. In this specific case, ideals regarding the manner in which one can live ethically framed how this struggle unfolded, guiding the desire to create spaces of justice and order that conformed to the ideal visions articulated within completing claims for the right to the city.

Understanding the city within the framework of these ideals generated the concrete experiences of area residents and the practices of both the local Brickfields communities and the state. Examples of these concrete aspects of everyday life are the empirical basis of this work. Understood in relation to a concept of rights rooted in experience and belief as well as with authoritative institutions such as the state or the law, the presented ethnographic information requires us to rethink the possibilities regarding what constitutes struggle over law and justice and where these struggles unfold. The engagements over the right to the city in Brickfields largely did *not* take place within the formal domains of the state, the law, or the political. I argued that, despite this fact, the engagements among communities in Brickfields and between these communities and institutions of the state and its proxies were a struggle over the law, forms of justice in everyday life, and the possibilities for action within this complex social terrain.

Lefebvre's notion of the right to the city locates this struggle primarily within everyday urban spaces rather than in the overt workings of institutions. According to Lefebvre (2003), the right to the city implies the right to *inhabit* city spaces. Throughout this work I have understood this to mean not only that individuals have the right to enter and circulate in particular spaces but also that these spaces must be experienced as open and stable within the larger geography of the city. This sought-after experience of stability does not exclude change, but does imply that the pace and trajectory of change must be anticipatable and that the process is to some degree open to input and action from the community. In this sense the right to the city is established through the possibilities that arise through the *habits* of individual urban dwellers in relation to space. During the time of extensive transformation that took place in Brickfields, however, it was often not possible to bring forth *action* rooted in these possibilities, due to the manner in which change was generated from above by the state and its proxies such as property developers. This lack made living in Brickfields an uncertain, ambiguous experience for residents during the time that I conducted fieldwork there. As I have demonstrated in this ethnography, attempts by individuals in Brickfields to engage these events were seldom explicitly articulated as a matter of rights guaranteed by law. The "right to the city" that Lefebvre defines allows us to better understand how attempts to assert understandings of local justice in Brickfields would often unfold outside of the formal institutional structures of the courts or the state.

Although they seldom articulated a slogan or an organized political platform, the citizens of Brickfields consistently attempted to assert their right to the city in the face of the dislocating effects of urban development in Brickfields. This right was often not explicitly linked to the operations of the law or the state, but rather was rooted in the expectation that the city is a social configuration that arises out of the relationships that exist between its residents. In this conception of the right to place, however, local concepts of justice and proper relatedness must engage the state and the formal institutions of law, even when these institutions are not seen as the sources of ethical living. During the time that I lived and conducted fieldwork in Brickfields, residents sought engagements with the state and its proxies and among themselves that produced a sense of place commensurate with the history of the neighborhood and the moral understandings of proper living held by members of the community.

Throughout this book I have advanced a threefold thesis. First, that the experience of the state and urban life in Brickfields often takes place in the gap between formal legality and local understandings of justice and relatedness. Second, I have argued that local residents struggled to establish concrete modes of ethical living in Brickfields due to the pace and scale of efforts to transform the neighborhood. Within this unstable environment it was at times impossible for residents to form a mental image of the world that was believable and generated the possibility for moral action in the world. Finally, largely lacking access to the state through formal legal channels, members of the Brickfields community pursued alternative avenues of engagement with the state, particularly through religious idioms and institutions. Through this complex set of interactions, Brickfields residents were able to articulate the right to public space and community on a limited basis. Through a careful consideration of the issues raised by the Brickfields case I have sought to address critical questions regarding the anthropology of law, religion, the state, and the urban.

Through a focus on critical domains of experience and belief in everyday life, I have argued for a revised understanding of how urban spaces are constituted, imagined, and inhabited. While not seeking to undermine the critical importance of institutions such as the law or the state as key factors in the creation of such spaces, I have sought to demonstrate empirically how *belief*, based in vectors of experience of the world and the possibilities of thought and action regarding such experience, occupies a critical place in the process of locating, inhabiting, and concretely *living* urban life. This has required an understanding of the concept of belief that transgresses received notions of faith as exclusively a phenomenon related to religion or magic; this revised understanding generates two specific claims within my overall argument. First, there is no aspect of human life that does not at some level require the presence and operation of a system of belief. No person, family, neighborhood, community, or nation exists "above" faith; even the secular claim to "faithlessness" is concretely embedded in the operations of belief. Second, it is incorrect to understand religious belief and practice itself as an epiphenomenal, secondary experience of being in the world or of difference. It is quite possible to establish empirically how specific religious beliefs, discourses, and practices are distinct from one another and work to frame and limit the experience of being in unique ways that can be identified, categorized, and compared. It is a mistake, however, to understand such visible differences through the idea that such operations rooted in belief serve to categorically distinguish religious confrontations with the ambivalence, uncertainty, and diversity of life from secular attempts to formulate concepts of human life through science or reason. This notion misrepresents the central function of *faith* embedded in techno-rational modes of living in the world (Asad 2003; Connolly 2005). Although it is critically important to understand the differences between religious and secular frameworks of understanding, I have not drawn a sharp distinction between religious faith and secular reason in this book. Rather, I have sought to empirically establish the commonalities, links, and engagements between the two within the concrete, observable domain of everyday life in Brickfields between 2000 and 2002.

The problem of belief in everyday life is not a new issue. Deliberation regarding this difficult domain of human existence has a long pedigree in philosophical debates, with engagements by Cavell, Derrida, and Levinas standing as only the most recent entries within a long-standing discussion (de Vries 1999). Among these attempts to provide some understanding of the "body/brain/culture" nexus and the place of belief within the common vectors of these domains, one finds an unexpected ally in the work of Deleuze. I say "unexpected" in that Deleuze's overarching suspicion of orthodoxy, opinion, and transcendental illusion in philosophy and thought would seem to place him at odds with a framework of understanding that privileges belief as an essential aspect of being in the world. Yet it is precisely Deleuze's attention to the links between sensory-motor perception, thought, and the social formations that emerge out of these domains that make his ideas particularly amenable to challenging established definitions of belief and its concrete operations in everyday life. His long-standing attempt to pose the problem of modern living as located in the disjuncture between time and history and his careful attention to demonstrating precisely how one is able to establish links between oneself and the world led Deleuze to acquire what Paola Marrati has described as "unanticipated allies"; these allies are belief, immanent conversion of faith, and (nondogmatic) images of thought (Marrati 2003).

The renovation of Brickfields explicitly ruptured habitual sensory-motor links between Brickfields residents and their world in the present. Largely excluded from formal processes of law and municipal planning, Brickfields residents actively sought to create other links with their world out of the radical, aggressive change that was taking place around them. Local strategies to create such links were rooted in overcoming events in everyday life that worked to prevent residents from forming an image of the world that allowed for action within horizons of possible meaning. In other words, they sought to create new worlds of possibility or becoming rooted in an image of the world that they could believe in. Belief therefore cannot be wholly associated with religious orthodoxies, practices, or a transcendent divine sphere. The object of belief in this context is the world itself.

Although often disadvantaged or excluded from the processes of law and governance that directly shaped both the physical and demographic character of the neighborhood, Brickfields residents nevertheless consistently sought new ways of claiming, defining, expanding, and *believing in* their right to the city. Although often faced with an experience of place and of self that was inconsistent, ambivalent, and under threat of disappearance, the people of Brickfields creatively engaged agents of the state, its proxies, and each other over precisely what sort of space Brickfields could and should become. Such engagements are, by definition, *ethical*. As in most communities that anthropologists live in and attempt to understand, Brickfields residents experienced civil society and modernity in equally complex, ambiguous ways. For these reasons Brickfields stands as an important case study not only within the anthropological literature regarding Malaysia and Southeast Asia, but also within ongoing efforts to understand the nature of the state, the workings of the law in the everyday, and the role of belief within the general experience of modern urban life in the early years of the twenty-first century.

Notes

1. Despite its importance in neighborhood narratives regarding the history of Brickfields, this site did not possess a stable name in these stories. As it was often described as "the lot behind the Hundred Quarters" or "the field on Chan Ah Tong," I refer to the space as the "Jalan Chan Ah Tong field."

2. This story was told to me on numerous occasions during my residence in Brickfields. I was unable to confirm the story, however, as the available archival materials related to Nehru's 1937 visit do not mention this event.

3. Kuala Lumpur Sentral, "About Us," http://www.klsentral.com.my/aboutUs .html. Kuala Lumpur Sentral is being developed by a consortium, Kuala Lumpur Sentral Sdn Bhd, owned by Malaysian Resources Corporation Bhd (64.38%), Keretapi Tanah Melayu Berhad (26%), and Pembinaan Redzai Sdn Bhd (9.62%). Joint ventures regarding specific aspects of the project have been formed with developers from Singapore (Capitaland) and Japan (Daito Trust Corporation). Kuala Lumpur Sentral, "Corporate Information," http://www.klsentral.com.my/ corpInfo.html.

4. KL Monorail does not publicly present itself in the grandiose manner deployed by KL Sentral, noting merely that "[t]he project involves the development, operation and maintenance of a monorail system that will provide inner-city public transportation to the central business, employment, hotel, shopping and tourism district of Kuala Lumpur." KL Monorail, "About the Company," http:// www.monorail.com.my/about.htm. KL Monorail is owned by the KL Monorail Systems Sdn Bhd (which is a subsidiary of KL Infrastructure Group Bhd, itself a subsidiary of MTrans Holdings Sdn Bhd) and headquartered in Brickfields. The construction of the enormous elevated tracks for the trains was equally disruptive to everyday life in the neighborhood during the time that I conducted fieldwork there.

5. As my ethnography demonstrates, these attempts were seldom explicitly articulated as a matter of rights guaranteed by law. Considering that I have drawn my examples from the words and observed practices of neighborhood residents in

Brickfields rather than from the courts or other locations explicitly defined as "spaces of the law," we must consider Tushnet's (1984) assertion that an analytic focus on rights in concrete urban situations distracts from the realities of everyday life and the "concreteness" of struggles for justice. Although I clearly am in agreement with Tushnet regarding the distinction he draws between "law" and "justice," I demonstrate throughout this book that articulations of local forms of justice always engage abstract understandings of law as well. As I will show, the "right to the city" that Lefebvre asserts is an appropriate concept to apply in this case, even though most attempts to assert understandings of local justice in Brickfields did not directly address themselves to The Law.

6. Victor Turner (1986) originally used this formulation in reference to such a circuit as it pertained to dance and performance.

7. My use of the term "governmentality" follows Foucault's definition of the concept. For a fuller explanation of my use of this concept see Baxstrom (2000). See also Foucault (1978, 1991).

8. The boundaries listed are also used to distinguish Brickfields from its neighbors by the Office of the Prime Minister (primarily for the purpose of census taking) and the Dewan Bandaraya Kuala Lumpur (Kuala Lumpur City Hall).

9. "Tamil" in Malaysia refers to the descendents of South Indian immigrants. Members of the "Ceylonese" community trace their origins to what is today Sri Lanka. Although many "Ceylonese" speak Tamil and would be classified as Tamils in Sri Lanka, Malaysians tend to distinguish between the two communities.

10. This period is generally referred to as "the Emergency."

CHAPTER 1

1. Numerous studies of urbanization in Malaysia explain urban growth as either a natural process of industrial development (Goh 1979; Hirschman 1976; McGee 1967, 1971; Ooi 1975; Rimmer and Cho 1981; Saw 1988) or as a "culturalist" problem related to ethnic and religious difference (Brookfield, Hadi, and Mahmud 1991, Provencher 1971). Several scholars, including Goh Beng Lan (2001), Patrick Guinness (1992), and Judith Nagata (1979, 2001), critique the onesidedness of these frameworks and have argued for an approach that emphasizes the interrelationships between colonial policies, economic factors, and identity processes related to ethnicity and religion. Benedict Anderson (1983, 1990), Clifford Geertz (1980), Rudolf Mrazek (2002), and John Pemberton (1994) also critique such dichotomies with reference to Indonesia.

2. Swettenham's early, and very public, displeasure with the Malayan Union in 1946 was a critical factor in its eventual transformation to the Federation of Malaya in 1948 (Mohamed 1974, 21–29). It seems that the only thing that could

keep Sir Frank out of Malayan affairs was death itself, as he died on June 11, 1946, just as the opposition to the Malayan Union was coming to a climax in both Britain and Malaya.

3. Before this time the area was identified as "Batu Lima Belas," the Malay translation of "Milestone 15," referring to where the area was situated on the still-incomplete Damansara Road.

4. Little is known regarding what the Brickfields area was like before Yap Ah Loy began building his brick kilns there, although there is a general consensus that much of the area was marshland, and J.H.M. Robson noted in an article entitled "Memories of Kuala Lumpur" published in the *Malay Mail* in 1905 that when he arrived in 1882 much of the area was "covered in tapioca" (Robson 2001, 224).

5. It is also possible that the motivation underpinning the move was a direct attempt to establish a center of power in the state entirely separate from the Malay Sultanate. The wholesale uprooting of the state capital in Selangor was not an isolated occurence, as the state capital of Perak was moved from Bandar Bahru to Taiping around the same time (Dewan Bandaraya Kuala Lumpur 1990, 10). In both instances the move was not only to a more central inland location vis-à-vis the economic activities of the respective states but also a clear move away from coastal towns at the mouths of major rivers, historically the sites of Malay power.

6. Swettenham remembered that "owing to the distance and the absence of any kind of road, the Captain China [Yap Ah Loy] was allowed to continue his benevolent despotism over his countrymen in and around Kuala Lumpor [*sic*] and the mines" (Swettenham 1907, 220).

7. The organization of central Kuala Lumpur as a defensible space was still explicit into the 1930s (Dick and Rimmer 2003; McGee 1963).

8. This assessment refers to the fact that the compound was situated on high ground with clear lines of sight and a secure escape route, the installation of artillery batteries, and the fact that the Klang River separated it from the town proper. The buildings themselves were not, however, actually enclosed within a thick wall.

9. Regarding the importance of Swettenham's road expansion plan and the development of Kuala Lumpur, Lim writes "Roads were constructed between the mines and the nearest navigable points on the main rivers of [Selangor]. Although the mines were scattered, they represented the most important points of population concentration. The construction of roads therefore had the effect of integrating the inhabitants, the settlements and the economy into a more tightly knit spatial system." He further notes that road construction was the catalyst by which controlled urban planning generally came into effect in the state (Lim 1978, 87).

10. Swettenham's plan to phase out wooden structures in the center of town was not a new one; his predecessor Bloomfield Douglas had proposed a prohibition

on erecting new wooden buildings in Kuala Lumpur to the State Council in September 1881 (Dewan Bandaraya Kuala Lumpur 1990, 14).

11. It was not unusual for government officials in Malaya to buy up large tracts of land at this time, although the potential conflicts of interest worried officials in Singapore and Whitehall. Even in this relatively relaxed atmosphere regarding such practices, however, Swettenham's numerous land deals caught the attention, and occasional censure, of his superiors. His aggressiveness in this arena may have contributed to Swettenham's early retirement in 1904, and the controversy over his acquisition of a 25,000-acre concession in Johor (along a proposed railway line that only an insider would have known about—the full import of the land deal and extent of Swettenham's profits were not known until 1906) immediately after his retirement may have prevented Sir Frank's elevation to the House of Lords upon his return to Britain (Barlow 1995, 423–437, 599; Robson 2001, 14).

12. *Attap* (also spelled *atap*) is thatched palm leaf, commonly used for roofing.

13. For example, note the concern expressed in Point 38 in Ridges, Robson, and Travers' "Memorandum of the Future Policy of Municipal Schemes in Kuala Lumpur" (originally published in the *Malay Mail* in 1905), which stated that "many people who now live in shophouses would gladly live in compound houses [but] it is well known among business people that 'bungalow property does not pay' . . . although the building of compound houses is not likely to prove a great attraction to the capitalist, there is no reason why it should not do so for individuals who would gladly live amid healthy surroundings and own their own houses" (Khoo 1996, 53–54). Although the authors couched their remarks in terms of making the "proper" choice available to rational residents, the shophouse design was by this time marked as a serious problem by colonial city planners and architects. Throughout the Crown Colonies and the FMS officials were attempting to remake and further domesticate the now-unruly shophouse space. These attempts were primarily articulated through the idioms of hygiene and public health, a discourse that the authors here allude to as well. See Yeoh (1996) for a detailed account of attempts by colonial authorities to reorder and domesticate the "Chinese shophouse" in Singapore in the context of growing concerns over public hygiene and proper public order.

14. Gullick notes that Yap Ah Loy was quite open to the reorganization of the space as it made his brick kilns profitable and raised the property values of his considerable holdings in the center of town (Gullick 2000, 51). Yap Ah Loy was not around to enjoy these improvements, however, as he died in 1885, causing a crisis for local officials when a nasty battle developed over what actually constituted his holdings at the time of his death. As a systematic procedure for determining property ownership was still in its infancy at this time, the issue proved to be a nuisance for town officials for several years after Yap Ah Loy's death.

15. Swettenham is quoting a circular sent to the newly installed British Residents in 1876 by the Secretary of State for the Colonies, Lord Carnavan, warning

them as to the limits of their powers in relation to the everyday governance of the "protected" states. The irony of Swettenham's remarks here is the fact that at roughly the same time as Lord Carnavan's circular, the governor in Singapore issued a similarly worded statement that Barlow claims was actually drafted by Swettenham. Barlow, correctly in my view, attributes Swettenham's "support" for cautious governance at this time to the fact that the governor's circular was primarily aimed at reining in W.E. Maxwell, Swettenham's arch-rival in the colonial government and a man with grand "civilizing" plans of his own, primarily related to the institution of the Torrens System as the basis for the Land Code in Malaya (Barlow 1995, 202).

16. Looking back after nearly sixty years, Swettenham rhapsodized that although it was difficult to find good officers to come to Malaya in the 1880s, it was a delight to find that some had "interest in the work; the intense satisfaction of construction; of making waste places habitable; of cutting roads and constructing bridges; of gathering people together into villages, and persuading them to build better houses; to vie with each other in planting gardens and orchards; and then getting the boys to join in games and teaching them to be useful" (Swettenham 1942, 83).

17. Andaya and Andaya (1982) note that indirect rule as a more formal strategy of governance was a modified version of Brooke's approach in Borneo. Although the authors primarily cite Hugh Low's administration in Perak between 1877–89 as the model for indirect rule, Swettenham's administration in Selangor during roughly the same years must also be regarded as an important prototype for the development of indirect rule as policy.

18. Kuala Lumpur's population in 1884 was 4,054. By 1895 that figure had risen to an estimated 25,000 (Lim 1978, 89).

19. The crucial role played by this factory in the early development of Kuala Lumpur is evident in Public Works Department reports of the time. The Director of Public Works Report for 1900, for example, notes that "the bricks still continue to be the best made in the State, and the Government could not erect the class of buildings, erected and under erection, without the Government Brickfields Establishment" (as cited in Kuala Lumpur Municipal Council 1959, 19).

20. This presumed location roughly corresponds to the large, irregular block currently bordered by Jalan Tun Sambanthan (formerly Brickfields Road) to the west, Jalan Tun Sambanthan 3 to the north, Jalan Padang Belia to the east, and Jalan Tun Sambanthan 4 to the south.

21. At this time "Indian" was purely a colonial designation as the clerks and laborers themselves identified as "Tamils," or "Ceylonese," clearly distinguishing themselves internally. Therefore, although the area came to appear quite homogeneously "Indian" to the colonial census takers, the growing resident population was already quite diverse. The fact that the area was now being associated with immigrants from the Indian subcontinent is clear, however, as Brickfields was also

coming to be known as *Sinnayarlpanam* or Little Jaffna among the Ceylonese (Selvaratnam 2002, 251).

22. Dick and Rimmer (2003) and Gullick (1983, 2000) explore the links between nineteenth-century understandings of race, occupational aptitude, and the proper organization of urban space in the thinking of colonial officials in Malaya.

23. The first phase of the project was estimated to cost $714,740, while the actual revenue of the Selangor government in 1883 was $450,664, increasing to $494,483 in 1884 (Kaur 1985, 16–19).

24. Swettenham himself somewhat smugly noted in a memorandum to the Resident of Perak in 1895 that "the lesson to be learned from these facts and figures is, I think, a very plain one. It is, that in the administration of a Malay State, revenue and prosperity follow the liberal but prudently-directed expenditure of public funds, especially when they are invested in high-class roads, in railways, telegraphs, waterworks, and everything likely to encourage trade and private enterprise; in this the Malay State is probably not peculiar" (Swettenham 1907, 294).

25. Malayan Railways also provided housing in nearby *Kampung Attap* and on Watkins Street behind the main train station.

26. The extension of the line to the north also led to the establishment of a railway yard in Sentul, three miles north of Kuala Lumpur, with a branch line being constructed specifically for this purpose. As with Brickfields, this area quickly came to be primarily an Indian neighborhood. Through the first decade of the twentieth century Sentul became perhaps even more important to the operation of the FMS Railways, as a larger central workshop than the one located in Brickfields that was constructed there between 1904 and 1906. In this workshop most of the actual coaches in operation on FMS Railways lines were assembled on metal frames imported from England (Kaur 1985, 49, 143).

27. The name of this society was changed to its present name, the Sasana Abhiwurdhi Wardhana Society, in June 1918 (de Silva 1998, 26).

28. The Societies Regulations Act of 1894 formally came into force on January 1, 1895. This act required all social, political, cultural, or religious organizations in Selangor to be registered with, and approved by, the British Resident.

29. In some cases the ethnic segregation of Kuala Lumpur was de jure as well, such as the urban Malay reservation of *Kampung Baru*. Originally established in 1899 as an agriculture settlement for Malays living around the city, *Kampung Baru* was quickly assimilated into the city as "the" Malay urban neighborhood (Concannon 1955; Dick and Rimmer 2003; Gullick 1983; Harrison 1985).

30. De Silva correctly points out that the factory itself was well over 100 yards from the lots granted to the Sasanabhi Wurdhi Wardhana Society, although it is possible that the reporter was referring to the home of the PWD factory manager W.A. Leach as a "PWD building." From Venning's sketch it can be estimated that Leach's home was about eighty yards from the site of the temple (de Silva 1998, 41).

31. The original temple was radically remodeled in the mid-1990s, and it reopened in its current incarnation in 1997 (Sri Kandaswamy Temple 2002, 161–162).

32. Tickell's own term.

33. Unofficial member Chow Kit was finally coerced into seconding the motion, although he did so "with grave headshaking as to what would follow in the way of reprimand" (Gullick 2000, 177). Gullick is unclear as to whether Chow Kit feared a reprimand from "more responsible" colonial officials or from the Chinese community that he represented on the board, although it is safe to say that Chow Kit anticipated opposition from both quarters.

34. J.H.M. Robson, who founded the *Malay Mail* in 1896 and published it until the Japanese Occupation, attempted something of a rehabilitation of Tickell when he wrote in his 1934 memoir: "I think that [Tickell] was the best Chairman the Board ever had. But he was in advance of his times; his work was not appreciated; he was looked upon as somewhat too daring an innovator and possibly there was some jealousy behind the official opposition to many of his plans and suggestions. Kuala Lumpur would have been a finer town to-day if Tickell's services had been retained and his efforts supported instead of thwarted" (Robson 2001, 18). Bear in mind that Robson himself was a staunch advocate of rationalized city planning along the lines Tickell suggested, and he used the *Malay Mail* to advance his own ideas of how urban planning should unfold in Kuala Lumpur (especially the "Memorandum on the Future Policy of Municipal Schemes in the Town of Kuala Lumpur," *Malay Mail*, January 26, 1905). As Robson himself was an unofficial member of the Sanitary Board at this time he, like Tickell, found himself in direct conflict with Resident H.C. Belfield and with the Chinese members of the board.

35. The prices of rubber and tin, Malaya's primary exports, remained relatively high during the war years. However, the end of the war brought an imbalance between demand and output in both of these markets; by 1921 the price of rubber had gone from wartime highs of three shillings per pound to less than one and the price of tin had declined by almost half since 1920 (Gullick 2000, 244).

36. The *Malay Mail* published a street-by-street description of the city in July 1913. The tone of these articles retained an air of bemusement, bordering on the paternalistic affection more common in turn-of-the-century descriptions. What is described is "disorderly," but the street sellers, rickshaw pullers, dhobis, etc., are depicted as quaint, somewhat charming figures in a growing town—a far cry from the soul searching that was going on in the same paper nearly a decade later regarding the same scenes.

37. The Garden City movement in urban planning was based on ideas articulated by Ebenezer Howard in his book *Garden Cities of To-morrow* (1965). Howard's notion of rationalized single-use urban space encircled by parks and other green zones has retained its power with Malaysian government officials and

city planners. The new capital Putrajaya explicitly exhibits aspects of Howard's original understanding of "healthy" and "efficient" urban design (Dick and Rimmer 2003, 336).

38. Due to hardships related to the economic slowdown, a government Retrenchment Committee recommended that Reade's post be abolished. The recommendation was ignored, and Reade would remain in Malaya through 1930.

39. Nearly all early city planning documents have been lost, mainly due to the destruction of records during the British retreat from the peninsula in December 1941 and January 1942, and during the Japanese Occupation (1942–1945). Goh Ban Lee notes that the biggest task for town planners in the immediate postwar period was the reconstitution (mostly from memory) of every town plan that had been drawn up since 1921. A number of these original plans are presumed to date from Reade's tenure in Malaya (Goh 1991, 49–50).

40. This was particularly true in Singapore (Yeoh 1996).

41. Despite these efforts to found a separate branch of municipal government devoted to city planning, the Sanitary Board continued to formally administer land law and oversee town planning until widespread municipal reforms were undertaken in the period immediately following the close of World War II and the return of the British to Malaya (Concannon 1960, Dick and Rimmer 2003).

42. This was a complex of government bungalows reserved for low-level state bureaucrats. It still existed in September 2002.

43. Neither this marsh nor the stream exist today; land reclamation projects in the late 1950s and early 1960s led to the draining and filling of the swampy land, the diversion of the stream, and the deepening and straightening of the Klang's channel. The formerly marshy area (stabilized with landfill consisting primarily of Kuala Lumpur's rubbish) was thus available for building by the mid-1960s.

44. Most oral accounts of long-time residents that I collected utilized the metaphor of "the jungle" to explain what it felt like for outsiders to enter this space.

45. In their discussion of Foucault's writings on power, Dreyfus and Rabinow highlight the fact that "languages of reform" are essential aspects of political technologies of control. Resistance or failure in these instances only serves to prove the need for further reform and reinforces the power of experts (Dreyfus and Rabinow 1984). This cyclical relationship between the need for "reform" and its failures is particularly evident in the history of Brickfields. See also Chatterjee (1993), Escobar (1995), Ferguson (1994), Holston (1989), Mitchell (1989), Rabinow (1989), Scott (1998), and Starrett (1998).

46. The origins and size of the Malay population in Brickfields are quite unclear from available information. Most oral accounts that I collected date the presence of Malays in the neighborhood to the Japanese Occupation. According

to these accounts, rural Malays were brought to the area by the Japanese in order to cultivate tapioca. There is some evidence, however, that there was a small number of Malays living in the area from the 1920s, and it is clear that there were a number of long-established Malay settlements (mainly *Kampung Kerinchi* and *Kampung Abdullah Hukum*) located south of Brickfields. One author dates the establishment of *Kampung Abdullah Hukum* around 1850, predating the establishment of Brickfields as a discrete area of the town (Adnan 1997, 2).

CHAPTER 2

1. Major scholarly works that begin with this assumption include Crouch (1996), Enloe (1973), Hilley (2001), Means (1991), Milne (1981), Milne and Mauzy (1999), Ratnam (1965), and Von Vorys (1975). As this partial list illustrates, the elite accommodation framework has dominated the political theory of Malaysia for nearly fifty years.

2. The original Alliance coalition that emerged during the municipal elections held in the mid-1950s comprised the United Malays National Organization (UMNO) representing Malays, the Malayan Chinese Association (MCA) representing Chinese, and the Malayan Indian Congress (MIC) representing Indians. The Alliance today is known as the Barisan Nasional (National Front) and has included a host of smaller political parties over time.

3. I cite Means (1991) here as a "typical" example of a fairly standard characterization of Malaysian political life due to the wide influence his work carries among scholars of Malaysia.

4. "Malaya" before 1963.

5. See Chapter 1.

6. The treaty signaling the formal end to hostilities between the Malaysian Government and the Malaysian Communist Party (MCP) was not actually signed until 1989. Although a second Emergency was never declared, low-intensity guerilla fighting resumed in the late 1960s and continued through the next decade. A comprehensive history of this second phase of fighting has yet to be written, although several popular and first-person accounts of this period have been published (Chin 1995; Lim 2000; Navaratnam 2001).

7. Stubbs cites official statistics that estimated the strength of the MRLA peaked in early 1952 with just under 6,000 active fighters, 10,000–15,000 active workers, and perhaps as many as 150,000 who sympathized with the rebels in some way (Stubbs 1989, 187). Short claims that there were 8,000 active members at the end of 1951 and Renick estimates that the network of active workers could claim as many as 25,000 members (Renick 1965, 4; Short 2000, 472).

8. "Squatter" is the generally accepted term in Malaysia for unregistered urban residents in both official and popular narratives. Although I dislike this term

due to its negative connotation and avoid using it elsewhere in the text, for the sake of clarity I deploy the term in this chapter while discussing the discourses surrounding the "squatter problem" that were evident during the Emergency and in the 1960s and 1970s.

9. *Orang asli* is the general term for indigenous tribal minority groups. The practice of resettling *orang asli* outside of their normal areas of residence was altered in 1953 to allow for their resettlement into "Jungle Forts" constructed within their normal spheres of residence. This change was undertaken primarily due to the fact that the mortality rate in *orang asli* New Villages was extraordinarily high and proving to be an embarrassment to the government. Also, given that large numbers of Semoi, Temiar, and other groups would evade the military's efforts to locate (and then relocate) them and, out of fear and bitterness over the campaign, join the ranks of the MRLA, it was decided that the New Villagization of *orang asli* was proving to be counterproductive from a strategic standpoint. When the MRLA was driven deep into the forest from 1953, cut off from most Min Yuen groups due to their relocation, it was their relationship with the *orang asli* that allowed the remaining MRLA units to survive and sustain the conflict for another seven years (Leary 1995, 96–139).

10. Some scholars estimate the affected population at closer to one million (Sidhu 1978, 65).

11. This area was so named due to the fact that it bordered the Bungsar Estate, which no longer exists. The accepted spelling at present is "Bangsar," although this change did not become common until the 1970s. Although the neighborhood has grown dramatically since the 1952 election, the historic "Bungsar" and the current "Bangsar" are essentially the same area.

12. This candidate, Mrs. (now bestowed with the honorific title Tan Sri) Devaiki Krishnan, was a Brickfields resident at that time and remained so at the time that I conducted fieldwork. Her victory represented the first time a woman attained elected office in Malaya. Although considered an independent at that time, Krishnan has been a long-time member of the Malaysian Indian Congress and remained active in politics during the years 2000–2002. During the election campaign of 1952, Krishnan recalled in our interview, she had to campaign quite aggressively (primarily by bike or on foot) throughout the newly formed ward, noting that her ability to form alliances across communities enabled her to win the seat. Looking back in 2002 on the election, Krishnan felt that her success was in large part due to her ability to win the endorsement of the local Malay leaders in the *kampungs* to the south, especially that of Dato Tata.

13. Dato Sir Onn bin Ja'afar was a founding member of UMNO and served as its first president (1946–1951). Uneasy with the direction of communal politics and increasingly isolated within the party, Onn resigned from UMNO in August 1951 and founded the noncommunal Independence of Malaya Party (IMP) the

following month. The strategic alliance between UMNO and the Malayan Chinese Association (MCA) during the 1952 municipal elections was formed primarily to prevent the IMP from displacing these parties as the leading representatives of the Malay and Chinese communities, and the success of their strategy effectively neutralized the IMP as a viable national political organization (Andaya and Andaya 1982; Harper 1999; Mohamed 1974; Ong Siew Im 1998).

14. The Barisan Nasional after 1973.

15. Malayan Railway after 1948.

16. As late as the mid-1950s the official position of both the Malayan Railways and the Public Works Department was that once a worker retired he would simply return to "his home," i.e., India. Coupled with the fact that the rubber estates essentially took the same line, many retired South Indian laborers had no choice but to set up a residence in an already established Indian *kampung* community. The fact that the citizenship status for many of these workers was also ambiguous, because of ongoing negotiations related to preparations for Malaya's independence, also contributed to the problem of what these former laborers could expect in terms of long-term status in the country.

17. Sen's assumption that squatters engage in goal-oriented, maximizing behavior based on self-interest is similar to Becker's articulation of rational actor theory in economics (Becker 1976).

18. A more generous explanation for Sen's statement regarding these statistics could be that although the government kept relatively precise statistics regarding those forcibly relocated during the Emergency, much of the data may still have been unavailable to the public at this time (although a number of studies had already appeared with some of this statistical data included). Also, Sen may be distinguishing between those who were forcibly relocated into New Villages and those who packed up for the city on their own initiative, although he does not state this. If he had this distinction in mind, then it severely weakens his argument, since the movement of all populations was quite tightly controlled during the Emergency and there is little evidence of a mass movement to Kuala Lumpur aside from the forced relocations undertaken by the government.

19. Nearly every work on the squatter problem during this period, Sen included, specifically cites Brickfields as one of the most problematic areas.

20. DBKL began to prepare its structure plan in 1978 but it was not until the passage of the Federal Territory (Planning) Act in 1982 that it actually had the legal standing to publish it.

21. Despite *Al-Imam*'s influence, the periodical is largely excluded from historical accounts of the development of journalism in Malaysia Mohd. Safar Hasim's well-known *Akhbar dan Kuasa: Perkembangan Sistem Akhbar di Malaysia Sejak 1806* (1996), for example, does not mention *Al-Imam* once or discuss the development of the Muslim press.

22. A full explanation of *adat* is found later in this section.

23. The Malayan Union was the first attempt on the part of the British to institutionalize a single Malayan state that would standardize the administrative apparatus, create one standard of common citizenship, and clarify the confused political loyalties of the old system of indirect rule in the colony. Malays, feeling forced to accept a plan that would undermine their status within the colony, strongly resisted the union until the British agreed to scrap the framework in 1948 (Harper 1999; Lau 1991; Mohamed 1974; Stockwell 1979).

24. Both the colonial government and the insurgents attempted to link Islamic reform initiatives to their own aims during the Emergency. The MCP, seeking to draw Malay support to its cause, claimed in its propaganda that British control of religious affairs in Malaya was an attempt to "Christianize" the peninsula. In Pahang the insurgents went so far as to declare their struggle a "jihad" again the state government and attempted to form an all-Malay regiment. Colonial officials responded to these moves by asserting in their own propaganda that the British Empire had historically acted as the "defender" of Islam and claimed that Communism sought to destroy Islam and all religions. In several states, particularly Pahang and Johor, Islam became a dominant theme in colonial propaganda (Chin 1995; Harper 1999; Lim 2000; Miller 1972).

25. The Indonesian *Muhammadiyah* has no connection to the underground Sufi movement of the same name that is popular with many wealthy Malays in contemporary Malaysia.

26. S.V.R. Nasr (1996) and Muhammad Qasim Zaman (2002) offer detailed discussions of Mawdudi's ideas and his influence on international discourses of reformist Islam.

27. Although ABIM was the larger of the two organizations, *Darul Arqam* represented a more fundamental challenge to government authority because the group sought to build a self-sufficient economic organization, based entirely on strict Islamic principles and free of government controls (although from 1978 its retail stores were legally registered as business organizations with municipal authorities). Led by founder Ustaz Ashaari, *Darul Arqam* opened small grocery stores offering their own halal foodstuffs, a medical clinic, several schools, and a commune. Plagued by harassment from the government, internal dissension, and a general paranoia regarding the outside world, *Darul Arqam* was officially banned in 1994.

28. Introduced by Prime Minister Tun Abdul Razak in 1971, the New Economic Policy sought to reduce economic disparities between the minority Chinese and majority Malay populations, through a series of mandated economic set-aside programs favoring Malays.

29. Efforts to fuse capitalist development and Islamic morality analytically in the local academic literature were increasingly common by the late 1990s. The 1998 volume *Prinsip dan Kaedah Dakwah dalam Arus Pembangunan Malaysia* (*Dakwah Principles and Methods in the Flow of Malaysian Development*), edited by Abdullah Muhammad Zin, Che Yusoff Che Mamat, and Ideris Endot, is one example of this growing body of work.

30. After meeting in the United States with President George W. Bush, Mahathir returned to Malaysia and amended the proclamation to include the word "fundamentalist." During the meetings in Washington, Bush had praised Malaysia's "moderate" Islam, leading to some criticism in the local Malaysian press as to how "Islamic" Mahathir's Islamic state was. Upon returning, Mahathir angrily rebutted these criticisms, noting that Malaysia is truly a "Fundamentalist Islamic State" (*Malaysiakini.com*, June 19, 2002).

31. This summary of Mahathir's views regarding Islam, modernity, and development is based on public speeches that have been published in the volumes *Globalisation and the New Realities* (2002) and *Islam and the Muslim Ummah* (2000). Writings, speeches, or statements from other sources are cited separately in the text.

32. Mahathir often uses the word "cosmopolitan" to refer to this openness.

33. I am referring specifically to section 298 of the Penal Code, which states: "Uttering words, etc., with deliberate intent to wound the religious feelings of any person is prohibited," and section 298A, which states: "Causing, etc., disharmony, disunity, or feelings of enmity, hatred or ill-will, of predudicing [*sic*], etc., the maintenance of harmony or unity, on grounds of religion is prohibited."

34. Malaysian scholars and political commentators are increasingly accused by both the state and the Islamic opposition of engaging in inappropriate religious debates. In early 2002 six Malaysian intellectuals were accused by the Persatuan Ulama Malaysia (Association of Malaysian Ulama; PUM) of insulting the Prophet and disgracing Islam. Although the PUM was an organization dominated by PAS stalwarts, its petition to the sultans demanding an authoritative fatwa condemning the intellectuals could have resulted in heavy prison sentences for them, because PUM's accusations were keyed to the fact that insulting the Prophet and disgracing Islam are formal offenses under Malaysian law (Peletz 2005). In the end the sultans did not issue a formal condemnation of any of the six individuals. However, the fact that two academics, a well-known feminist leader, two journalists, and a human rights lawyer were accused of religious offenses illustrated that public critique of any kind in Malaysia must, at some level, refer to religion.

35. Although a number of other governments have praised Mahathir's ability to promote and enact a "modern" version of Islam that is, by traditional standards of development and progress, quite successful. This admiration on the part of governments in the Muslim world has resulted in Mahathir being awarded a

number of prestigious prizes, awards, and recognitions, including the King Faisal International Prize for Service to Islam in Riyadh on March 22, 1997.

36. The difference between *adat perpatih* and *adat temenggong* is primarily rooted in local notions of kinship, with *adat perpatih* signifying a social structure that utilizes matrilineal descent. This variant of *adat* is associated with groups that trace their ancestry to Minangkabau communities in what is now West Sumatra, Indonesia. In Malaysia, *adat perpatih* is primarily associated with Malays living in Negeri Sembilan. *Adat temenggong,* which is much more widespread throughout the peninsula and is not so strongly linked to any particular state or region, exists in communities that practice a bilateral (i.e., cognatic, where every type of known biological relation is also socially recognized) form of kinship and, although communities identified with *adat temenggong* also trace their lineage back to Palembang, Sumatra, they consider themselves distinct from Minangkabau groups (Peletz 1996, 13–15).

37. Butcher (2001), Comber (1983), Means (1991), and von Vorys (1975) offer detailed accounts and analyses of the ethnic riots that engulfed Kuala Lumpur on May 13, 1969.

38. Directly translating the world *negara* into English is difficult, as *negara* is commonly used to refer both to the ensemble of institutions we would refer to as "the state" and the more abstract notions of shared community and "country" that are implied by "nation." The popular *Minerva Malay-English Dictionary* offers the definition of *negara* as "a nation, a state," although the Echols-Shadily *Kamus Indonesia-Inggris* attempts a more precise definition, asserting that *negara* translates as "state" and *negeri* as "country." In my experience, *negara* is used interchangeably to refer to both nation and state, with *negeri* sometimes used to more directly denote "country" or "nation."

CHAPTER 3

1. Laura Nader's extensive scholarship regarding the anthropology of law is generally associated with this approach, particularly the anthology *The Disputing Process: Law in Ten Societies* (coedited with H.F. Todd, 1978) and her ethnography of law, disputes, and "harmony ideologies" in Mexico, *Harmony Ideology* (1990). Works by Collier (1988), Merry (1990), Parnell (1989), and Starr (1978) also make the disputing process the center of their analyses of law.

2. Previous efforts to eradicate "squatter" colonies in Kuala Lumpur had resulted in a great deal of protest and the formation of a number of political groups organized explicitly to oppose the state's policies regarding land development in the 1980s and 1990s. Local accounts of these struggles circulated widely in Kuala Lumpur and other urban areas in Malaysia in the form of pamphlets such as "*Peneroka Bandar Menuntut Keadilan*" [Urban Pioneers Demand Justice] (Mohd 1994).

3. The notion of right as rooted in possibility is also important in Lefebvre's notion of urban residents "right to the city" (Lefebvre 1996, 2003). Lefebvre's concept of rights in relation to everyday city life is dealt with in detail in Chapter 4.

4. Following Bergson's understanding of the material experience of time (Bergson 1991, 2001).

5. These enactments were in force in the Federated Malay States (Perak, Selangor, Negeri Sembilan, and Pahang). The Unfederated Malay States (Perlis, Terengganu, Kelantan, Kedah, and Johor) had their own land enactments that remained in force until the unified Malayan Land Code was passed in 1965, eight years after independence. Complicating matters further, the English Deeds systems prevailed in the former Straits Settlements of Penang and Melaka until 1965 as well (Andaya and Andaya 1982, 182–184; Salleh 2001, 11–13).

6. Section 340(2) of the National Land Code of 1965 states that title shall not be defensible in cases of fraud, misrepresentation, forgery, insufficient or void instrument, or unlawful acquisition.

7. Individual exceptions due to Malay custom are not specifically cited in the National Land Code of 1965, but certain precedents established through judicial review have established *adat* as a legitimate contextual factor in challenging the supremacy of land title. See *Kiah v. Som* [1953] 19 M.L.J. 82, and *Roberts vs. Ummi Khalthom* [1966] 1 M.L.J. 163.

8. Constitutionally the state authority is the absolute owner of all land within its territory. Alienation of land, therefore, is the authority's power to dispose of land to any grantee deemed fit. The authority's powers of disposal are: (1) to alienate land for a term not exceeding ninety-nine years or, in certain cases, in perpetuity; (2) to reserve state land and grant leases of reserved land; (3) to grant temporary occupation licenses in respect to state land, reserved land, and mining land; (4) to permit the extraction and removal of rock material; (5) to permit the use of air space on or above state land or reserved land (Land Acquistion [Amended] Act of 1991, s.42; see also Harding 1996; Salleh 2001).

9. "Scheduled" in this usage refers to the specific parcel of land subject to acquisition by the state for the public good.

10. Section 8(3) of the amended act is essentially the same as in previous versions of the law, therefore precedents established before 1991 remain citable.

11. The plaintiffs in *Syed* asserted that the Johore State Authority must make a more specific citation of intended use and its relation to the land under declaration before any mandated acquisition could be enforced. Viscount Dilhorne, in his judgment, clearly rebuffed this line of argument, stating that "the Act imposed no obligation on the acquiring authority to produce a plan for inspection which shows how the land to be acquired is to be zoned." Leaving nothing to chance, the presiding judge emphasized the point: "In the absence of bad faith, which in the instant case is negatived by concurrent findings of fact in the courts

below, this subsection renders it not possible to challenge its validity by asserting that some of the land to which it relates is not needed for the purposes stated or that the land is in fact wanted for purposes other than those specified." See *Syed Omar bin Abdullah Rahman Taha Alsagoff and Anor. v. Government of Johore* [1979] 1 M.L.J. 49.

12. The state authority, under section 3 of the act, must give public notice of its intent to acquire a tract of land. This notice must be published in the *Gazette*, posted in the District Land Office, and (in theory) in a public place in the *mukim* or township in which the land to be acquired is situated. Once announced, the land must be surveyed and then, with twenty-one days' notice, the authority must schedule an inquiry regarding proper compensation. Affected landowners can raise objections over the measurement of the land, the amount of compensation, the person to whom the compensation is to be paid, and/or the apportionment of the compensation. Objections must be made in writing and referred to the state collector, whose decisions regarding such claims are considered final (Salleh 2001, 267–272). It is important to note that this process only refers to proper compensation and does not allow for broader challenges regarding the acquisition itself. Decisions regarding acquisition are not subject to public debate (a position upheld by the courts in *S. Kulasingam and Anor. v. Commission of Lands, Federal Territory and Ors.* [1982] 1 M.L.J. 204), and only in instances of utterly incompetent execution of formal procedure have claims of bad faith against the authority been upheld (see *Pemungut Hasil Tanah Daerah Barat Daya, Pulau Pinang v. Ong Gaik Khoo* [1983] 2 M.L.J. 35, where the justices invalidated a compensation settlement due to the fact that the valuation of the land was carried out in 1974 but not actually paid to the claimant until 1981).

13. A pseudonym.

14. The name of this neighborhood has been changed.

15. Dr. Kurukkal is referring to the widespread belief that major development projects are often conceived and approved according to their potential to make money for the government ministers involved with such projects.

16. Dr. Kurukkal's estimate. I could not locate any official documents or media reports that verified his claim.

17. The independently produced pamphlet *Peneroka Bandar Menuntut Keadilan* (Urban Pioneers Demand Justice) details the struggle over land in Kuala Lumpur between urban *kampung* residents, activists, property developers, and government officials (Mohd 1994). Written on behalf of the Support Committee for Urban Pioneers, the pamphlet explains and promotes the organization's explicit strategy of mixing public protest with attempts to seek relief through the Malaysian judiciary. Openly critical of the government and quick to highlight the successes of the group's efforts, the pamphlet provides a blueprint for action that community organizations dominated by the middle class tend to distance themselves from. Although sometimes successful in their opposition to the demolition

of urban *kampung* communities, members of the Support Committee and Save Our Selves (Penang) had also been arrested under the Internal Security Act due to their political activism (Suarat Rakyat Malaysia 2000). Dr. Kurukkal's efforts to work closely with the local Brickfields police should be understood in this context.

18. A pseudonym.

19. Ethnographic studies regarding bureaucrats and bureaucratic processes also include Alexander (2002), Brunn and Williams (1993), Gilboy (1991), Pardo (1996), and Rosen (1989).

20. A pseudonym.

21. A pseudonym.

22. Goh Ban Lee confirms Dr. Lim's statement, writing: "Generally, it is fair to say that Malaysians do not have access to important and useful information primarily because the government, which is the biggest source of data, is rather stringent in disseminating them. There is a high degree of fetishism for the *sulit* stamp among Malaysian civil servants as evidenced by its generous usage. Furthermore, the amendment to the Official Secrets Act in 1986 only serves to cement the widespread belief that politicians want secrecy" (Goh 1991, 110). The reference to the use of the "*sulit* stamp" is significant. The term *rahasia* more directly captures the connotation of "secret" or "confidential" in English. *Sulit* can mean both "secret" and "difficult." This duality seems to mirror the ambiguous situation both bureaucrats and residents face in dealing with information pertaining to urban development projects.

23. The name of the restaurant has been changed.

24. This restaurant was then operating with more than twice the staff needed, as the owners felt it would be unduly harsh to fire anyone, even under these circumstances.

25. It is understandable that residents in *Kampung Khatijah* would be unable or unwilling to talk at length during the actual time of their removal from Brickfields, particularly with the police standing watch over the event. One can reasonably assume that they were feeling a combination of shock and mistrust of the researcher at this time. The inability to narrate what was happening/had happened remained strong well after these removals, however, for both unregistered residents and those whose legal homes or businesses disappeared. The owners of Sri Radha were still unable or unwilling to talk at length about their sudden move ten months after the fact.

26. For more regarding the general issue of how the interplay of how institutions organize space and the ability of those inhabiting such spaces to imagine future possibilities, see Desjarlais (1997), Massumi (2002), and Poole (2004).

27. Bowen (2004) and Peletz (2002) have observed similar strategies in Islamic courts in Indonesia and Malaysia. Questions of equality and process unfold differently in these settings, however, due to the fact the dispute processing in these courts is governed by Islamic legal codes that conceptualize justice and

the proper execution of the law in markedly different terms than their "secular" counterparts.

28. The fact that many who operate in informal business sectors attempt to simultaneously evade the law and to restructure their enterprise as an openly legal business is discussed at greater length in works by Ferme (2001, 2004), Guyer (2004), Tsai (2002), and Winn (1994).

29. Despite Najwa's semi-authoritative claim regarding the building's imminent disappearance, the structure in question remained standing as of December 2006.

30. The "five-foot way" refers to the narrow area between colonial-era shophouses and the street. British city planners mandated a distance of five feet between the entrance to the building and the street during colonial times to provide a space for pedestrians to safely circulate on foot. Use of these frontage areas was a continued source of conflict between business owners and the colonial government, since traders would often crowd these areas with goods for sale or obstruct the path in some other manner (Yeoh 1996).

31. The women's branch of the United Malays National Organization.

32. Due to heat and vehicular traffic during the day, most heavy construction related to KL Monorail took place in the evening and early morning hours.

33. The financial crisis of 1997–98.

CHAPTER 4

1. Ethnicity is often cited in academic works as the primary factor shaping the character of urban space in Malaysia generally as well (Brookfield, Hadi, and Mahmud 1991; Jesudason 1989; Provencher 1971).

2. According to the 2000 census Indians (38%), Chinese (25%), and Malays (23%) were all numerically significant ethnic communities in Brickfields. For a more detailed analysis of census data for Brickfields since 1980 see the chart provided in the Introduction.

3. See Chapter 3 for a more detailed discussion of the threat of displacement in Brickfields.

4. For discussion of this phenomenon in other locations see Fortier (1999) and Guano (2004).

5. Rorty's concept of the figure also resonates with Lévi-Strauss' assertion that figures associated with myths provide a means to express one's identity through the creation of borders between nature and culture (Lévi-Strauss 1969). The process of "othering" in this sense is confronting persons or institutions who simultaneously appear to be natural and unnatural and finding a means of indexing oneself in relation to such problematic figures. While Hannerz (1980) warns us that we should not read Lévi-Strauss too literally into contemporary urban settings, his understanding of mythic figures and their role in the creation of boundaries resembles Rorty's theorization of personhood and cultural practices.

6. This reworking of the outsider figure by Brickfields residents resembles Desjarlais' description of the ways in which residents in Boston's Station Street Shelter reformulated the figures of the mentally ill homeless person and the "normal" (Desjarlais 1997).

7. Federal Constitution of Malaysia, Article 153(1). Martinez (2001) and Nagata (1997) have argued that in recent times Islam has become the most salient characteristic in legally defining who is a Malay. The other two characteristics cited by the constitution are language and custom.

8. I understand the tendency of my interlocutors attempts to "imagine how outsiders imagine us" as a form of *intimacy* in much the same way that Hannerz (invoking Simmel) describes how intersecting fields of social practice produce feelings of belonging for individual subjects that cut across racial, linguistic, religious, or occupational identities. Although Hannerz implies that such intimacy displaces the importance of face-to-face contacts, Herzfeld notes that this intimate space may actually intensify the felt solidity of "insider/outsider" borders in urban settings (Hannerz 1980, 1992; Herzfeld 2001; Simmel 1964).

9. Scholarly works that engage the perception that Malaysian Indians are "outsiders" within mainstream Malaysian society include studies of religious practice (Ackerman and Lee 1988; Collins 1997; Willford 2006a), urban life (Mearns 1995), economic life (Jain 1970; Jomo 1988; Ramachandran 1994; Ramasamy 1994), and general studies of Indians and ethnic identity in Malaysian society (Arasaratnam 1970; Mearns 1986; Sandhu 1969; Stenson 1980; Wiebe and Mariappan 1978). Sababathy Venugopal (1996) also points out that this perception often serves as a backdrop in many Tamil-language novels written by Malaysian Tamil writers since 1957 and claims that the figure of the outsider is a strong theme in K.S. Maniam's English-language novels (*The Return*, 1981; *In a Far Country*, 1993) and short stories (collected in *Haunting the Tiger*, 1996).

10. In this section I focus primarily on my interview with Chandra, although those who I interviewed for this project commonly held many of the same ideas and sentiments that he expressed.

11. Ground was broken on Petaling Jaya in February 1952.

12. "Ceylonese" is a term in common use in Malaysia for families or individuals whose ancestors originally emigrated from colonial Ceylon. Despite the fact that Ceylon is presently known as Sri Lanka, the original term is still used. This group is also sometimes referred to as "Jaffna Tamils."

13. Sentul is an area located north of downtown Kuala Lumpur that was undergoing a similar process of urban development. Like Brickfields, Sentul was historically populated by Malaysian Railway workers and is generally believed to be a predominantly Indian neighborhood.

14. The tension between welcoming urban development projects as modes of improving everyday life in cities and resisting the same development strategies due to their potentially disruptive and homogenizing impact is not limited to the ex-

perience of urban development in Kuala Lumpur. Judith Nagata's work regarding city planning and heritage preservation efforts in Penang clearly illustrates a similar tension (Nagata 2001; see also Goh 2001; Khoo 1993).

15. Deleuze traces the shifting terrain of the Good in relation to the law when he marks the transition from the law being a secondary power related to a notion of a higher good in classical conceptions to the modern understanding of law as the foundational source of the Good. He writes that "this means that the law no longer has its foundation in some higher principle from which it would derive its authority, but that is it self-grounded and valid solely by virtue of its own form. For the first time we can now speak of the law, regarded as an absolute, without further specification or reference to an object." Deleuze notes that one concrete result of this shift is that, without reference to a superior principle of the Good, subjects of the law cannot know what the Good is. Thus, simply obeying the law becomes the highest Good (Deleuze 1989b, 81–90; capitalization in original). For Chandra and many other Brickfields residents, articulating a fidelity to the Good as articulated by the state and the Good as understood through local principles of justice generated the potential of being estranged from both and from a sense of the Good generally.

16. Because Mr. Rama often worked seven days a week in his food stall, home interviews were impossible to arrange with him. When he did take a day off, Mr. Rama understandably guarded his time off and never agreed to allow me to interview him at home. Like many of the interviews cited in this book, my encounters with Mr. Rama were structured by the fact that our conversations had to be folded into the rhythm of my interlocutor's schedule.

17. The fundamental importance of seeing and knowing one's neighbors resonates with Cavell's claim that "being human is aspiring to be seen as human" (Cavell 1999, 399). Regarding Southeast Asia, the *slematan* (ritual feast) has been discussed as an important practice in Malay social life by which individuals can "see and be seen" in public contexts (Geertz 1960; Robinson 1995). More recently, Klima engages Thai funerary rites and modes of commemoration as the "simultaneous demand for and impossibility of recognition"(Klima 2002, 15), linking the desire to be recognized to complex ethical and political negotiations in Thai national politics.

18. Poole's work regarding the "endless and unpredictable circulation of juridical paperwork" (2004) within the Peruvian judicial system and the ambiguity of individual subjects in relation to the processes of the state is a similar example of this phenomenon in Latin America.

19. Malaysian scholar Syed Hussein Alatas has written at length about the nature and function of "corruption" in society (1990). Arguing for a universal definition of corruption (1–4, 109), Alatas offers a systematic typology of what he understands as the forms of corruption found in all societies. Although his work offers a passionate argument against corruption at the state level, Alatas's types are inadequately tuned to understanding how the institution of the law and local un-

derstandings of justice and association constitute everyday practice for individual subjects. In particular, the fact that Alatas clearly relies on a notion of "the moral" (11) without defining either "the Good" or "the law" severely limits the usefulness of his framework in discussing local practices.

20. Khan and Jomo define rent seeking as "activities which seek to create, maintain or change the rights and institutions on which particular rents are based" (Khan and Jomo 2000, 5). "Rent" refers to incomes which are "above normal" in some sense. The concept of "normal" functions as the benchmark for what an individual or firm should receive in a competitive market. As the authors admit, "rent" is an unstable concept, because the determination of what a normal income "should" be is rooted in social factors that cannot be analyzed solely in terms of economic science. Thus, rent seeking can refer to both legal and illegal practices and produce different effects across countries and regions.

21. Tsai's account of how business owners in China mobilize complex financial and social resources in relation to formal state institutions regarding economic development and financial regulation stands out as an exception to my claim regarding the literature on rent seeking and corruption (Tsai 2002).

22. Bitterness regarding the "unfair" advantage such practices could yield was generally expressed when my interlocutors described someone perceived to be a competitor. In such contexts "illegality" was cited from a strategic point of view rather than as a categorical moral differentiation.

23. Schwartz (1996) observes that "forgery is but the extreme of copying: the extreme of fair copying, when what is forged is indiscernible from the original; the extreme of foul copying, when what is forged is a fabrication passed off in the name or style of another person or era" (219). Schwartz's insight highlights the ambiguously performative aspect of the practices of counterfeiting that I am focusing on in this section. In particular, these forms of counterfeiting are simultaneously a reenactment of the law (fair copy, 224) and an appropriation of it (foul copy, 225), making it difficult at the level of everyday life to separate forms of copying and documentation *required* by the law from those acts of copying or forgery that formally *violate* the law.

24. The essays found in *Ethnography at the Edge: Crime, Deviance, and Field Research* (Ferrell and Hamm eds. 1998), explore the difficulties in conducting fieldwork related to homelessness (Fleisher, Arrigo), the military and state terror (Kraska, Hamm), sex work (Kane, Mattley), drug use (Jacobs, Weisheit), and dangerous criminal activities generally (Tunnell, Lyng).

25. All proper names and the name of the business have been changed.

26. Most of the specific contextual and biographical information regarding this business and its owner is intentionally withheld here because I am describing a transaction that took place in their shop that could make them vulnerable to legal action or harassment by the authorities if they were identified.

27. The irony that the professional tools for the legal duplication of documents on hand in the print shop were used to produce an alternate version of the negotiated contract should be noted here. The fact that "real" copies attesting to a "fake" version of an agreement to produce "fair" reproductions of college test booklets reinforces the "copy/forgery" connection that Schwartz makes regarding the "culture" of the copy generally (Schwartz 1996). The technological capacity to duplicate these documents *at every stage of the process* understandably complicated matters further for both parties in that they had to forge a unitary documentary record of a negotiation that was explicitly being conducted on multiple levels.

28. "In modern thought irony and humor take on a new form: they are now directed at a subversion of the law. . . . Irony is [the] process or movement which bypasses the law as a merely secondary power and aims at transcending it toward a higher principle. But what if the higher principle no longer exists, and if the Good can no longer provide a basis for the law or a justification of its power?" (Deleuze 1989b, 86). Deleuze wrote these lines specifically in reference to the relation of the law and the Good to the works of Sade and Sacher-Masoch. In my view, his general insight applies here as well.

29. Mrs. Ramachandran switched to English when speaking directly with me.

30. I omitted proper names and identifying information when discussing this case with Tan Piow.

31. Popular shock over the connections between Chinese and Indian gangs was, for many Brickfields residents, itself surprising, as many explained in interviews that such connections had existed for at least the previous decade among criminal groups active in Brickfields.

32. Tafe College, an unaccredited vocational school loosely associated with the Malaysian Indian Congress and located in the nearby city of Seremban, had been plagued with accusations of improper management by students in the six months prior to the destruction of the hostel. Several less serious acts of vandalism, linked to protests over management issues and the fact that the school remained unrecognized by the Education Ministry, had taken place during the time leading up to the incident at the hostel in July 2002. Despite the obvious link between student dissatisfaction with the school and the increasingly serious vandalism that took place (mentions of both the mismanagement and student dissatisfaction did appear in media reports), the "hook" for the popular media and the line of investigation for the police was the fact that young Indian men engaging in violent acts "must" be gangsters.

33. Similar situations of informal or illegal social groups providing an alternative local order have been observed in relation to drug gangs (Bourgois 1995), and informal networks among the urban homeless (Desjarlais 1997) and migrant workers (Ferguson 1999).

34. I do not name these sites here because doing so and identifying their connection to the local drug trade could endanger those who frequent them. Given

the presence of legal homes and businesses and the fact that it is nearly impossible to live in Brickfields and not at some point circulate through these sites, such detail would only serve to incriminate everyone, whether involved in illegal activity or not. Raymond's specific information matched the accounts of others I interviewed who have some knowledge of these organizations and practices, and also matched my own observations.

35. Tan Piow told me his version of the fruit seller's biography on condition that I not approach the man for an interview directly. He convincingly argued that it could be dangerous for both of us if the subject of our conversations were more widely known and would, at the very least, cause considerable embarrassment for the old man. Due to the fact that it was widely known that I spoke at length with Tan Piow about Brickfields, I agreed to this request and did not interview the fruit seller, making independent confirmation of Tan Piow's story from the seller himself impossible.

36. Tan Piow was one of the few persons I interviewed who would talk in great detail about the contemporary relationship between the gangs and everyday life in Brickfields. Although nearly every person I interviewed would vaguely acknowledge such relationships, they were understandably reluctant to provide specific information or to speak more personally about their own experiences with these groups. It was much more common for my interlocutors to direct the conversation away from the details of the present toward the recounting of "legendary" stories from the 1950s and 1960s. The personal risk of talking to the researcher about these issues was evident in these interactions, and Tan Piow would only speak with some degree of detail after I had known him for over a year.

37. Sally Engle Merry (1981) has detailed how perceptions of criminality, authority, and danger are markedly different between residents of "dangerous" neighborhoods and outsiders who know of the area's reputation. Merry found that resident insiders in the American neighborhood she examined often explicitly attempted to "manage" contacts with potentially dangerous people and groups and reports that many of the residents she surveyed felt that these strategies of engagement made the area feel safer overall. In a later study, Philippe Bourgois (1995) maps the organizational hierarchy of an East Harlem group engaged in selling crack cocaine and details how the internal discipline of the group was known to, and engaged by, local residents. While these engagements were often ambiguous and unpredictable, Bourgois marks the complex perceptions held by neighborhood insiders of local groups that sold drugs, compared to the relatively general and consistently negative perceptions of outsiders.

38. A diverse range of anthropologists have asserted that the individual self should not be understood as a unitary entity, including Desjarlais (1992, 1997, 2003), Ewing (1990), Geertz (1973), Herzfeld (1997), Klima (2002), and Mauss (1973).

39. My understanding of how abstract figures of identity shape local understandings of self and place in Brickfields is similar to that of Nagata (1979), Goh (2001), and Guinness (1992), who emphasize the interrelationships between capitalism, ethnic identity, and political life in their characterizations of Malaysian urban transformations.

CHAPTER 5

1. The issue of Islamic reform efforts that concretely engage institutions commonly understood as secular has also been discussed in reference to Afghanistan (Barfield 2005), Egypt (Hirschkind 2006; Singerman 2005; Starrett 1998; Wickham 2002), Indonesia (Bowen 2004; Hefner 2000, 2005) Pakistan (Khan 2006; Nasr 1996; Zaman 2002, 2005), and Turkey (Göle 1996; Mehmet 1990; Navaro-Yashin 2002; White 2005).

2. A number of important works in recent years have carefully illustrated the decisive conjunctures of colonial economies, governmental strategies, and concepts regarding "traditional" religious and cultural practices that resulted in the violent and irreversible separation of large populations from their birthplaces in India, including Arasaratnam (1970), Baxstrom (2000), Breman (1989), Jain (1970), Kaur (2001), Kelly (1991), Sandhu (1969), Sandhu and Mani (1993), Tinker (1974), and van der Veer (1995).

3. The Special Branch is the federal investigative police unit, roughly equivalent to the Federal Bureau of Investigation in the United States.

4. The Federal Constitution of Malaysia was ratified in 1957. For discussion of the complex process of negotiation that took place over ethnic, linguistic, and religious issues in the process leading up to the ratification of the document see Fernando (2002); Harding (1996); Harper (1999); Mohamed (1974); Ongkili (1985).

5. *Hudud* law generally refers to crimes such as theft, adultery, and apostasy. Punishment is most often corporal, including amputations, whippings, imprisonment, and for the most serious crimes, death by stoning.

6. PAS attempted to enact *hudud* laws in Kelantan in 1993 and in Terengganu in 2002.

7. After meeting in the United States with President George W. Bush in June 2002, Mahathir unilaterally amended the proclamation to include the word "fundamentalist." During the meetings in Washington, Bush had praised Malaysia's "moderate" Islam, leading to some criticism in the local Malaysian press regarding how "Islamic" Mahathir's Islamic state really was. Upon returning to Malaysia, Mahathir angrily rebutted these criticisms, noting that Malaysia is actually a "Fundamentalist Islamic State" (*Malaysiakini.com*, June 19, 2002).

8. Munisvaran and Mariamman are the most popular village deities in South India and, hence, are quite commonly worshipped by Malaysian Hindus well.

Munisvaran is a male guardian deity who is generally associated with Kali and the mode of worship in temples or shrines devoted to him is generally non-agamic and at times involves mediums, states of possession, and the sacrifice of animals (in Malaysia the sacrificial animal is normally a goat). Mariamman is a female deity identified with Sakti and is sought out, among other things, to ward off sickness (especially smallpox) and, in rural areas, crop failure. Ackerman and Lee (1988) provide an analysis of the "Sanskritization" of village temples in Malaysia. Although not mentioned directly by Ackerman and Lee, the role of monastic orders in relation to issues of caste and the role of the Brahman is considered a crucial link in much of the scholarship regarding the division that the writers are addressing here (Dumont 1970). For a critique of Dumont's understanding of the everyday and the role of caste and the Brahman see Das (1982). Arasaratnam (1970), Jain (1970), Rajah (2000), Ramasamy (1994), and Ramasamy (1984) address various aspects of everyday practice and the transformation of caste among Malaysian Tamils.

9. Badawi was elevated to prime minister in October of 2003.

10. Malaysia came into being in 1963, replacing the previous name "Malaya" with the addition of Singapore (which then separated from Malaysia in 1965) and the Borneo territories of Sabah and Sarawak.

11. Iyngkaran and Kunaletchumy (2002) and Santhiram (1999) examine the specific situation of Tamil students in Malaysian public schools, focusing particularly on issues of Tamil medium primary schools and purported links between student creativity and the specificity of Tamil culture, religion, and language. Both texts are published locally in Malaysia through the private CHILD (Child Information, Learning, and Development) Center and are often cited as support for educational initiatives that specifically target Malaysian Tamil schoolchildren.

12. Collins argues that Thaipusam constitutes a form of submerged protest against the relative exclusion of Malaysian Indians from public life. Willford disagrees with this assessment, noting that Thaipusam serves to more unambiguously mark out its participants as Hindus within Malaysian public life, with its more extreme modes of observance representing the community as quite safely Other and thus not a threat at all as long as Muslims themselves do not attempt to observe the festival. As the argument of this chapter makes clear, my own position is closer to Willford's view (Collins 1997; Willford 2006a).

13. A pseudonym.

14. This concept of signature related to the writing technologies of the state is borrowed from Das (2007). See also Derrida (1988).

15. A pseudonym. This interview was conducted in English.

16. It is extremely important to emphasize the irregular, dispersed nature that this form of recognition often takes, particularly in light of events regarding the demolition of Hindu temples that have taken place in the years since I completed the fieldwork for this project. According to media reports between February 22

and November 31, 2006, 74 Hindu temples had been demolished throughout Malaysia (*The Star*, December 19, 2006). Several media commentators, particularly Farish A. Noor, have consistently decried these demolitions and have argued that the destruction of the temples constitutes an example of the increasing "Arabization" of Malaysian society (a relatively new term used to describe the increasing importance of Islam in Malaysian governance) and an impoverished, racist notion of what constitutes a "real" Malaysian. Even though this was not precisely the case in Brickfields during the time I lived there, I generally agree with the analyses offered by Noor and others regarding the recent acceleration of temple demolitions throughout the country. It is critical to point out, however, that the response to these efforts to "cleanse" the countryside of nominally illegal Hindu temples has generally been a strategy of asserting rights under the law for citizens and the assertion of a broad Malaysian Indian identity politics. As I argue throughout this chapter, these positions are unfortunately the weakest from which to mount an effective defense of homes, property, and community for minorities in contemporary Malaysia, and were not the basis of the ability of the Brickfields temples to gain some recognition from the state and remain in the neighborhood in 2002. I would like to thank S. Nagarajan for his continued help in passing on articles and information regarding this issue.

17. Formally, the "State Authority" is defined in Section 5 of the Malaysian Constitution to mean the ruler or *Yang Dipertuan Negeri* (Sultan) of the state. In practical terms, the state authority refers to the individual state government (Salleh 2001, 25).

18. *Adat* is a broad concept that has come to refer to the "local customs" of Malays. Although *adat* is a concept that ranges across Malay communities, it also marks certain contrasts between local communities and it generally refers to a distinctive set of local practices, such as *adat perpatih* as commonly practiced in Negeri Sembilan, or variants of *adat temenggong* found throughout the rest of the peninsula and further localized through reference to "Kelantanese *adat*," "Terengganu *adat*," and so forth. Although most everyday Malays do not find *adat* practices to be in conflict with the tenets of Islam, many Islamic reformers cite *adat* as evidence of the "pre-Islamic" past of Malays (see Bowen 1993; Peletz 1997; Wazir 1992).

19. Precedents regarding "Malay custom or *adat*" relate primarily to differing concepts of movable property (*Kiah v. Som* [1953] 19 M.L.J. 82) and the division of matrimonial property under local notions of *harta sepencarian* (*Roberts v. Ummi Kalthon* [1966] 1 M.L.J. 163). In both cases, the dictates of local *adat*, rooted in interpretations of Islamic law (such as *hibah* in the Roberts case) were found to constitute limited exceptions to the Torrens rule that the "register is everything" (Salleh 2001, 17–19). See Chapter 2 for a more detailed discussion of *adat*.

20. This statement does not imply that every person who worshipped at these small Hindu temples was displaced in this process, as many working-class Tamil

Hindus who lived in and around Brickfields in legally registered apartments continued to visit the temples on a regular basis.

21. For general surveys regarding the ordering of urban space and populations in Southeast Asia see Dale (1999), Evers and Korff (2000), Goh (2001), Kusno (2000), Nagata (2001), Sirat and Ghazali (1999), Sullivan (1992), and Yeoh (1996).

22. Hanuman is the popular monkey deity worshipped primarily in North India; Murugan is a warrior deity commonly worshipped in South India. In actuality, both of these temples more resemble Muniswaran temples, but have adopted more Sanskritic deities as part of the process of Sanskritization, cited by Ackerman and Lee (1988) whereby these village temples now possess the "veneer" of more widely accepted Sanskritic practices. The "village" roots of the Hanuman temple are unclear, but the local character of the Murugan temple is made clear by the fact that it is named *Kuil Muniswaran Murugan* (Muniswaran Murugan Temple). See also Bastin (2002) and Clothey (1978).

23. In general terms, the rites of divination that were reportedly used strongly resemble those common throughout the region. See Bowen (1993), Endicott (1970), Peletz (1993), and Skeat (1965).

24. Authors who explore Tamil worship and ritual practice in Malaysia include Arasaratnam (1970), Collins (1997), Jain (1970), Rajah (2000), and Willford (2006a, 2006b). Ritual practices among Tamils in India are the subject of works by Clothey (1978), Nabokov (2000), and Whitehead (1921), among others.

25. This perception of physical danger was shaped by rumors about events that occurred during the attempted demolition of an unregistered temple on the current site of the Mid-Valley MegaMall, which borders the south end of Brickfields. Construction on the MegaMall was plagued by a number of unusual accidents and persistent equipment failures that were commonly held to be the work of the temple deity. Some local versions of this story recount that the private developer, after having a vision of the deity in his dreams, agreed to reconstruct the temple next to the mall. While these rumors circulated, officials at Mid-Valley refused to offer an alternative explanation (or any explanation at all) as to why a large Hindu temple was constructed at the developer's expense on the north side of the structure. This temple was formally consecrated and opened in June 2002. The force of these rumors was striking in the local context of the construction being carried out in Brickfields, as an official from KL Monorail cited these stories in the course of explaining the corporation's relationship to local temples.

26. See previous section.

27. Mearns (1995) provides a detailed account of Hindu temple practices in Melaka. Daniel (1984), Hancock (2002), Schulman (1980), Trawick (1990), and Younger (2002) examine similar practices in South India. For a study of the consecration of Hindu temples outside of India see Nye (1995).

28. As of October 2001 more than thirty Hindu temples in Kuala Lumpur and Selangor had either been demolished or issued a notice that they were to be de-

molished. Most of these temples were in outlying rural districts, and at one time served nearby communities of Tamil estate laborers. Public Works Minister (and president of the Malaysian Indian Congress) S. Samy Vellu complained publicly that the lack of clear procedures in this matter made it impossible for nominally illegal temples even to attempt to comply with the law. Seemingly unaware of the laws regarding the alienation of land and the legal precedents regarding possessory rights, he was quoted in the *Sun* on October 26, 2001, as saying "How can you say [the temples] are illegal? These temples have been there a long time, why have they been deemed illegal suddenly?"

29. This figure is based on verbal estimates provided to me by members of the temple committees, a KL Monorail representative, and regular members of the temple and its neighbors. The actual figure has not, to my knowledge, ever been publicly announced and no documentation regarding the settlement was forthcoming from official sources.

30. At the time the statement was made to me a final settlement had not been reached.

31. *Tokong* is the term used to denote a small Chinese temple or shrine in Malaysia, as opposed to the word *kuil* that more literally means "temple" in Malay. *Kuil* tends to refer more specifically to Hindu temples or shrines. As both terms would generally be rendered as "temple" in English, I am using "*tokong*" to specifically refer to the *Seng Hong Tokong* here, although I translate the Malay term *kuil* for the other temples mentioned in my narrative.

32. The same Krishna temple discussed previously.

33. All proper names in this section are pseudonyms.

34. I have reconstructed this particular conversation from notes made after the fact. I have chosen to render the conversation in this manner rather than as paraphrased speech in order to give the reader a feel for the casual offhandedness of the conversation and the informal manner in which the question of religious identity was treated in response to my questions.

35. It is possible that one of David's parents is a Christian and the other a Hindu, although he did not relate this directly to me.

36. Normally this small building was not open. Devotees who came to perform daily prayers would do so at the outdoor altars.

37. As the *Seng Hong Tokong* was not registered under the Societies Act of 1966, it possessed no legal right to undertake public possessions. Therefore, the annual Wesak Day procession was technically illegal.

38. He made this statement in English.

39. The members of the *Tokong* allowed me to videotape several spirit possessions and the burning of the ship that culminated the Festival of the Hungry Ghosts over several days in late July 2002. Tan approached me during the ceremony and, while describing the ghosts as they emerged from the river one by one, asked if I was getting them on film.

40. The orientation of present-day rites regarding the removal of hungry ghosts from the human realm represents a transition relative to earlier understandings of the place and utility of these spirits articulated in medieval China, India, and Japan. Originally hungry ghosts were essential to everyday human life because, due to their voracious hunger, they would "consume" waste, especially human waste. In the era of modern urban life and rationalized modes of maintaining hygienic conditions, hungry ghosts now occupy a liminal space between divine and profane worlds and pose a problem of categorization for human believers. See LaFleur (1989) and Orzech (1996).

41. A pseudonym.

42. Ironically, this restaurant was located on the grounds of the Palm Court complex.

43. I met Ramalingam with two other Tamil men I know, one of whom was a graduate student. This student translated the Tamil passages quoted here for me as Ramalingam spoke. This interview with Ramalingam is the only one I conducted that required the use of a translator.

44. Although he could not recall exact dates, Ramalingam's chronology of these events in Brickfields roughly corresponded to a series of widely publicized events that took place in September 1995 in India in which various Shaiva statues were reported to have been accepting offerings of milk.

45. Form 5 is equivalent to the eleventh grade in the American educational system.

Bibliography

Abbas, A. (1997). *Hong Kong: Culture and the Politics of Disappearance*. Minneapolis, University of Minnesota Press.

Abdullah, M.Z., Y.C.M. Che et al., eds. (1998). *Prinsip dan Kaedah Dakwah dalam Arus Pembangunan Malaysia*. Bangi, Penerbit Universiti Kebangsaan Malaysia.

Abel, R.L. (1982). The Contradictions of Informal Justice. *The Politics of Informal Justice*. R.L. Abel, ed. New York, Academic: 1, 2.

Abu-Lughod, J. (1987). "The Islamic City: Historic Myth, Islamic Essence, and Contemporary Relevance." *International Journal of Middle Eastern Studies* 19: 155–176.

Ackerman, S.E. and R.L.M. Lee (1988). *Heaven in Transition: Non-Muslim Religious Innovation and Ethnic Identity in Malaysia*. Kuala Lumpur, Forum.

Adnan, H.N. (1997). *Kuala Lumpur dari Perspektif Haji Abdullah Hukum*. Kuala Lumpur, Berita Publishing.

Ahmad, I. (1978). *Family Law in Malaysia and Singapore*. Singapore, Malayan Law Journal.

Ahmed, A. (1992). *Postmodernism and Islam: Predicament and Promise*. New York, Routledge.

Alatas, S.H. (1990). *Corruption: Its Nature, Causes, and Functions*. Brookfield, VT, Avebury.

Alexander, C. (2002). *Personal States: Making Connections Between People and Bureaucracy in Turkey*. New York, Oxford University Press.

Allen, J.D.V. (1967). *The Malayan Union*. New Haven, CT, Yale University Press.

Andaya, B.W. and L.Y. Andaya (1982). *A History of Malaysia*. London, Macmillan.

Anderson, B. (1983). *Imagined Communities: Reflections on the Origin and Spread of Nationalism*. New York, Verso.

Anderson, B. (1990). *Language and Power: Exploring Political Cultures in Indonesia*. Ithaca, NY, Cornell University Press.

Ang, I. (1993). "To Be or Not to Be Chinese: Diaspora, Culture, and Postmodern Ethnicity." *Southeast Asian Journal of Social Science* 21 (1): 1–17.

Appadurai, A. (1996). *Modernity at Large: Cultural Dimensions of Globalization*. Minneapolis, University of Minnesota Press.

Arasaratnam, S. (1970). *Indians in Malaysia and Singapore*. Kuala Lumpur, Oxford University Press.

Arthurs, H.W. (1985). *Without the Law: Administrative Justice and Legal Pluralism in Nineteenth Century England*. Toronto, University of Toronto Press.

Asad, T. (1993). *Genealogies of Religion: Discipline and Reasons of Power in Christianity and Islam*. Baltimore, MD, Johns Hopkins University Press.

Asad, T. (2003). *Formations of the Secular: Christianity, Islam, Modernity*. Stanford, CA, Stanford University Press.

Asad, T. (2006). Responses. *Powers of the Secular Modern: Talal Asad and His Interlocutors*. D. Scott and C. Hirschkind, eds. Stanford, CA, Stanford University Press: 206–242.

Axel, B.K. (1996). "Time and Threat: Questioning the Production of the Diaspora as an Object of Study." *History and Anthropology* 9(2): 415–443.

Axel, B.K. (2001). *The Nation's Tortured Body: Violence, Representation, and the Formation of a Sikh Diaspora*. Durham, NC, Duke University Press.

Barfield, T. (2005). An Islamic State Is a State Run by Good Muslims: Religion as a Way of Life and Not an Ideology in Afghanistan. *Remaking Muslim Politics: Pluralism, Contestation, Democratization*. R.W. Hefner, ed. Princeton, NJ, Princeton University Press: 213–239.

Barlow, H.S. (1995). *Swettenham*. Kuala Lumpur, Southdene.

Bastin, R. (2002). *The Domain of Constant Excess: Plural Worship at the Munnesvaram Temples in Sri Lanka*. New York, Berghahn Books.

Baxstrom, R. (2000). "Governmentality, Bio-power, and the Emergence of the Malayan-Tamil Subject on the Plantations of Colonial Malaya." *Crossroads: An Interdisciplinary Journal of Southeast Asian Studies* 14(2): 49–78.

Becker, G. (1976). *The Economic Approach to Human Behavior*. Chicago, University of Chicago Press.

Benda-Beckmann, K.V. and F. Strijbosch, eds. (1986). *Anthropology of Law in the Netherlands: Essays in Legal Pluralism*. Dordrecht, Foris.

Benjamin, W. (1968). Theses on the Philosophy of History. *Illuminations: Essays and Reflections*. H. Arendt, ed. New York, Schocken.

Bentley, C. (1984). "Hermeneutics and World Construction in Maranao Disputing." *American Ethnologist* 11: 642–655.

Bergson, H. (1991). *Matter and Memory*. New York, Zone Books.

Bergson, H. (1998). *Creative Evolution*. Mineola, NY, Dover Books.

Bergson, H. (2001). *Time and Free Will*. Mineola, NY, Dover Books.

Bestor, T.C. (1989). *Neighborhood Tokyo*. Stanford, CA, Stanford University Press.

Bhabha, H. (1994). *The Location of Culture*. New York, Routledge.

Blythe, W.L. (1969). *The Impact of Chinese Secret Societies in Malaya*. London, Oxford University Press.

Bohannan, P. (1957). *Justice and Judgement Among the Tiv*. London, Oxford University Press.

Bourdieu, P. (1980). *The Logic of Practice*. Stanford, CA, Stanford University Press.

Bourgois, P. (1995). *In Search of Respect: Selling Crack in El Barrio*. Cambridge, Cambridge University Press.

Bowen, J.R. (1993). *Muslims Through Discourse: Religion and Ritual in Gayo Society*. Princeton, NJ, Princeton University Press.

Bowen, J.R. (2004). *Islam, Law, and Equality in Indonesia: An Anthropology of Public Reasoning*. Cambridge, Cambridge University Press.

Breman, J. (1989). *Taming the Coolie Beast: Plantation Society and the Colonial Order in Southeast Asia*. New Delhi, Oxford University Press.

Brenner, S.A. (1998). *The Domestication of Desire: Women, Wealth, and Modernity in Java*. Princeton, NJ, Princeton University Press.

Brookfield, H., A.S. Hadi and Z. Mahmud. (1991). *The City in the Village: The In-Situ Urbanization of Villages, Villagers and Their Land Around Kuala Lumpur, Malaysia*. Singapore, Oxford University Press.

Brunn, S.D. and J.F. Williams (1993). *Cities of the World: World Regional Urban Development*. New York, Harper Collins College Publishers.

Butcher, J.G. (1979). *The British in Malaya 1880–1941: The Social History of a European Community in Colonial South-East Asia*. Kuala Lumpur, Oxford University Press.

Butcher, J.G. (2001). May 13: A Review of Some Controversies in Accounts of the Riots. *Reinventing Malaysia: Reflections on Its Past and Future*. K.S. Jomo, ed. Bangi, Malaysia, Penerbit Universiti Kebangsaan Malaysia: 35–56.

Caldeira, T. (1996). "Fortified Communities." *Public Culture* 8: 303–328.

Caton, S.C. (1990). *"Peaks of Yemen I Summon": Poetry as Cultural Practice in a North Yemeni Tribe*. Berkeley, University of California Press.

Cavell, S. (1999). *The Claim of Reason: Wittgenstein, Skepticism, Morality, and Tragedy*. Cambridge, MA, Harvard University Press.

Chai, H.C. (1967). *The Development of British Malaya 1896–1909*. Kuala Lumpur, Oxford University Press.

Chakrabarty, D. (2000). *Provincializing Europe: Postcolonial Thought and Historical Difference*. Princeton, NJ, Princeton University Press.

Chan, K.B. and C.S.N. Chiang (1994). *Stepping Out: The Making of Chinese Entrepreneurs*. Singapore, Simon and Schuster.

Chandra, M. (1987). *Islamic Resurgence in Malaysia*. Kuala Lumpur, Fajar Bakti.

Chatterjee, P. (1993). *The Nation and Its Fragments: Colonial and Postcolonial Histories*. Princeton, NJ, Princeton University Press.

Cheah, B.K. (1979). "The Japanese Occupation of Malaya, 1941–45: Ibrahim Yaacob and the Struggle for Indonesian Raya." *Indonesia* 28 (October).

Chen, H.S. (1992). *Chinatown No More: Taiwan Immigrants in Contemporary New York*. Ithaca, NY, Cornell University Press.

Chin, A. (1995). *The Communist Party of Malaya: The Inside Story*. Kuala Lumpur, Vinpress.

Chin, C.B.N. (1998). *In Service and Servitude: Foreign Female Domestic Workers and the Malaysian "Modernity" Project*. New York, Columbia University Press.

Chin, K.O. (1976). *Malaya Upside Down*. Singapore, Federal Press.

Clothey, F.W. (1978). *Many Faces of Murukan: The History and Meaning of a South Indian God*. The Hague, Mouton Publishers.

Coates, J. (1992). *Suppressing Insurgency: An Analysis of the Malayan Emergency, 1948–54*. Boulder, CO, Westview Press.

Cohn, B.S. (1996). *Colonialism and Its Forms of Knowledge: The British in India*. Princeton, NJ, Princeton University Press.

Collier, J.F. (1988). *Marriage and Inequality in Classless Societies*. Stanford, CA, Stanford University Press.

Collins, E.F. (1997). *Pierced by Murugan's Lance: Ritual, Power, and Moral Redemption Among Malaysian Hindus*. DeKalb, Northern Illinois University Press.

Comaroff, J. (1997). "The Portrait of an Unknown South African: Identity in a Global Age." *Macalester International* 4(Spring).

Comaroff, J. and J.L. Comaroff (1997). *Of Revelation and Revolution: The Dialectics of Modernity on a South African Frontier*. Chicago, University of Chicago Press.

Comaroff, J.L. and S. Roberts (1981). *Rules and Processes: The Cultural Logic of Dispute in an African Context*. Chicago, University of Chicago Press.

Comber, L. (1959). *Chinese Secret Societies in Malaya*. New York, Association for Asian Studies.

Comber, L. (1983). *13 May 1969: A Historical Survey of Sino-Malay Relations*. Singapore, Graham Brash.

Concannon, T.A.L. (1955). "A New Town in Malaya: Petaling Jaya, Kuala Lumpur." *The Malayan Journal of Tropical Geography* 5: 39–43.

Concannon, T.A.L. (1960). *Building a City Within a City*. Kuala Lumpur, Caxton Press.

Connolly, W.E. (1999). *Why I Am Not a Secularist*. Minneapolis, University of Minnesota Press.

Connolly, W.E. (2002). *Neuropolitics: Thinking, Culture, Speed*. Minneapolis, University of Minnesota Press.

Connolly, W.E. (2005). *Pluralism*. Durham, NC, Duke University Press.

Connolly, W.E. (2006). Europe: A Minor Tradition. *Powers of the Secular Modern: Talal Asad and His Interlocutors*. D. Scott and C. Hirschkind, eds. Stanford, CA, Stanford University Press: 75–92.

Coronil, F. (1997). *The Magical State: Nature, Money, and Modernity in Venezuela*. Chicago, University of Chicago Press.

Cowan, C.D. (1961). *Nineteenth-Century Malaya: The Origins of British Political Control*. London, Oxford University Press.

Crouch, H. (1996). *Government and Society in Malaysia*. Ithaca, NY, Cornell University Press.

Dale, O.J. (1999). *Urban Planning in Singapore: The Transformation of a City*. Kuala Lumpur, Oxford University Press.

Dalton, C. (1942). *Men of Malaya*. London, Eldon Press.

Daniel, E.V. (1984). *Fluid Signs: Being a Person the Tamil Way*. Berkeley, University of California Press.

Das, V. (1982). *Structure and Cognition: Aspects of Hindu Caste and Ritual*. Delhi, Oxford University Press.

Das, V. (2000). The Practice of Organ Transplants: Networks, Documents, Translations. *Living and Working with the New Medical Technologies: Intersections of Inquiry*. M. Lock, A. Young and A. Cambrosio, eds. Cambridge, Cambridge University Press: 263–287.

Das, V. (2007). *Life and Words: Violence and the Decent into the Ordinary*. Berkeley, University of California Press.

Das, V., A. Kleinman et al., eds. (2000). *Violence and Subjectivity*. Berkeley, University of California Press.

Das, V., A. Kleinman et al., eds. (2001). *Remaking a World: Violence, Social Suffering, and Recovery*. Berkeley, University of California Press.

Das, V. and D. Poole (2004). The State and Its Margins: Comparative Ethnographies. *Anthropology in the Margins of the State*. V. Das and D. Poole, eds. Santa Fe, School of American Research.

de Silva, H.M.A. (1998). *100 Years of the Buddhist Maha Vihara*. Kuala Lumpur, Sasana Abhiwurdhi Wardhana Society.

de Vries, H. (1999). *Philosophy and the Turn to Religion*. Baltimore, Johns Hopkins University Press.

de Vries, H. (2001). Introduction. *Religion and Media*. H. de Vries and S. Weber, eds. Stanford, CA, Stanford University Press.

Deeb, L. (2006). *An Enchanted Modern: Gender and Public Piety in Shi'i Lebanon*. Princeton, NJ, Princeton University Press.

Deleuze, G. (1986). *Cinema 1: The Movement-Image*. Minneapolis, University of Minnesota Press.

Deleuze, G. (1989a). *Cinema 2: The Time-Image*. Minneapolis, University of Minnesota Press.

Deleuze, G. (1989b). *Masochism: Coldness and Cruelty*. New York, Zone Books.

Deleuze, G. (1990). *The Logic of Sense*. New York, Columbia University Press.

Deleuze, G. (1991a). *Bergsonism*. New York, Zone Books.

Deleuze, G. (1991b). *Empiricism and Subjectivity: An Essay on Hume's Theory of Human Nature*. New York, Columbia University Press.

Deleuze, G. (1994). *Difference and Repetition*. New York, Columbia University Press.

Deleuze, G. (1997). *Essays Critical and Clinical*. Minneapolis, University of Minnesota Press.

Deleuze, G. (2000). *Proust and Signs: The Complete Text*. Minneapolis, University of Minnesota Press.

Deleuze, G. (2001). *Pure Immanence: Essays on a Life*. New York, Zone Books.

Deleuze, G. and F. Guattari (1994). *What Is Philosophy?* New York, Columbia University Press.

Derrida, J. (1988). *Limited, Inc.* Evanston, IL, Northwestern University Press.

Desjarlais, R. (1992). *Body and Emotion: The Aesthetics of Illness and Healing in the Nepal Himalayas*. Philadelphia, University of Pennsylvania Press.

Desjarlais, R. (1997). *Shelter Blues: Sanity and Selfhood Among the Homeless*. Philadelphia, University of Pennsylvania Press.

Desjarlais, R. (2003). *Sensory Biographies: Lives and Deaths Among Nepal's Yolmo Buddhists*. Berkeley, University of California Press.

Devji, F. (2005). *Landscapes of the Jihad: Militancy, Morality, Modernity*. Ithaca, NY, Cornell University Press.

Dewan Bandaraya Kuala Lumpur (1982). *Kuala Lumpur Draft Structure Plan*. Kuala Lumpur, Dewan Bandaraya Kuala Lumpur.

Dewan Bandaraya Kuala Lumpur (1990). *Album Kuala Lumpur: 100 Years as a Local Authority*. Kuala Lumpur, Penerbitan Puteries.

Dick, H. and P.J. Rimmer (2003). *Cities, Transport and Communications: The Integration of Southeast Asia since 1850*. New York, Palgrave.

Dillon, R.A. (1991). People in Transition: A Case Study of Indian Squatters in Urban Malaysia: Responses to the Need for Shelter, Livelihood and Their Forced Resettlement. Ph.D. diss., Australian National University.

Dreyfus, H.L. and P. Rabinow (1984). *Michel Foucault, Beyond Structuralism and Hermeneutics*. Chicago, University of Chicago Press.

Dumont, L. (1970). *Homo Hierarchicus: An Essay on the Caste System*. Chicago, University of Chicago Press.

Durkheim, E. (1984). *The Division of Labor in Society*. New York, Free Press.

Eck, D.L. (1998). *Darsan: Seeing the Divine Image in India*. New York, Columbia University Press.

Eck, D.L. (2001). *A New Religious America: How a "Christian Country" Has Now Become the World's Most Religiously Diverse Nation*. San Francisco, HarperSanFrancisco.

Eickelman, D.F. and J. Piscatori (1996). *Muslim Politics*. Princeton, NJ, Princeton University Press.

Endicott, K. (1970). *An Analysis of Malay Magic*. Oxford, Clarendon Press.

Engel, D.M. (1978). *Code and Custom in a Thai Provincial Court: The Interactions of Formal and Informal Systems of Justice*. Tucson, University of Arizona Press.

Englund, H. and J. Leach (2000). "Ethnography and the Meta-Narratives of Modernity." *Current Anthropology* 41(2): 225–248.

Enloe, C.H. (1973). *Ethnic Conflict and Political Development*. Boston, Little, Brown & Co.

Escobar, A. (1995). *Encountering Development: The Making and Unmaking of the Third World*. Princeton, NJ, Princeton University Press.

Euben, R.L. (1999). *Enemy in the Mirror: Islamic Fundamentalism and the Limits of Modern Rationality*. Princeton, NJ, Princeton University Press.

Evers, H.-D. and R. Korff (2000). *Southeast Asian Urbanism: The Meaning and Power of Social Space*. Singapore, Institute of Southeast Asian Studies.

Ewing, K. (1990). "The Illusion of Wholeness: Culture, Self, and the Experience of Inconsistency." *Ethos* 18: 251–278.

Ewing, K. (1997). *Arguing Sainthood: Modernity, Psychoanalysis and Islam*. Durham, NC, Duke University Press.

Ferguson, J. (1994). *The Anti-Politics Machine: "Development," Depoliticization, and Bureaucratic Power in Lesotho*. Minneapolis, University of Minnesota Press.

Ferguson, J. (1999). *Expectations of Modernity: Myths and Meanings of Urban Life on the Zambian Copperbelt*. Berkeley, University of California Press.

Ferme, M.C. (2001). *The Underneath of Things: Violence, History and the Everyday in Sierra Leone*. Berkeley, University of California Press.

Ferme, M.C. (2004). Deterritorialized Citizenship and the Resonances of the Sierra Leone State. *Anthropology in the Margins of the State*. V. Das and D. Poole, eds. Santa Fe, School of American Research: 81–116.

Fernando, J.M. (2002). *The Making of the Malayan Constitution*. Kuala Lumpur, The Malaysian Branch of the Royal Asiatic Society.

Ferrell, J. and M.S. Hamm, eds. (1998). *Ethnography at the Edge: Crime, Deviance, and Field Research*. Boston, Northeastern University Press.

Fleming, S. (1996). Trading in Ambiguity: Law, Rights and Realities in the Distribution of Land in Northern Mozambique. *Inside and Outside the Law: Anthropological Studies of Authority and Ambiguity*. O. Harris, ed. London, Routledge: 56–74.

Fong, T.P. (1994). *The First Suburban Chinatown: The Remaking of Monterey Park, California*. Philadelphia, Temple University Press.

Forbes, D. (1996). *Asian Metropolis: Urbanisation and the Southeast Asian City*. Melbourne, Oxford University Press.

Fortier, A.M. (1999). "Re-Membering Places and the Performance of Belonging(s)." *Theory, Culture and Society* 16(2): 41–64.

Foucault, M. (1977). *Discipline and Punish: The Birth of the Prison*. New York, Vintage.

Foucault, M. (1978). *The History of Sexuality: An Introduction*. New York, Vintage.

Foucault, M. (1988). Technologies of the Self. *Technologies of the Self: A Seminar with Michel Foucault.* L.H. Martin, H. Gutman and P.H. Hutton, eds. Amherst, University of Massachusetts Press.

Foucault, M. (1991). Governmentality. *The Foucault Effect: Studies in Governmentality.* G. Burchell, C. Gordon and P. Miller, eds. Chicago, University of Chicago Press.

Foucault, M. (2003). *"Society Must Be Defended": Lectures at the Collège de France, 1975–1976.* New York, Picador.

Fukuyama, F. (1992). *The End of History and the Last Man.* New York, Free Press.

Gaonkar, D.P. (2002). "Toward New Imaginaries: An Introduction." *Public Culture* 14(1): 1–19.

Geertz, C. (1960). *The Religion of Java.* Chicago, University of Chicago Press.

Geertz, C. (1963). *Peddlers and Princes: Social Development and Economic Change in Two Indonesian Towns.* Chicago, University of Chicago Press.

Geertz, C. (1973). *The Interpretation of Cultures.* New York, Basic Books.

Geertz, C. (1980). *Negara: The Theatre State in Nineteenth-Century Bali.* Princeton, NJ, Princeton University Press.

Geertz, C. (1983). *Local Knowledge.* New York, Basic Books.

Ghannam, F. (2002). *Remaking the Modern: Space, Relocation, and the Politics of Identity in a Global Cairo.* Berkeley, University of California Press.

Gilboy, J.A. (1991). "Deciding Who Gets In: Decisionmaking by Immigration Inspectors." *Law and Society Review* 25(3): 574–599.

Gluckman, M. (1955). *The Judicial Process Among the Barotse of Northern Rhodesia.* Manchester, Manchester University Press.

Goh, B.L. (1979). Patterns of Landownership: Case Studies in Urban Inequalities. *Malaysia: Some Contemporary Issues in Socio-Economic Development.* K.C. Cheong, S.M. Khoo and R. Thillainathan, eds. Kuala Lumpur, Malaysian Economic Society.

Goh, B.L. (1991). *Urban Planning in Malaysia: History, Assumptions and Issues.* Petaling Jaya, Malaysia, Tempo Publishing.

Goh, B.L. (2001). Rethinking Urbanism in Malaysia: Power, Space and Identity. *Risking Malaysia: Culture, Politics and Identity.* M. Maznah and S.K. Wong, eds. Bangi, Penerbit Universiti Kebangsaan Malaysia: 159–178.

Göle, N. (1996). *The Forbidden Modern: Civilization and Veiling.* Ann Arbor, University of Michigan Press.

Gomez, E.T. and K.S. Jomo (1999). *Malaysia's Political Economy: Politics, Patronage and Profits.* Cambridge, Cambridge University Press.

Greenbaum, S.D. (1993). Housing Abandonment in Inner-City Black Neighborhoods: A Case Study of the Effects of the Dual Housing Market. *The Cultural Meaning of Urban Space.* R. Rotenberg and G.W. McDonogh, eds. Westport, CT, Bergin and Garvey: 139–156.

Greenhouse, C. (1986). *Praying for Justice: Faith, Order, and Community in an American Town*. Ithaca, NY, Cornell University Press.

Gregory, S. (1992). "The Changing Significance of Race and Class in an African-American Community." *American Ethnologist* 19: 255–274.

Gregory, S. (1998). *Black Corona*. Princeton, NJ, Princeton University Press.

Griffiths, A. (1997). *In the Shadow of Marriage: Gender and Justice in an African Community*. Chicago, University of Chicago Press.

Guano, E. (2004). "The Denial of Citizenship: 'Barbaric' Buenos Aires and the Middle-Class Imaginary." *City and Society* 16(1): 69–97.

Guinness, P. (1992). *On the Margins of Capitalism: People and Development in Mukim Plentong, Johor, Malaysia*. Singapore, Oxford University Press.

Gullick, J.M. (1983). *Kuala Lumpur 1880–1895: A City in the Making*. Kuala Lumpur, Pelanduk Publications.

Gullick, J.M. (1993). *Glimpses of Selangor 1860–1898*. Kuala Lumpur, The Malaysian Branch of the Royal Asiatic Society.

Gullick, J.M. (1994). *Old Kuala Lumpur*. Kuala Lumpur, Oxford University Press.

Gullick, J.M. (2000). *A History of Kuala Lumpur 1856–1939*. Kuala Lumpur, The Malaysian Branch of the Royal Asiatic Society.

Gupta, A. (1997). The Song of the Nonaligned World: Transnational Identities and the Reinscription of Space in Late Capitalism. *Culture, Power, Place: Explorations in Critical Anthropology*. A. Gupta and J. Ferguson, eds. Durham, NC, Duke University Press: 179–199.

Gupta, A. and J. Ferguson, eds. (1997). *Culture, Power, Place: Explorations in Critical Anthropology*. Durham, NC, Duke University Press.

Guyer, J.I. (2004). *Marginal Gains: Monetary Transactions in Atlantic Africa*. Chicago, University of Chicago Press.

Hallward, P. (2006). *Out of This World: Deleuze and the Philosophy of Creation*. New York, Verso.

Hancock, M. (2002). "Modernities Remade: Hindu Temples and Their Publics in Southern India." *City and Society* 14(1): 5–35.

Handler, J.F. (1986). *The Conditions of Discretion: Autonomy, Community, Bureaucracy*. New York, Russell Sage Foundation.

Hannerz, U. (1980). *Exploring the City*. New York, Columbia University Press.

Hannerz, U. (1992). *Cultural Complexity: Studies in the Organization of Meaning*. New York, Columbia University Press.

Harding, A. (1996). *Law, Government and the Constitution in Malaysia*. London, Kluwer Law International.

Harper, T.N. (1999). *The End of Empire and the Making of Malaya*. Cambridge, Cambridge University Press.

Harris, O., ed. (1996). *Inside and Outside the Law: Anthropological Studies of Authority and Ambiguity*. London, Routledge.

Harrison, C.W. (1985). *An Illustrated Guide to the Federated Malay States*. Kuala Lumpur, Oxford University Press.

Harvey, D. (1989). *The Condition of Postmodernity*. Oxford, Basil Blackwell.

Hefner, R.W. (2000). *Civil Islam: Muslims and Democratization in Indonesia*. Princeton, NJ, Princeton University Press.

Hefner, R.W. (2005). Introduction: Modernity and the Remaking of Muslim Politics. *Remaking Muslim Politics: Pluralism, Contestation, Democratization*. R.W. Hefner, ed. Princeton, NJ, Princeton University Press: 1–36.

Herzfeld, M. (1997). *Cultural Intimacy: Social Poetics in the Nation-State*. New York, Routledge.

Herzfeld, M. (2001). *Anthropology: Theoretical Practice in Culture and Society*. Oxford, Blackwell Publishers.

Heussler, R. (1981). *British Rule in Malaya: The Malayan Civil Service and Its Predecessors 1867–1942*. Westport, CT, Greenwood Press.

Hilley, J. (2001). *Malaysia: Mahathirism, Hegemony and the New Opposition*. London, Zed Books.

Hiro, D. (1989). *Holy Wars: The Rise of Islamic Fundamentalism*. New York, Routledge.

Hirsch, S. (1998). *Pronouncing and Persevering: Gender and the Discourse of Disputing in an African Islamic Court*. Chicago, University of Chicago Press.

Hirschkind, C. (2006). *The Ethical Soundscape: Cassette Sermons and Islamic Counterpublics*. New York, Columbia University Press.

Hirschman, C. (1976). "Recent Urbanization Trends in Peninsula Malaysia." *Demography* 13(4): 445–461.

Holston, J. (1989). *The Modernist City: An Anthropological Critique of Brasilia*. Chicago, University of Chicago Press.

Holston, J. (1999). The Modernist City and the Death of the Street. *Theorizing the City: The New Urban Anthropology Reader*. S.M. Low, ed. New Brunswick, NJ, Rutgers University Press: 245–276.

Holston, J. and A. Appadurai (1996). "Cities and Citizenship." *Public Culture* 8: 187–204.

Horowitz, D.L. (1985). *Ethnic Groups in Conflict*. Berkeley, University of California Press.

Horvath, R.J. (1969). "In Search of a Theory of Urbanization: Notes on the Colonial City." *East Lakes Geographer* 5: 69–82.

Howard, E. (1965). *Garden Cities of To-morrow*. Cambridge, MA, MIT Press.

Hume, D. (2000). *A Treatise of Human Nature*. Oxford, Oxford University Press.

Huntington, S. (1996). *The Clash of Civilizations and the Remaking of World Order*. New York, Simon and Schuster.

Husin, M. (1993). *Islam in Malaysia: From Revivalism to Islamic State?* Singapore, Singapore University Press.

Hwa, Y. and R. Hunt (1992). The Methodist Church. *Christianity in Malaysia: A Denominational History.* R. Hunt, K.H. Lee and J. Roxborogh, eds. Petaling Jaya, Malaysia, Pelanduk Publishers: 142–198.

Ibrahim, B.A.B. (1994). *Islamic Modernism in Malaya: The Life and Thought of Sayid Syekh al-Hadi 1867–1934.* Kuala Lumpur, University of Malaya Press.

Irschick, E.F. (1969). *Politics and Social Conflict in South India.* Berkeley, University of California Press.

Irschick, E.F. (1994). *Dialogue and History: Constructing South India, 1795–1895.* Berkeley, University of California Press.

Ishak, S. (1977). Squatters: The Urban Poor in Kuala Lumpur. *Some Case Studies on Poverty in Malaysia: Essays Presented to Professor Ungku A. Aziz.* B. Mokhzani and S.M. Khoo, eds. Kuala Lumpur: University of Malaya Press, 109–125.

Iyngkaran, N. and P. Kunaletchumy (2002). *Cultural Cross-Currents and Creativity: The Plus Factor in Multi-Cultural Societies.* Kuala Lumpur, Child Information, Learning and Development Centre.

Jackson, R. (1991). *The Malayan Emergency: The Commonwealth's Wars, 1948–1966.* London, Routledge.

Jain, R.K. (1970). *South Indians on the Plantation Frontier in Malaya.* New Haven, CT, Yale University Press.

Jesudason, J.V. (1989). *Ethnicity and the Economy: The State, Chinese Business, and Multinationals in Malaysia.* Singapore, Oxford University Press.

Jomo, K.S. (1988). *A Question of Class: Capital, the State, and Uneven Development in Malaya.* New York, Monthly Review Press.

Jomo, K.S. and A.S. Cheek (1992). Malaysia's Islamic Movements. *Fragmented Vision: Culture and Politics in Contemporary Malaysia.* J.S. Kahn and F.L.K. Wah, eds. Honolulu, University of Hawaii Press.

Just, P. (2001). *Dou Donggo Justice: Conflict and Morality in an Indonesian Society.* New York, Rowman and Littlefield.

Kant, I. (1914). *Critique of Judgement.* London, Macmillan.

Kaur, A. (1985). *Bridge and Barrier: Transport and Communications in Colonial Malaya, 1870–1957.* Singapore, Oxford University Press.

Kaur, A. (2001). *Historical Dictionary of Malaysia.* Lanham, MD, Scarecrow Press.

Keith, M. and M. Cross (1993). *Racism, the City and the State.* New York, Routledge.

Kelly, J.D. (1991). *A Politics of Virtue: Hinduism, Sexuality, and Countercolonial Discourse in Fiji.* Chicago, University of Chicago Press.

Kessler, C.S. (1978). *Islam and Politics in a Malay State: Kelantan 1838–1969.* Ithaca, NY, Cornell University Press.

Kessler, C.S. (1980). "Malaysia: Islamic Revivalism and Political Disaffection in a Divided Society." *Southeast Asia Chronicle* 75: 3–11.

Khan, M.H. and K.S. Jomo (2000). *Rents, Rent-Seeking and Economic Development: Theory and Evidence in Asia.* Cambridge, Cambridge University Press.

Khan, N. (2006). "Of Children and Jinn: An Inquiry into an Unexpected Friendship During Uncertain Times." *Cultural Anthropology* 21(2): 234–264.

Khoo, B.T. (1995). *Paradoxes of Mahathirism: An Intellectual Biography of Mahathir Mohamad.* Kuala Lumpur, Oxford University Press.

Khoo, K.K. (1996). *Kuala Lumpur: The Formative Years.* Kuala Lumpur, Berita Publishing.

Khoo, S.N. (1993). *Streets of Georgetown, Penang.* Penang, Malaysia, Janus Publishers.

King, A.D. (1990). *Urbanism, Colonialism, and the World Economy: Cultural and Spatial Foundations of the World Urban System.* London, Routledge.

King, A.D., ed. (1997). *Culture, Globalization, and the World-System: Contemporary Conditions for the Representation of Identity.* Minneapolis, University of Minnesota Press.

King, V.T. (1999). *Anthropology and Development in South-East Asia: Theory and Practice.* Kuala Lumpur, Oxford University Press.

Kleinman, A., V. Das et al., eds. (1997). *Social Suffering.* Berkeley, University of California Press.

Klima, A. (2002). *The Funeral Casino: Meditation, Massacre, and Exchange with the Dead in Thailand.* Princeton, NJ, Princeton University Press.

Kondo, D. (1990). *Crafting Selves: Power, Gender, and Discourse.* Chicago, University of Chicago Press.

Kratoska, P. (1998). *The Japanese Occupation of Malaya.* Sydney, Allen and Unwin.

Kratoska, P., ed. (1995). *Malaya and Singapore During the Japanese Occupation.* Singapore, Singapore University Press.

Kuala Lumpur Municipal Council (1959). *Kuala Lumpur—100 Years.* Kuala Lumpur, Kuala Lumpur Municipal Council.

Kusno, A. (2000). *Behind the Postcolonial: Architecture, Urban Space and Political Cultures in Indonesia.* London, Routledge.

Kwong, P. (1987). *The New Chinatown.* New York, Hill & Wang.

Laderman, C. (1993). *Taming the Wind of Desire: Psychology, Medicine, and Aesthetics in Malay Shamanistic Performance.* Berkeley, University of California Press.

LaFleur, W.R. (1989). Hungry Ghosts and Hungry People: Somaticity and Rationality in Medieval Japan. *Fragments for a History of the Human Body, Part One.* M. Feher, R. Naddaff and N. Tazi, eds. New York, Zone Books.

Lau, A. (1991). *The Malayan Union Controversy, 1942–1948.* Singapore, Oxford University Press.

Leary, J. (1995). *Violence and the Dream People: The Orang Asli in the Malayan Emergency, 1948–1960.* Athens, Ohio University Press.

Lefebvre, H. (1991). *The Production of Space*. Oxford, Blackwell.

Lefebvre, H. (1996). *Writings on Cities*. Oxford, Blackwell.

Lefebvre, H. (2003). *The Urban Revolution*. Minneapolis, University of Minnesota Press.

Levi-Strauss, C. (1969). *The Raw and the Cooked: Introduction to a Science of Mythology, Vol. 1*. New York, Harper and Row.

Levy, R. (1990). *Mesocosm: Hinduism and the Organization of a Traditional Newar City in Nepal*. Berkeley, University of California Press.

Lewis, B. (2003). *The Crisis of Islam: Holy War and Unholy Terror*. New York, Modern Library.

Lijphart, A. (1977). *Democracy in Plural Societies*. New Haven, CT, Yale University Press.

Lim, C.L. (2000). *The Story of a Psy-Warrior: Tan Sri Dr. C.C. Too*. Kuala Lumpur (Batu Caves), Lim Cheng Leng.

Lim, H.K. (1978). *The Evolution of the Urban System in Malaya*. Kuala Lumpur, Penerbit Universiti Malaya.

Lim, K.S. (2002). *No to 929*. Kuala Lumpur, Democratic Action Party.

Low, S.M. (1999). Introduction: Theorizing the City. *Theorizing the City: The New Urban Anthropology Reader*. S.M. Low, ed. New Brunswick, NJ, Rutgers University Press: 1–36.

Luhrmann, T. (1996). *The Good Parsi: The Fate of a Colonial Elite in a Postcolonial Society*. Cambridge, MA, Harvard University Press.

Mahathir, M. (1970). *The Malay Dilemma*. Singapore, Times Books International.

Mahathir, M. (1986). *The Challenge*. Kuala Lumpur, Pelanduk Publications.

Mahathir, M. (2000). *Islam and the Muslim Ummah: Selected Speeches of Dr. Mahathir Mohamad, Prime Minister of Malaysia*. Subang Jaya, Malaysia, Pelanduk Publishers.

Mahathir, M. (2002). *Globalisation and the New Realities*. Kuala Lumpur, Pelanduk Publications.

Mahmood, S. (2001). "Feminist Theory, Embodiment, and the Docile Agent: Some Reflections on the Egyptian Islamic Revival." *Cultural Anthropology* 16(2): 202–236.

Mahmood, S. (2005). *Politics of Piety: The Islamic Revival and the Feminist Subject*. Princeton, NJ, Princeton University Press.

Majid, A. (2000). *Unveiling Traditions: Postcolonial Islam in a Polycentric World*. Durham, NC, Duke University Press.

Malaysian Association for the Blind (2001). *Golden Jubilee Charity Banquet Souvenir Program, 1951–2001*. Kuala Lumpur, Malaysian Association for the Blind.

Malinowski, B. (1985). *Crime and Custom in Savage Society*. Totowa, NJ, Rowan and Littlefield.

Maniam, K.S. (1981). *The Return*. London, Skoob Books.

Maniam, K.S. (1993). *In a Far Country*. London, Skoob Books.

Maniam, K.S. (1996). *Haunting the Tiger: Contemporary Stories from Malaysia*. London, Skoob Books.

Margolis, M.L. (1994). *Little Brazil: An Ethnography of Brazilian Immigrants in New York City*. Princeton, NJ, Princeton University Press.

Markowitz, F. (1993). *A Community in Spite of Itself: Soviet Jewish Emigres in New York*. Washington DC, Smithsonian Institution Press.

Marrati, P. (2003). *Gilles Deleuze: Cinéma et Philosophie*. Paris, Presses Universitaires de France.

Martinez, P. (2001). Mahathir, Islam, and the New Malay Dilemma. *Mahathir's Administration: Performance and Crisis in Governance*. H.K. Leong and J. Chin, eds. Singapore, Times Books International.

Massey, D. and N. Denton (1993). *American Apartheid: Segregation and the Making of the Underclass*. Cambridge, MA, Harvard University Press.

Massumi, B. (2002). *Parables for the Virtual: Movement, Affect, Sensation*. Durham, NC, Duke University Press.

Mauss, M. (1973). "Techniques of the Body." *Economy and Society* 2: 70–88.

McDonogh, G.W. (1993). The Geography of Emptiness. *The Cultural Meaning of Urban Space*. R. Rotenberg and G.W. McDonogh, eds. Westport, CT, Bergin and Garvey: 3–16.

McGee, T.G. (1963). "The Cultural Role of Cities: A Case Study of Kuala Lumpur." *Journal of Tropical Geography* 17: 178–196.

McGee, T.G. (1967). *The Southeast Asian City: A Social Geography of the Primate Cities of Southeast Asia*. London, G. Bell and Sons.

McGee, T.G. (1971). *The Urbanization Process in the Third World: Explorations in Search of a Theory*. London, G. Bell and Sons.

McGee, T.G. and W.D. McTaggart (1967). *Petaling Jaya: A Socio-Economic Survey of a New Town in Selangor, Malaysia*. Pacific Viewpoint Monograph, No. 2. Wellington, New Zealand: Victoria University Department of Geography.

Means, G.P. (1991). *Malaysian Politics: The Second Generation*. Singapore, Oxford University Press.

Mearns, D.J. (1986). Do Indians Exist? The Politics and Culture of Ethnicity. *Ethnicity and Ethnic Relations in Malaysia*. R.L.M. Lee, ed. DeKalb, Northern Illinois University Press: 73–103.

Mearns, D.J. (1995). *Shiva's Other Children: Religion and Social Identity Amongst Overseas Indians*. New Delhi, Sage Publications.

Mehmet, O. (1990). *Islamic Identity and Development: Studies of the Islamic Periphery*. Kuala Lumpur, Forum Press.

Merry, S.E. (1981). *Urban Danger: Life in a Neighborhood of Strangers*. Philadelphia, Temple University Press.

Merry, S.E. (1990). *Getting Justice and Getting Even: Legal Consciousness Among Working-Class Americans*. Chicago, University of Chicago Press.

Merry, S.E. (1992). "Anthropology, Law, and Transnational Processes." *Annual Review of Anthropology* 21: 357–379.

Messick, B. (1992). *The Calligraphic State: Textual Domination and History in a Muslim Society.* Berkeley, University of California Press.

Middlebrook, S.M. and J.M. Gullick (1989). *Yap Ah Loy.* Kuala Lumpur, The Malaysian Branch of the Royal Asiatic Society.

Miller, H. (1972). *Jungle War in Malaya: The Campaign Against Communism, 1948–60.* London, Barker.

Milne, R.S. (1981). *Politics in Ethnically Bipolar States: Guyana, Malaysia, Fiji.* Vancouver, University of British Columbia Press.

Milne, R.S. and D.K. Mauzy (1999). *Malaysian Politics under Mahathir.* New York, Routledge.

Milner, A. (1986). "Rethinking Islamic Fundamentalism in Malaysia." *Review of Indonesian and Malaysian Affairs* 20(2): 48–75.

Milner, A. (1995). *The Invention of Politics in Colonial Malaya.* Cambridge, Cambridge University Press.

Mitchell, D. (2003). *The Right to the City: Social Justice and the Fight for Public Space.* New York, Guilford Press.

Mitchell, T. (1989). *Colonising Egypt.* Berkeley, University of California Press.

Mohamed, N.S. (1974). *From Malayan Union to Singapore Separation: Political Unification in the Malaysia Region 1945–65.* Kuala Lumpur, Penerbit Universiti Malaya.

Mohammad, H.K. (1995). *Punishment in Islamic Law: An Enquiry into the Hudud Bill of Kelantan.* Kuala Lumpur, Ilmiah Publishers.

Mohammad, H.K. (2000). *Islamic Law in Malaysia: Issues and Developments.* Kuala Lumpur, Ilmiah Publishers.

Mohd, N.H. (1994). *Peneroka Bandar Menuntut Keadilan.* Kuala Lumpur, Daya Komunikasi.

Mohd, S.H. (1996). *Akhbar dan Kuasa: Perkembangan Sistem Akhbar di Malaysia Sejak 1806.* Kuala Lumpur, Penerbit Universiti Malaya.

Moore, S.F. (1978). *Law as Process: An Anthropological Approach.* London, Routledge & Kegan Paul.

Moore, S.F. (1986). *Social Facts and Fabrications: Customary Law on Kilimanjaro, 1880–1980.* Cambridge, Cambridge University Press.

Moore, S.F. (2001). "Certainties Undone: Fifty Turbulent Years of Legal Anthropology, 1949–1999." *Journal of the Royal Anthropological Institute* 7(1): 95–116.

Moore, S.F., ed. (2005). *Law and Anthropology: A Reader.* Oxford, Blackwell Publishing.

Morshidi, S. and G. Suriati (1999). *Globalisation of Economic Activity and Third World Cities: A Case Study of Kuala Lumpur.* Kuala Lumpur, Utusan Publications.

Mrazek, R. (2002). *Engineers of Happy Land: Technology and Nationalism in a Colony.* Princeton, NJ, Princeton University Press.

Munro-Kua, A. (1996). *Authoritarian Populism in Malaysia*. London, Macmillan Press.

Mutalib, H. (1990). *Islam and Ethnicity in Malay Politics*. Singapore, Oxford University Press.

Myrdal, G. (1968). *Asian Drama: An Inquiry into the Poverty of Nations*. New York, Pantheon.

Nabokov, I. (2000). *Religion Against the Self: An Ethnography of Tamil Rituals*. Oxford, Oxford University Press.

Nader, L. (1990). *Harmony Ideology: Justice and Control in a Zapotec Mountain Village*. Stanford, CA, Stanford University Press.

Nader, L. (2005). *The Life of the Law: Anthropological Projects*. Berkeley, University of California Press.

Nader, L., ed. (1980). *No Access to Law: Alternatives to the American Judicial System*. New York, Academic Press.

Nader, L. and H.F. Todd, eds. (1978). *The Disputing Process: Law in Ten Societies*. New York, Columbia University Press.

Nagata, J. (1979). *Malaysian Mosaic: Perspectives from a Poly-Ethnic Society*. Vancouver, University of British Columbia Press.

Nagata, J. (1984). *The Reflowering of Malaysian Islam: Modern Religious Radicals and Their Roots*. Vancouver, University of British Columbia Press.

Nagata, J. (1997). "Ethnonationalism versus Religious Transnationalism: Nation-Building and Islam in Malaysia." *The Muslim World* 87(2).

Nagata, J. (2001). Heritage as a Site of Resistance: From Architecture to Political Activism in Urban Penang. *Risking Malaysia: Culture, Politics and Identity*. M. Maznah and S.K. Wong, eds. Bangi, Penerbit Universiti Kebangsaan Malaysia: 179–202.

Nasr, S.V.R. (1996). *Mawdudi and the Making of Islamic Revivalism*. New York, Oxford University Press.

Navaratnam, A. (2001). *The Spear and the Kerambit: The Exploits of the VAT 69, Malaysia's Elite Fighting Force 1968–1989*. Kuala Lumpur, Utusan Publications.

Navaro-Yashin, Y. (2002). *Faces of the State: Secularism and Public Life in Turkey*. Princeton, NJ, Princeton University Press.

Nawang, A.H. (1997). *Kuala Lumpur dari Perspektif Haji Abdullah Hukum*. Kuala Lumpur, Berita Publishing.

Nonini, D. (1997). Shifting Identities, Positioned Imaginaries: Transnational Traversals and Reversals by Malaysian Chinese. *Ungrounded Empires: The Cultural Politics of Modern Chinese Transnationalism*. A. Ong and D. Nonini, eds. New York, Routledge: 203–227.

Nonini, D. and A. Ong (1997). Introduction: Chinese Transnationalism as an Alternative Modernity. *Ungrounded Empires: The Cultural Politics of Modern Chinese Transnationalism*. A. Ong and D. Nonini, eds. New York, Routledge: 3–36.

Noor, F.A. (2002). *The Other Malaysia: Writings on Malaysia's Subaltern History.* Kuala Lumpur, Silverfish Books.

Nye, M. (1995). *A Place for Our Gods: The Construction of an Edinburgh Hindu Temple Community.* Richmond, UK, Curzon Press.

O'Ballance, E. (1966). *Malaya: The Communist Insurgent War, 1948–60.* Hamden, CT, Archon Books.

Ong, A. (1987). *Spirits of Resistance and Capitalist Discipline: Factory Women in Malaysia.* Albany, State University of New York Press.

Ong, A. (1995). State Versus Islam: Malay Families, Women's Bodies, and the Body Politic in Malaysia. *Bewitching Women, Pious Men: Gender and Body Politics in Southeast Asia.* A. Ong and M.G. Peletz, eds. Berkeley, University of California Press: 159–194.

Ong, A. (1999). *Flexible Citizenship: The Cultural Logics of Transnationality.* Durham, NC, Duke University Press.

Ong, A. and D. Nonini, eds. (1997). *Ungrounded Empires: The Cultural Politics of Modern Chinese Transnationalism.* New York, Routledge.

Ong Siew Im, P. (1998). *One Man's Will: A Portrait of Dato' Sir Onn bin Ja'afar.* Kuala Lumpur, Island Printers.

Ongkili, J.P. (1985). *Nation-Building in Malaysia 1946–1974.* Singapore, Oxford University Press.

Ooi, J.B. (1975). "Urbanization and the Urban Population in Peninsular Malaysia." *Journal of Tropical Geography* 40: 40–47.

Orzech, C. (1996). Saving the Burning-Mouth Hungry Ghost. *Religions of China in Practice.* D.S. Lopez, ed. Princeton, NJ, Princeton University Press.

Pardo, I. (1996). *Managing Existence in Naples: Morality, Action, and Structure.* Cambridge, Cambridge University Press.

Parnell, P.C. (1989). *Escalating Disputes: Social Participation and Change in the Oaxacan Highlands.* Tucson, University of Arizona Press.

Peacock, J. (1978). *Muslim Puritans: Reformist Psychology in Southeast Asian Islam.* Berkeley, University of California Press.

Peletz, M.G. (1993). Knowledge, Power, and Personal Misfortune in a Malay Context. *Understanding Witchcraft and Sorcery in Southeast Asia.* C.W. Watson and R. Ellen, eds. Honolulu, University of Hawaii Press.

Peletz, M.G. (1995). Neither Reasonable nor Responsible: Contrasting Representations of Masculinity in a Malay Society. *Bewitching Women, Pious Men: Gender and Body Politics in Southeast Asia.* A. Ong and M.G. Peletz, eds. Berkeley, University of California Press: 76–123.

Peletz, M.G. (1996). *Reason and Passion: Representations of Gender in a Malay Society.* Berkeley, University of California Press.

Peletz, M.G. (1997). "Ordinary Muslims" and Muslim Resurgence in Contemporary Malaysia: Notes on an Ambivalent Relationship. *Islam in the Era of*

Nation-States: Politics and Religious Renewal in Muslim Southeast Asia. R.W. Hefner and P. Horvatich, eds. Honolulu, University of Hawaii Press.

Peletz, M.G. (2002). *Islamic Modern: Religious Courts and Cultural Politics in Malaysia.* Princeton, NJ, Princeton University Press.

Peletz, M.G. (2005). Islam and the Cultural Politics of Legitimacy: Malaysia in the Aftermath of September 11. *Remaking Muslim Politics: Pluralism, Contestation, Democratization.* R.W. Hefner, ed. Princeton, NJ, Princeton University Press.

Pemberton, J. (1994). *On the Subject of "Java."* Ithaca, NY, Cornell University Press.

Pessar, P. (1995). "The Elusive Enclave: Ethnicity, Class and Nationality among Latino Entrepreneurs in Greater Washington D.C." *Human Organization* 54: 383–392.

Poole, D. (2004). Between Threat and Guarantee: Justice and Community in the Margins of the Peruvian State. *Anthropology in the Margins of the State.* V. Das and D. Poole, eds. Santa Fe, School of American Research.

Portes, A. and A. Stepick (1993). *City on the Edge: The Transformation of Miami.* Berkeley, University of California Press.

Pospisil, L. (1971). *Anthropology of Law: A Comparative Theory.* New York, Harper and Row.

Pospisil, L. (1978). *The Ethnology of Law.* New Haven, CT, Human Relations Area Files.

Provencher, R. (1971). *Two Malay Worlds: An Urban-Rural Comparison of Social Interaction.* Berkeley, University of California Press.

Rabinow, P. (1989). *French Modern: Norms and Forms of the Social Environment.* Cambridge, MA, MIT Press.

Rabinow, P. (2003). *Anthropos Today: Reflections on Modern Equipment.* Princeton, NJ, Princeton University Press.

Rajah, S. (2000). *Folk Hinduism: A Study on the Practice of Blood Sacrifice in Peninsular Malaysia from a Christian Perspective.* Manila, ATESEA.

Ramachandran, S. (1994). *Indian Plantation Labour in Malaysia.* Kuala Lumpur, S. Abdul Majeed & Co.

Ramasamy, P. (1994). *Plantation Labour, Unions, Capital, and the State in Peninsular Malaysia.* Kuala Lumpur, Oxford University Press.

Ramasamy, R. (1984). *Caste Consciousness Among Indian Tamils in Malaysia.* Petaling Jaya, Malaysia, Pelanduk Publishers.

Ramaswamy, S. (1997). *Passions of the Tongue: Language Devotion in Tamil India, 1891–1970.* Berkeley, University of California Press.

Ratnam, K.J. (1965). *Communalism and the Political Process in Malaya.* Kuala Lumpur, University of Malaya Press.

Read, C. (1909). *The Revelation of Britain: A Book for Colonials.* Auckland, Gordon and Gotch.

Read, C. (1922). *Town Planning and Development in the Federated States: Preliminary Report and General Survey with Recommendations to the Acting Under Secretary to Government Federated Malay States by the Government Town Planner Federated Malay States.* Kuala Lumpur, Federated Malay States Government Press.

Rehman, R. (1993). *A Malaysian Journey.* Petaling Jaya, Malaysia, Rehman Rashid.

Renick, R. (1965). Emergency Regulations of Malaya: Background, Organisation, Administration and Use as a Socializing Technique. M.A. diss., Tulane University.

Riddell, P. (2001). *Islam and the Malay-Indonesian World: Transmission and Responses.* Singapore, Horizon Books.

Rimmer, P.J. and G.C.H. Cho (1981). "Urbanization of the Malays Since Independence: Evidence from West Malaysia, 1957 and 1970." *Journal of Southeast Asian Studies* 12(2): 349–363.

Robinson, G. (1995). *Dark Side of Paradise: Political Violence in Bali.* Ithaca, NY, Cornell University Press.

Robson, J.H.M. (2001). *Records and Recollections 1889–1934.* Kuala Lumpur, The Malaysian Branch of the Royal Asiatic Society.

Rofel, L. (1999). *Other Modernities: Gendered Yearnings in China after Socialism.* Berkeley, University of California Press.

Roff, W.R. (1994). *The Origins of Malay Nationalism.* Kuala Lumpur, Oxford University Press.

Rorty, A. (1976). A Literary Postscript: Characters, Persons, Selves, Individuals. *The Identities of Persons.* A. Rorty, ed. Berkeley, University of California Press: 301–323.

Rosen, L. (1989). *The Anthropology of Justice: Law as Culture in Islamic Society.* Cambridge, Cambridge University Press.

Sacks, K.B. (1997). *Race, Class, Gender and the Jewish Question.* New Brunswick, NJ, Rutgers University Press.

Sadka, E. (1968). *The Protected Malay States, 1874–1895.* Kuala Lumpur, University of Malaya Press.

Said, E. (1978). *Orientalism.* New York, Vintage.

Salleh Hj. Buang, H. (2001). *Malaysian Torrens System.* Kuala Lumpur, Dewan Bahasa dan Pustaka.

Sandhu, K.S. (1969). *Indians in Malaya: Some Aspects of Their Immigration and Settlement.* Cambridge, Cambridge University Press.

Sandhu, K.S. and A. Mani, eds. (1993). *Indian Communities in Southeast Asia.* Singapore, Times Academic Press.

Santhiram, R. (1999). *Education of Minorities: The Case of Indians in Malaysia.* Kuala Lumpur, Child Information, Learning and Development Centre.

Sarat, A., L. Douglas, and M. Umphrey, eds. (2003). *The Place of Law*. Ann Arbor, MI, University of Michigan Press.

Sarat, A. and T. Kearns, eds. (1993). Editorial Introduction. *Law in Everyday Life*. Ann Arbor, MI, University of Michigan Press, 1–21.

Sardar, Z. (2000). *The Consumption of Kuala Lumpur*. London, Reaktion Books.

Sarkesian, S. C. (1993). *Unconventional Conflicts in a New Security Era: Lessons from Malaya and Vietnam*. Westport, CT, Greenwood Press.

Sassen, S. (2001). *The Global City: New York, London, Tokyo*. Princeton, NJ, Princeton University Press.

Sato, S. (1994). *War, Nationalism, and Peasants: Java under the Japanese Occupation 1942–1945*. Sydney, Allen and Unwin.

Saw, S.H. (1988). *The Population of Peninsular Malaysia*. Kuala Lumpur, Oxford University Press.

Schulman, D.D. (1980). *Tamil Temple Myths: Sacrifice and Divine Marriage in the South Indian Saiva Tradition*. Princeton, NJ, Princeton University Press.

Schwartz, H. (1996). *The Culture of the Copy: Striking Likenesses, Unreasonable Facsimiles*. New York, Zone Books.

Scott, D. and C. Hirschkind, eds. (2006). *Powers of the Secular Modern: Talal Asad and His Interlocutors*. Stanford, CA, Stanford University Press.

Scott, J.C. (1985). *Weapons of the Weak: Everyday Forms of Peasant Resistance*. New Haven, CT, Yale University Press.

Scott, J.C. (1990). *Domination and the Arts of Resistance: Hidden Transcripts*. New Haven, CT, Yale University Press.

Scott, J.C. (1998). *Seeing Like a State: How Certain Schemes to Improve the Human Condition Have Failed*. New Haven, CT, Yale University Press.

Selvaratnam, T. (2002). Railways, Brickfields and Jaffna Tamils. *Centenary Celebration 1902–2002*. Kuala Lumpur, Sri Kandaswamy Temple.

Sen, M.K. (1973). *The Rehabilitation and Resettlement of Squatters: The Kuala Lumpur Experience*. Kuala Lumpur, Malaysian Institute of Planners.

Shamsul, A.B. (1999). From Orang Kaya Baru to Melayu Bara: Cultural Construction of the Malay "New Rich." *Culture and Privilege in Capitalist Asia*. M. Pinches, ed. New York, Routledge.

Shiraishi, S. and T. Shiraishi, eds. (1993). *The Japanese in Colonial Southeast Asia*. Ithaca, NY, Cornell University Press.

Short, A. (2000). *In Pursuit of Mountain Rats: The Communist Insurrection in Malaya*. Singapore, Cultured Lotus.

Sidhu, M.S. (1978). *Kuala Lumpur and Its Population*. Kuala Lumpur, Surinder Publications.

Sidhu, R.J.H. (1978). *Administration in the Federated Malay States 1896–1920*. Kuala Lumpur, Oxford University Press.

Siegel, J.T. (1986). *Solo in the New Order: Language and Hierarchy in an Indonesian City*. Princeton, NJ, Princeton University Press.

Siegel, J.T. (1997). *Fetish, Recognition, Revolution*. Princeton, NJ, Princeton University Press.

Siegel, J.T. (1998). *A New Criminal Type in Jakarta: Counter-Revolution Today*. Durham, NC, Duke University Press.

Siegel, J.T. (2006). *Naming the Witch*. Stanford, CA, Stanford University Press.

Simmel, G. (1964). *Conflict: The Web of Group-Affiliations*. New York, Free Press.

Simon, D. (1984). "Third World Colonial Cities in Context: Conceptual and Theoretical Approaches with Particular Reference to Africa." *Progress in Human Geography* 8: 493–514.

Singerman, D. (2005). Rewriting Divorce in Egypt: Reclaiming Islam, Legal Activism, and Coalition Politics. *Remaking Muslim Politics: Pluralism, Contestation, Democratization*. R.W. Hefner, ed. Princeton, NJ, Princeton University Press: 161–188.

Sirat, M. and S. Ghazali (1999). *Globalisation of Economic Activity and Third World Cities: A Case Study of Kuala Lumpur*. Kuala Lumpur, Utusan Publications.

Sjoberg, G. (1960). *The Preindustrial City, Past and Present*. New York, Free Press.

Sjoberg, G. (1965). Cities in Developing and in Industrial Societies: A Cross-Cultural Analysis. *The Study of Urbanization*. P.M. Hauser and L.F. Schnore, eds. New York, John Wiley and Sons.

Skeat, W.W. (1965). *Malay Magic: An Introduction to the Folklore and Popular Religion of the Malay Peninsula*. London, Cass.

Sloterdijk, P. (1988). *Critique of Cynical Reason*. New York, Verso.

Snyder, F.G. (1981). *Capitalism and Legal Change: An African Transformation*. New York, Academic Press.

Soong, K.K., ed. (1998). *Mother Tongue Education of Malaysian Ethnic Minorities*. Kuala Lumpur, Dong Jiao Zong Higher Learning Centre.

Sri Kandaswamy Temple (2002). *Centenary Celebration 1902–2002*. Kuala Lumpur, Sri Kandaswamy Temple.

Sri Murugan Centre (2001). *Pelancaran Program Pendidikan*. Kuala Lumpur, Sri Murugan Centre.

Starr, J. (1978). *Dispute and Settlement in Rural Turkey*. Leiden, Brill.

Starr, J. and J.F. Collier, eds. (1989). *History and Power in the Study of Law: New Directions in Legal Anthropology*. Ithaca, NY, Cornell University Press.

Starrett, G. (1998). *Putting Islam to Work: Education, Politics, and Religious Transformation in Egypt*. Berkeley, University of California Press.

Stenson, M.R. (1980). *Class, Race and Colonialism in West Malaysia: The Indian Case*. St. Lucia, University of Queensland Press.

Stewart, I. (2003). *The Mahathir Legacy: A Nation Divided, A Region at Risk*. Sydney, Allen and Unwin.

Stockwell, A.J. (1979). *British Policy and Malay Politics During the Malayan Union Experiment, 1945–1948*. Kuala Lumpur, Malaysian Branch of the Royal Asiatic Society.

Stubbs, R. (1989). *Hearts and Minds in Guerrilla Warfare: The Malayan Emergency 1948–1960*. Singapore, Oxford University Press.

Suara Rakyat Malaysia (2000). Malaysian Human Rights Report: Civil and Political Rights in 2000. Kuala Lumpur, Suaram Kommunikasi.

Sullivan, J. (1992). *Local Government and Community in Java: An Urban Case-Study*. Singapore, Oxford University Press.

Swettenham, F. (1907). *British Malaya: An Account of the Origin and Progress of British Influence in Malaya*. London, J. Lane.

Swettenham, F. (1942). *Footprints in Malaya*. London, Hutchinson and Co.

Tarling, N. (2001). *A Sudden Rampage: The Japanese Occupation of Southeast Asia 1941–1945*. Singapore, Horizon Books.

Taussig, M. (1997). *The Magic of the State*. New York, Routledge.

Taylor, C. (1998). Modes of Secularism. *Secularism and Its Critics*. R. Bhargava, ed. Delhi, Oxford University Press.

Tinker, H. (1974). *A New System of Slavery: The Export of Indian Labour Overseas, 1830–1920*. London, Oxford University Press.

Trawick, M. (1990). *Notes on Love in a Tamil Family*. Berkeley, University of California Press.

Tsai, K.S. (2002). *Back-Alley Banking: Private Enterprise in China*. Ithaca, NY, Cornell University Press.

Turner, V. (1986). "Body, Brain, and Culture." *Performing Arts Journal* 10(2): 26–34.

Tushnet, M. (1984). "An Essay on Rights." *Texas Law Review* 62: 1363–1412.

Unger, R.M. (1986). *The Critical Legal Studies Movement*. Cambridge, MA, Harvard University Press.

van der Veer, P., ed. (1995). *Nation and Migration: The Politics of Space in the South Asian Diaspora*. Philadelphia, University of Pennsylvania Press.

Varzi, R. (2006). *Warring Souls: Youth, Media, and Martyrdom in Post-Revolution Iran*. Durham, NC, Duke University Press.

Venugopal, S. (1996). *Malaysian Tamil Novels after Independence*. Kuala Lumpur, University of Malaya Press.

Verkaaik, O. (2004). *Militants and Migrants: "Fun" and Urban Violence in Pakistan*. Princeton, NJ, Princeton University Press.

Verma, V. (2002). *Malaysia: State and Civil Society in Transition*. Boulder, CO, Lynne Rienner Publishers.

Virilio, P. (1991). *The Aesthetics of Disappearance*. New York, Semiotext(e).

von Vorys, K. (1975). *Democracy Without Consensus: Communalism and Political Stability in Malaysia*. Princeton, NJ, Princeton University Press.

Wacquant, L. and W. Wilson (1989). "The Cost of Racial and Class Exclusion in the Inner City." *Annals of the American Academy of Political and Social Science* 501: 8–25.

Wan Mohd, N.W.D. (1998). *The Educational Philosophy and Practice of Syed Muhammad Naquib al-Attas: An Exposition of the Original Concept of Islamization*. Kuala Lumpur, International Institute of Islamic Thought and Civilization.

Watson, C.W. and R. Ellen, eds. (1993). *Understanding Witchcraft and Sorcery in Southeast Asia*. Honolulu, University of Hawaii Press.

Wazir, J.K. (1992). *Women and Culture: Between Malay Adat and Islam*. Boulder, CO, Westview Press.

White, J.B. (2005). The End of Islamism? Turkey's Muslimhood Model. *Remaking Muslim Politics: Pluralism, Contestation, Democratization*. R.W. Hefner, ed. Princeton, NJ, Princeton University Press: 87–III.

Whitehead, H. (1921). *The Village Gods of South India*. London, Oxford University Press.

Whitehead, H. (1988). *The Village Gods of South India*. New Delhi, Asian Educational Services.

Wiebe, P.D. and S. Mariappan (1978). *Indian Malaysians*. Delhi, Manohar.

Willford, A.C. (2006a). *Cage of Freedom: Tamil Identity and the Ethnic Fetish*. Ann Arbor, MI, University of Michigan Press.

Willford, A.C. (2006b). "The 'Already Surmounted' Yet 'Secretly Familiar': Malaysian Identity as Symptom." *Cultural Anthropology* 21(1): 31–59.

Williams, B. (1992). "Poverty among African-Americans in the Urban United States." *Human Organization* 51: 164–174.

Winn, J.K. (1994). "Relational Practices and the Marginalization of Law: Informal Financial Practices of Small Businesses in Taiwan." *Law and Society Review* 28(2): 193–332.

Winstedt, R.O. (1982). *A History of Malaya*. Kuala Lumpur, Marican and Sons.

Witty, C.J. (1980). *Mediation and Society: Conflict Management in Lebanon*. New York, Academic Press.

Yeoh, B.S.A. (1996). *Contesting Space: Power Relations and the Urban Built Environment in Colonial Singapore*. Kuala Lumpur, Oxford University Press.

Young, I.M. (1990). *Justice and the Politics of Difference*. Princeton, NJ, Princeton University Press.

Younger, P. (2002). *Playing Host to Deity: Festival Religion in the South Indian Tradition*. New York, Oxford University Press.

Zaman, M.Q. (2002). *The Ulama in Contemporary Islam: Custodians of Change*. Princeton, NJ, Princeton University Press.

Zaman, M.Q. (2005). Pluralism, Democracy, and the Ulama. *Remaking Muslim Politics: Pluralism, Contestation, Democratization*. R.W. Hefner, ed. Princeton, NJ, Princeton University Press: 60–86.

Zhou, M. (1992). *Chinatown: The Socioeconomic Potential of an Urban Enclave*. Philadelphia, Temple University Press.

Jill Bennett, *Empathic Vision: Affect, Trauma, and Contemporary Art*

Ban Wang, *Illuminations from the Past: Trauma, Memory, and History in Modern China*

James Phillips, *Heidegger's* Volk: *Between National Socialism and Poetry*

Frank Ankersmit, *Sublime Historical Experience*

István Rév, *Retroactive Justice: Prehistory of Post-Communism*

Paola Marrati, *Genesis and Trace: Derrida Reading Husserl and Heidegger*

Krzysztof Ziarek, *The Force of Art*

Marie-José Mondzain, *Image, Icon, Economy: The Byzantine Origins of the Contemporary Imaginary*

Cecilia Sjöholm, *The Antigone Complex: Ethics and the Invention of Feminine Desire*

Jacques Derrida and Elisabeth Roudinesco, *For What Tomorrow . . . : A Dialogue*

Elisabeth Weber, *Questioning Judaism: Interviews by Elisabeth Weber*

Jacques Derrida and Catherine Malabou, *Counterpath: Traveling with Jacques Derrida*

Martin Seel, *Aesthetics of Appearing*

Nanette Salomon, *Shifting Priorities: Gender and Genre in Seventeenth-Century Dutch Painting*

Jacob Taubes, *The Political Theology of Paul*

Jean-Luc Marion, *The Crossing of the Visible*

Eric Michaud, *The Cult of Art in Nazi Germany*

Anne Freadman, *The Machinery of Talk: Charles Peirce and the Sign Hypothesis*

Stanley Cavell, *Emerson's Transcendental Etudes*

Stuart McLean, *The Event and Its Terrors: Ireland, Famine, Modernity*

Beate Rössler, ed., *Privacies: Philosophical Evaluations*

Ian Balfour, *The Rhetoric of Romantic Prophecy*

Martin Stokhof, *World and Life as One: Ethics and Ontology in Wittgenstein's Early Thought*

Gianni Vattimo, *Nietzsche: An Introduction*

Jacques Derrida, *Negotiations: Interventions and Interviews, 1971–2001*, edited by Elizabeth Rottenberg

Brett Levinson, *The Ends of Literature: The Latin American "Boom" in the Neoliberal Marketplace*

Timothy J. Reiss, *Against Autonomy: Global Dialectics of Cultural Exchange*

Hent de Vries and Samuel Weber, eds., *Religion and Media*

Niklas Luhmann, *Theories of Distinction: Redescribing the Descriptions of Modernity*, edited and with an introduction by William Rasch

Johannes Fabian, *Anthropology with an Attitude: Critical Essays*

Michel Henry, *I Am the Truth: Toward a Philosophy of Christianity*

Gil Anidjar, *"Our Place in Al-Andalus": Kabbalah, Philosophy, Literature in Arab-Jewish Letters*

Hélène Cixous and Jacques Derrida, *Veils*

F.R. Ankersmit, *Historical Representation*

F.R. Ankersmit, *Political Representation*

Elissa Marder, *Dead Time: Temporal Disorders in the Wake of Modernity (Baudelaire and Flaubert)*

Reinhart Koselleck, *The Practice of Conceptual History: Timing History, Spacing Concepts*

Niklas Luhmann, *The Reality of the Mass Media*

Hubert Damisch, *A Theory of /Cloud/: Toward a History of Painting*

Jean-Luc Nancy, *The Speculative Remark: (One of Hegel's Bons Mots)*

Jean-François Lyotard, *Soundproof Room: Malraux's Anti-Aesthetics*

Jan Patocka, *Plato and Europe*

Hubert Damisch, *Skyline: The Narcissistic City*

Isabel Hoving, *In Praise of New Travelers: Reading Caribbean Migrant Women's Writing*

Richard Rand, ed., *Futures: Of Jacques Derrida*

William Rasch, *Niklas Luhmann's Modernity: The Paradoxes of Differentiation*

Jacques Derrida and Anne Dufourmantelle, *Of Hospitality*

Jean-François Lyotard, *The Confession of Augustine*

Kaja Silverman, *World Spectators*

Samuel Weber, *Institution and Interpretation: Expanded Edition*

Jeffrey S. Librett, *The Rhetoric of Cultural Dialogue: Jews and Germans from Moses Mendelssohn to Richard Wagner and Beyond*

Ulrich Baer, *Remnants of Song: Trauma and the Experience of Modernity in Charles Baudelaire and Paul Celan*

Samuel C. Wheeler III, *Deconstruction as Analytic Philosophy*

David S. Ferris, *Silent Urns: Romanticism, Hellenism, Modernity*

Rodolphe Gasché, *Of Minimal Things: Studies on the Notion of Relation*

Sarah Winter, *Freud and the Institution of Psychoanalytic Knowledge*

Samuel Weber, *The Legend of Freud: Expanded Edition*

Aris Fioretos, ed., *The Solid Letter: Readings of Friedrich Hölderlin*

J. Hillis Miller / Manuel Asensi, *Black Holes / J. Hillis Miller; or, Boustrophedonic Reading*

Miryam Sas, *Fault Lines: Cultural Memory and Japanese Surrealism*

Peter Schwenger, *Fantasm and Fiction: On Textual Envisioning*

Didier Maleuvre, *Museum Memories: History, Technology, Art*

Jacques Derrida, *Monolingualism of the Other: or, the Prosthesis of Origin*

Andrew Baruch Wachtel, *Making a Nation, Breaking a Nation: Literature and Cultural Politics in Yugoslavia*

Niklas Luhmann, *Love as Passion: The Codification of Intimacy*

Mieke Bal, ed., *The Practice of Cultural Analysis: Exposing Interdisciplinary Interpretation*

Jacques Derrida and Gianni Vattimo, eds., *Religion*

CPSIA information can be obtained
at www.ICGtesting.com
Printed in the USA
LVHW101609211122
733707LV00003B/23